FileMaker Pro 4 and the World Wide Web

FileMaker Pro 4 and the World Wide Web

Jesse Feiler

AP PROFESSIONAL
AP PROFESSIONAL is a division of Academic Press

San Diego   London   Boston
New York   Sydney   Tokyo   Toronto

Find us on the Web! http://www.apnet.com

This book is printed on acid-free paper.

Copyright © 1999 by Academic Press.

Academic Press
A division of Harcourt Brace & Company
525 B Street, Suite 1900, San Diego, CA 92101-4495
http://www.apnet.com

ACADEMIC PRESS
24-28 Oval Road, London NW1 7DX
http://www.hbuk.co.uk/ap/

Library of Congress Cataloging-in-Publication Data

Feiler, Jesse.
        FileMaker Pro 4 and the World Wide Web / Jesse Feiler
                p.   cm.
        Includes index.
        ISBN 0-12-638055-4 (acid-free paper)
        1. FileMaker Pro.   2. Database management.   3. World Wide Web
                (Information retrieval system) I. Title
        QA76.9.D3F44   1998
        005.75'65--dc21   98-25950
                                                                                      CIP

Printed in the United States of America
98 99 00 01 02 IP 9 8 7 6 5 4 3 2 1

Contents

Part I. Overview   11

Part V. Setting Up and Maintaining Your Databases on the Web   407

Foreword

In purchasing this book, you are part of history in the making. The accessibility of information on the Internet is transforming us into a more global community. And now, its not just having information, but exchanging information that has furthered the Internets—and the marketplaces—evolution. The award-winning FileMaker Pro software has also evolved to its next stage: publishing database information on the Web, carrying forward all of the simplicity, power, and productivity found in FileMaker Pro.

FileMaker, Inc. has undergone an evolution of its own. Our transformation from Claris Corporation to FileMaker, Inc. focuses our undivided efforts and energies on the strong FileMaker Pro line of database software. Accordingly, FileMaker Press focuses on providing you with valuable information to help you take advantage of FileMaker Pro features and capabilities.

Jesse Feiler's *FileMaker Pro 4 and the WWW* will help you make the most out of bringing your FileMaker Pro database information to the Internet or an intranet. With this book, you can unlock the power of both the Internet and FileMaker Pro. Together, these two powerful entities will help you interactively distribute, gather, and modify the information important to you or your business, perhaps even evolving your own business to its next stage.

FileMaker Pro is rapidly becoming the desktop database of choice. The Internet is becoming the standard for electronic information exchange. Clearly, this book, FileMaker Pro, and the Internet will enhance your databases for their most rich, robust, and productive use. We thank you for using File-Maker Pro, and we wish you every success in this exciting new field of publishing databases on the Web.

DOMINIQUE GOUPIL
President
FileMaker, Inc.

Preface

Whether you come to FileMaker Pro as an experienced Web designer or you come to Web design as an experienced File-Maker Pro database designer—or both, or neither—this book is designed to help you quickly get databases up and running on the Web (or your intranet).

The basics are remarkably simple, and the book steps you through the processes involved in designing and creating FileMaker Pro database-driven Web sites. The examples in the book are based largely on the examples that ship with FileMaker Pro. You will quickly get the hang of things and be able to implement your own sites.

A Note on Platforms and Screenshots

FileMaker Pro is available on both Windows and Mac OS. Screenshots in this book are shown using those platforms interchangeably. Unless specifically noted, the differences between the platforms are purely cosmetic (e.g., scroll bars look different, window frames look different).

More Information, Updates, and Errata

Use these URLs to find out more about FileMaker Pro and the World Wide Web:

- FileMaker, Inc. —
  http://www.filemaker.com

- AP PROFESSIONAL (publisher)—
  http://www.apnet.com/approfessional

- Philmont Software Mill (author)—
  http://www.philmontmill.com/filemaker

Acknowledgments

At FileMaker, Inc. (and before that at Claris), a number of people have provided invaluable assistance on this project. Among them are Geri Hyde, Jill Holdaway, Tom Lloyd, Monet Thomson, and Marty Blaker.

Carole McClendon at Waterside Productions as usual helped to bring this project about.

AP PROFESSIONAL/FileMaker Press continues to be a wonderful group of people to work with. Ken Morton put this book in motion and saw it through to completion. Thanks are also due to Cindy Kogut (copy editor), Julie Champagne (production editor), and Phil Sibbet (cover production).

Thanks are also due to Digital Forest, a FileMaker Pro database-hosting site, for their assistance with real-life examples.

Despite the welcome assistance from so many people, any errors or omissions remain the sole handiwork of the author.

Introduction

Originally, FileMaker databases were simple repositories of data that lived on individual computers. Over the years, File-Maker grew and developed, adding more sophisticated database options as well as networking capabilities that allowed databases to be shared over local area networks. With its new World Wide Web features, FileMaker now lets you share databases across the Internet as well as on proprietary networks that use Internet standards (intranets).

This opens up a wealth of new opportunities. No longer are your users limited to people connected to your local area network: the millions of people on the Internet can now access your databases. This does not mean that those millions of people will be browsing your databases, but it does mean that the limited numbers of people who care about your data and who may be scattered around the world among the scores of millions of Internet users can now use your databases.

Individuals and organizations alike have quickly come to realize that it is this vast reach—literally global—that moves everyone onto the broader stage of the wired world. You can use your FileMaker Pro database to publish information, to collect information, to develop an online store, or to dynamically construct Web pages.

Integrating a FileMaker Pro database with your Web site immediately transforms it from the electronic equivalent of a printed brochure to a dynamic, interactive information desk, warehouse, and storefront. You can examine the static pages of a traditional Web site exhaustively; however, you cannot predict or examine the pages of a database driven Web site—those pages are created dynamically as users interact with the site. The third paragraph of a page labeled "Products for the Home" can be proofread and typset to within an inch of its life on static pages, but the third paragraph of a page labeled "Results of Your Search" depends on the user's selections and the state of the database at that particular moment (it may be changing in response to other users' additions and deletions).

Integrating FileMaker Pro and the World Wide Web

FileMaker Pro and the World Wide Web fit together perfectly. It is hard to imagine that they were not designed for one another, but the fact is that when FileMaker was first developed, the Web did not yet exist. In fact, when databases were first devised, the Internet itself was not even a reality.

On the other side, the designers of the World Wide Web recognized the importance of integrating databases with the

Web from the start.[1] However, this integration was put on the back burner in many cases as the Web itself—with primal data types such as text, graphics, sound, and video—was being developed, deployed, and explored by designers and users. After the Web's first half-decade of existence, more complex data types—Java applets, databases, and software components—started to come into their own and people "discovered" the benefits of integrating the Web with databases such as FileMaker Pro.

The integration of FileMaker Pro and the World Wide Web is such a logical development that it may come as no surprise to you that there are many ways to achieve this goal. You can choose the method that is most appropriate for you, your database, or your development environment—and you can mix and match them as you see fit.

Instant Web Publishing

This is the simplest and fastest way to put databases on the Web. For database designers without the experience or inclination to have much to do with Web authoring, this is a good way to get started. The Web pages are generated automatically as needed—you do not have to do any Web page design.

---

1. See *Information Management: A Proposal*, Tim Berners-Lee, CERN. March 1989, May 1990. Available on the Web at http://www.w3.org/History/1989/proposal.html.

Custom Web Publishing with CDML

This is the easiest way for Web designers who are adept at using HTML to put databases on the Web. Whereas Instant Web Publishing (IWP) is great for database types with limited Web experience, Custom Web Publishing (CWP) is ideal for their counterparts with lots of Web experience and limited database experience.

Custom Web Publishing with Home Page

This is the way to achieve more sophisticated Web effects than Instant Web Publishing can provide while still avoiding the nuts and bolts of HTML.

CGI Publishing

This requires a knowledge of databases, HTML, and CGI scripting. It is the only way to publish FileMaker Pro 3.0 databases, and it may be appropriate for installations that are hosting multiple types of databases (such as SQL databases as well as FileMaker Pro databases). CGI publishing requires the use of software in addition to FileMaker Pro, such as Tango, Lasso, Web FM, or Cuesta.

Note that FileMaker Pro 4.0 is needed for the first three methods; CGI publishing is available for FileMaker Pro 3.0 or FileMaker Pro 4.0.

As you can infer from the descriptions of the different ways of publishing databases on the Web, many different types of people are getting into the act. Database designers, Web page developers, software developers, programmers, and business consultants are all able to achieve comparable results using their own sets of skills.

Although different people approach the process in different ways and use different tools, the underlying process is fundamentally the same in all cases. Particularly when it comes to issues of design, testing, and maintenance (both of Web pages and of databases), many of the issues transcend the specific tools that are used.

Getting Starting with FileMaker Pro and the World Wide Web

Your FileMaker Pro product—including its documentation and examples—is the place to start if you want to jump in and try out a database on the Web. Experiment and explore without any worries—it's unlikely that you will cause any permanent damage to anything.

Follow the links and suggestions in advertising and promotional materials to see actual FileMaker Pro databases at work on the Web. (Those references are not given in this book since they change frequently.) If you attend trade shows or user group meetings, watch the demonstrations to see what can be done. Visit the FileMaker Web site (http://www.filemaker.com) for more information and samples.

Appendix A, "Appendix: FileMaker Pro Web Publishing Checklist" on page 501, provides a step-by-step guide to the mechanics of implementing FileMaker Pro databases on the Web.

How This Book Is Organized

This book provides detailed descriptions of the individual publishing methods mentioned previously as well as of the common design and maintenance concerns that apply in all cases. You may read it sequentially, or you may decide to jump back and forth to specific issues that interest you. Cross-references are provided to help you no matter which course you choose.

There are six parts to the book, described in the following sections.

Part I: Overview

This part of the book provides a high-level look at some of the possibilities available to you with FileMaker Pro and the World Web Web. If you are new to FileMaker Pro—or if you want to refresh and expand your knowledge—you will find a detailed chapter that summarizes the high points of the product.[2]

Home Page is the easiest tool to use to develop Web pages that are integrated with FileMaker Pro.[3] (Many people consider it the easiest tool to use to develop any Web pages.) As with FileMaker Pro, there is a chapter that provides an over-

---

2. For further information about FileMaker Pro, consult the online documentation (including the tutorial), the User's Guide, as well as other books from FileMaker Press.

3. For further information about Home Page, consult the online documentation as well as other books from FileMaker Press and Claris Press. Note that a sample version of Home Page often ships wiith FileMaker Pro and may be available for downloading at the FileMaker site—http://www.filemaker.com.

view of Home Page: you can use this as an introduction or refresher.

Part II: Instant Web Publishing with FileMaker Pro

This part—and the two that follow it—focuses on one of the three technologies that you can use to publish FileMaker Pro databases on the World Wide Web. (You may choose to use only one of the technologies, or you may choose to combine them in various ways.)

Instant Web Publishing is the simplest way to get a database up on a Web site, and the step-by-step instructions are provided here.

Once you have a database on your Web site, it needs to be tested, debugged, and maintained. Those instructions are also provided in this section.

Part III: Custom Web Publishing with CDML

This part of the book helps people who want to work with the basic HTML-type codes to integrate FileMaker Pro databases with Web pages. The issues involving testing, debugging, and maintenance are much the same as with Instant Web Publishing and are not repeated here.

This section also deals extensively with Web-based forms. You can use forms with any of the publishing techniques, but this is the primary location in which they are discussed.

Part IV: Custom Web Publishing with Home Page

The Home Page solution provides the most powerful and flexible way of publishing FileMaker Pro databases on the Web while giving the Web designer a graphical user interface that makes the work relatively easy. (Advanced users can use the basic designs created with Home Page and customize the Web pages and CDML using the techniques outlined in Part III.) This section describes the tools involved.

As with the previous section, the common testing, debugging, and maintenance issues are not repeated.

Part V: Setting Up and Maintaining Your Database on the Web

Beyond the basics described in Part II, there are more advanced issues that need to be addressed if you want your databases to function properly. In this section, you will find details about security, file maintenance, intranets, transaction processing, and site maintenance.

Part VI: Interface and Usability Design Concerns

The last part of the book deals with the way in which your Web site and your databases are presented to the world. These actually are the most fundamental issues that you must deal with in designing your site: the fact that they are presented at the end of the book is not meant to minimize their importance. They are presented at the end of the book because to address these issues you need to understand everything that has come before.

Overview

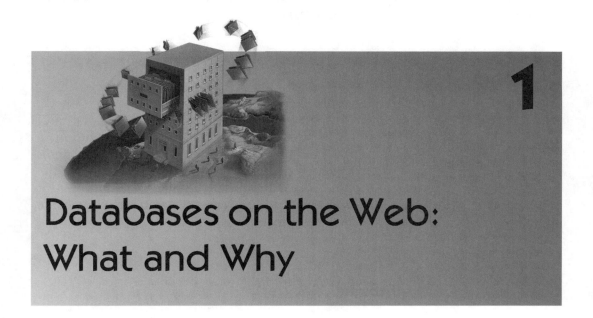

Databases on the Web: What and Why

What took so long? FileMaker Pro databases and the World Wide Web are a natural combination. This chapter provides an overview of what this combination means—and what you can do with it.

You will find an overview of database and Web concepts and how they relate to one another; you will see how FileMaker Pro databases are implemented on the Web. Details about FileMaker Pro, the Internet in general, and the Web in particular follow in the remaining chapters of this book.

Database Overview

"Database" is one of those words (like "multimedia" and even "computer") that everyone uses—generally without a clear definition in mind. This section presents the terminology used in this book. It is an introduction to databases of the sort that occupies many hundreds of pages in textbooks. If it is more than you want to know about databases now, come back to it as you read the book.

"Database" Defined

"Database" is one of those terms that is widely used without having a precise definition that is shared by all its users. At various times, it can refer to any, several, or all of the following:

- A database may be a body of data—often a large body of information—usually stored on a computer or other electronic device.

- A database may be the software (and sometimes hardware) that is used to store, retrieve, and manipulate data.

- A database may be a combination of data, software, and custom-written code and procedures that address a given problem. The database for a doctor's office can consist of patient records (data), FileMaker Pro (software), and custom-written layouts, reports, and procedures that provide operational and management guidance.

In this book, those concepts are expressed with three different terms:

- **Database** is used in the first sense: a collection of data.

- **Database software**—usually FileMaker Pro—is the term used for the second sense.

- **Database project** is used for the final sense—the combination of data, software, and the reports, layouts, and procedures that make everything work together for a given purpose.

If you want to make a further distinction among these three concepts, you can consider who owns or creates them:

- Databases are owned or created by users.

- Database software is created by software developers such as FileMaker, Oracle, and IBM.

- Database projects are created by consultants, end users, or others familiar with both the data in the database and the capabilities of the database software.

However you define them, certain characteristics of databases (and their associated database software and database projects) are commonly recognized. From a practical, real-life point of view, here are some of the generally accepted characteristics of databases.

Databases Handle Large Amounts of Structured Data

Individual values are not databases. Your name is a value, not a database, and its relationship to your address is not a database. A collection of names, however, can be a database. It makes sense to think of a database of the children in a class (or a school), or of a database of the securities that are in an individual's portfolio. Similarly, the aisle in which you have parked your car at the shopping mall is scarcely a database, but the collection of license plate tags and aisle numbers that a valet parking clerk maintains does sound like a database.

In each of these cases, the database is a collection not only of a relatively large amount of data, but also of data that has certain similarities within itself. A database consisting of the names of children in a class as well as the destinations to which an airline flies sounds—and would be—strange. (See "The Structure of Database Data" on page 21.)

Database Data Can Change Quickly (Often Unpredictably)

The databases suggested in the previous section contain different types of data. Although each would be large, given sufficient resources it is possible to present the data from the database in a nondatabase form, such as a printed list. In the case of the children in a class, a class list could be—and normally is—produced once a semester. The relatively few enrollments and dropouts can be marked in pencil on the printed list. Likewise, an airline's destinations can be presented in a printed schedule that is updated a few times a year.

In the case of a database of parked cars, however, the situation is likely to be impossible to handle with a printed list. Each time a car is parked or removed the list needs to be updated. The line of patrons waiting to park or retrieve their cars would quickly grow to unmanageable dimensions if a new list had to be prepared each time.

What is important to note is that although databases may contain relatively static data (such as the class list), their nature allows for rapidly changing data (such as the parked car directory).

Database Data Needs to Be Selected and Displayed in Different Ways (Sometimes Unpredictable)

Whether or not data changes, databases allow it to be selected and displayed in various ways. Whereas a printed list of the students in a class will always be presented one way—alphabetically by last name, in rows and columns corresponding to classroom seats, by birthdate, or by address—the fact that databases can present data on an ad hoc basis means that the way in which data is stored has little to do with the way in which it is retrieved.

These first three points—the fact that databases normally contain large amounts of data, that they can manage changes to the data, and that they can select and display the data (and parts of it) in different ways—are the most important characteristics of databases. The other characteristics follow from these.

Databases Have Tools to Manipulate Their Data

Database software is designed to perform the manipulations needed in storing, retrieving, updating, selecting, and displaying data. It is usually highly optimized for these purposes.

Data stored in standard computer files (**flat files**) must be manipulated by custom-written software that manipulates the data directly. This is usually less efficient and much more expensive than using software like FileMaker Pro. Much traditional programming is incorporated into FileMaker Pro.

Databases Contain Meta-data

In order to manipulate database data, FileMaker Pro (like all database software) stores **meta-data** in addition to the data. Meta-data (data about data) describes the data. Aspects of meta-data that are stored include

- A name for each data field ("birth date," "customer name," etc.). The name of the data field is distinct from the values in the database ("Rajiv," "Jan," "Carmen," "Joussef," etc.)

- A type for each data field—whether it is text, an integer, a date, or whatever.

- Additional information that can optimize storage and retrieval.

Databases Contain Data Validation and Integrity Features

Database software itself contains routines that can be invoked to edit data as it is entered. The types of validation and integrity features that are present in FileMaker Pro include the following rules:

- Values must be unique (as, for example, ID numbers).

- Values must correspond to other databases (if you enter an invoice, the account number must be valid).

- Values can be generated automatically (such as serial numbers).

- Values must be within a certain range (earlier than today, greater than 124, etc.).

- Values can be calculated automatically (total price = quantity *x* unit price).

FileMaker Pro provides the option for you to specify error messages to be displayed if these rules are not satisfied. Note that this is another example of the database software containing routines that otherwise would be programmed manually. In FileMaker Pro, you specify the validation rule and the message that is to be displayed if it fails. You do not write code such as

```
if (validation ≠ good) then
        display (error message)
```

The processing is handled for you by FileMaker Pro.

There is a very important distinction between procedural programming, in which the sequence of events *is paramount, and database programming, in which the* state of data *is paramount. An overly simplified rule of thumb is that in the procedural world, time is important—this happens, then that happens, then the other thing happens. In the database world, you do not know in which order things happen, but once they have happened (for example, once an entry has passed validation checks), you know that all of the rules have been satisfied.*

Databases Are Often Shared across Time and Space

If you consider the facts that databases usually have large amounts of data in them, that the data can change, and that the data can be excerpted and displayed in various ways, it is obvious that the database can appear—and be—different at various times. In fact, one way of thinking of a database is not as a static body of data, but as a static structure for the storage, retrieval, and manipulation of dynamic data. This means that the data in the database may be different today

(or may be presented differently today) than it was yesterday.

Although the technological underpinnings are quite sophisticated, there is little difference between one person accessing
a database on two different occasions and two people accessing a database from two different locations. The sharing of
data across time and space is an integral part of what people
think of when they think of databases.

Databases Can Be Related to One Another

Often, databases contain data that they share with one
another. A customer database may contain a list of a firm's
customers; an invoice database may contain current
invoices—including references to customers in the customer
database. Further, an inventory database may contain references to items in inventory that are referred to in the invoice
database.

There are a number of ways to formally link databases
together; FileMaker Pro uses the **relational** model—the ability to specify that a certain data field in one database matches
a data field in another. Thus, the customer-name data field in
a customer database may match the name-of-customer field
in an invoice database. This is part of the meta-data for both
databases.

Other models exist that allow databases to be linked
together. These can be implemented in database software or
they can be implemented using manual procedures. (Your
"customer database" might be a drawer of file cards, whereas
your "invoice database" is a FileMaker Pro database.)

Terminology varies when it comes to relationships among databases. In FileMaker Pro, the terminology is as it is used here: a database may be related to another one. In some other database systems—such as SQL (Structured Query Language)—a database is a collection of individual tables; the tables are analogous to FileMaker Pro databases, and the aggregate SQL database is roughly comparable to a FileMaker Pro database project. If you are used to SQL terminology, ratchet your thinking down one level so that you think of an SQL table as a FileMaker Pro database. If you aren't used to such terminology, don't sweat it.

The Structure of Database Data

Database data is more than just a large body of data that is able to be stored, retrieved, and manipulated easily by database software. Database data has certain structural characteristics that make those processes possible.

Databases Contain Multiple Instances of Similarly Structured Data

Databases are used to organize data (just as physical filing cabinets and bookshelves are). As in the physical world, the storage structures are often customized for what they will contain. Thus, the shelves on which you place books are likely to be different from the hooks from which you hang garden tools, and the freezer in which you store ice cubes and daiquiris is a far cry from the drawer in which you keep your socks.

In general, the more similar the data instances are, the more efficient a database can be. You can create a database into which you place the names and addresses of people, but if you know that the database will be used to store names and addresses of students rather than of clients, you can often construct a more efficient and logical database.

The following terms are used to describe the data in a database:

- A **record** is a given data instance—one student, client, inventory record, appointment, message, etc. Other terms that are sometimes used synonymously are instance, observation, row, and case. Each record within a database has the same structure as every other record.

- A **field** is a single piece of data within each record—the date of an appointment, the time of an appointment, the location of an appointment, etc. Other terms that are sometimes used synonymously are data point, column, and variable. All fields are present in each record of a database, but they need not have data within them. Furthermore, a record cannot have any data that is not part of a field.

- A **key** is a field that is used to retrieve data. Often keys are unique (identification numbers, for example); it is often necessary to construct such a field when the real-world data may not be unique (names are not unique).

- A **value** is the content of a field in a specific record—the name "John" in a student record or the name "Sari" in another student record.

Databases Can Be Normalized

As noted previously, the structural aspects of databases—multiple instances of similarly structured data objects—are not new. People have been categorizing and storing objects and information for millennia. There are many theories and techniques that have been developed to make information storage and retrieval more efficient; the methods of enumeration and identification that were used in ancient Egypt and Greece are far from out of date.

Some specific methods for structuring databases have been developed and are categorized under the general term of **normalization**. Your database does not have to be normalized—many are not. However, normalized databases function more efficiently than others, in large part because database software—like FileMaker Pro—is optimized to handle data that is structured in this way.

With the issue of normalization, one of the most important aspects of database design is raised: it is not a mechanical process or even a science. Developing an efficient and useful database is a matter of experience as well as of trial and error. It requires a knowledge of databases in general as well as of the data that is to be used and of the uses to which it will be put. No database designer can properly create a database without an understanding of the people who will use the database.

There are five forms of normalization. You probably normalize data now without knowing it; you need not normalize your data (and if you do, you need not say that you have done so). Nevertheless, it is useful to know the correct terminology. It is very easy to set up all of the database fields shown in this section. The five forms of normalization are:

1. The elimination of repeated groups.

2. The elimination of redundant data.

3. The elimination of fields not dependent on the key field (or, the separation of different types of data).

4. The elimination of multiple relations (another type of data separation).

5. The use of common sense.

You can use the basic FileMaker Pro documentation and online assistance to create databases like these; however, most people will find it more useful to use this section as background material. The processes of normalizing databases are covered in this book as they are needed in a step-by-step manner. If you are not interested in database theory, skip this section (and don't complain when your databases are slow and inefficient).

FIRST NORMAL FORM (ELIMINATE REPEATING GROUPS)   In Figure 1-1, you see a database record layout that lets you store your appointments for a given day.

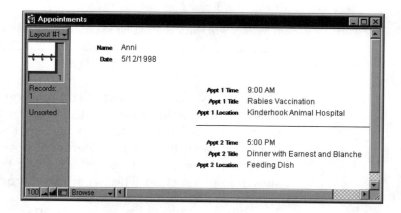

FIGURE 1-1. Appointments Database

The fields of this database are shown in Figure 1-2.

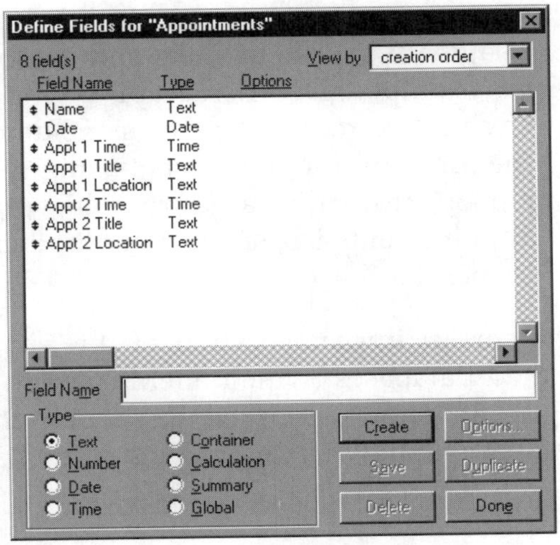

FIGURE 1-2. Fields for Appointments Database

This may look simple (and in fact it is the type of database layout that almost everyone creates when they are starting). Note, however, that there is a repeating group of fields—the time, title, and location for appointment 1, appointment 2, and so on. This is almost always a problem for the following reasons:

- Since each record contains all of the fields, if you ever need as many as 10 appointments for one day, every record must have space for the three fields of each of 10 appointments. This can be an enormous waste of space.

- It is very difficult to use search mechanisms efficiently on this structure. If you are looking for a specific appointment, you wind up searching for a condition in which, for example, Appointment 1 name = X or Appointment 2 name = X.

- Getting around this problem brings out the most imaginative ideas in users and database designers. In the example given here, typical workarounds include having two records for the same day (so as to double the limit for appointments), using two names for one person (for the same reason), piggybacking two appointments in one entry, and others too disturbing to mention.

The correct implementation of this structure is to use two related databases (which FileMaker Pro does very handily). Figure 1-3 shows what the user sees in this case. (The related database is shown in a scrolling portal.)

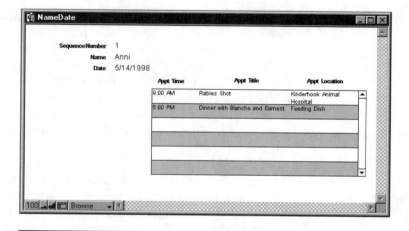

FIGURE 1-3. Normalized Appointments Database

In Figure 1-4, you can see the two databases that are used to produce the layout shown in Figure 1-3. The relationship between the two databases is provided by a sequence number that is unique for each record in the Name/Date database. Every appointment for that person and that date is stored in the Appointments database; each record in the Appointments database has a sequence number in it that matches a Name/Date database sequence number. (These sequence numbers are unique within the Name/Date database, identifying a single person and date; within the Appointments database, they are not unique, since many appointments can exist for a single person on a given date.)

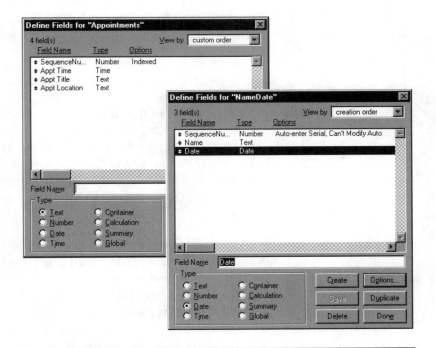

FIGURE 1-4. Database Structures for Normalized Appointments Database

Note that this structure doesn't waste space—there are only as many appointments for a given person on a given date as actually exist (if any). Furthermore, there is no limit to the number of appointments that can exist.

Violating the first normal form is the most common mistake that people make in designing databases. However (as always in database design, there is a "however"), you should remember two important points:

1. Not all databases support relations such as that used to link the sequence number in the two databases shown in Figures 1-3 and 1-4. (FileMaker Pro 2.0 and earlier did not.) If you are working with old databases—or databases derived from old databases—do not automatically assume that people didn't know what they were doing. They may not have had FileMaker Pro 3.0 or later.

2. The definition of a repeating group is far from clear. Table 1-1 shows two sets of data fields. Do you think that the fields in the first column represent a repeating group? (Three repetitions of a pair of data elements— phone number and type.) The same information can be presented in a way that appears to be a repeating group (the first column) and that appears to be unique data fields (the second column). This is a common situation.

In general, the trade-off is simply stated: repeated groups take up more disk space and are harder to work with, whereas non-repeating groups use slightly more processing time (to perform the relationship) and use less disk space. Although you may need to do some experiments for yourself in very time-critical applications, in most cases the cost of normalizing data is well worth it.

SECOND NORMAL FORM (ELIMINATE REDUNDANT DATA)   When you start creating a database project with several related databases, you will encounter the temptation of storing data in two places: don't do this. In the example shown in Figure 1-4, you can blithely violate the second normal form by add-

Structure A	Structure B
Phone I Number	Fax Phone Number
Phone I Type (fax, home, office etc.)	Home Phone Number
Phone 2 Number	Office Phone Number
Phone 2 Type	
Phone 3 Number	
Phone 3 Type	

TABLE 1-1. Identifying Repeating Groups

ing a Name field to the Appointments database. The sequence number lets you match up a Name/Date database record with the appropriate Appointments database records; using that relationship, you find the appropriate name from the Name/Date database for a given sequence number. Stashing the name in the Appointments database as well may seem like a good idea, but it is not.

The most common reason given for violating this rule is efficiency: "Why should I have to look up the name from another database, when I can just as easily keep a copy in the Appointments database?" The answer is that as soon as you have redundant data in your design, you need to worry about keeping it synchronized. Violation of the second normal form is what lets you have two different names at your bank, two different account numbers for a single credit card, or a multitude of different mailing addresses for a single mass marketer.

However, there is a reason for violating this rule—and it is a very important consideration. The advantages of storing each data value once (and only once) include not only reduced storage space but also the fact that a change to the data value—such as a change of address or change of name—

need only be entered once; it is propagated throughout the entire database project as various related databases pick up the revised data.

If you are using related data in an invoice database, it is important that the values not change after the invoice has been accepted. A change to your mailing address a week after you have ordered an item should not affect the records of a shipment that has already been dispatched. More important, a change in the price of an item that you have ordered and paid for should not be reflected on the invoice when it is subsequently printed and stuffed in the carton in which the goods are shipped.

There are two standard solutions to this problem:

1. When you want to freeze the value of related fields (such as a price at the moment when a sale is consummated), you can copy all of the data in the invoice record to a new database that contains all of the invoice's data with no relations. This violates a whole host of database design considerations but is a realistic and practical solution to the need to keep a copy of the data as it was at a given time.

2. You can add validity dates to the related data items, indicating that the price, item name, or address is valid from a certain date and time until another one. Then, when you request the related data, you get the data that falls within the appropriate range based on the invoice date and time. This is a more complicated method than the first one, and its failure can lead to the display of incorrect data. The first method—duplication of data when it is accepted for processing—cannot display incorrect data.

THIRD NORMAL FORM (ELIMINATE FIELDS NOT DEPENDENT ON THE KEY FIELD) There may be relationships within the data that you store in a database record (the most common is the relationship between a ZIP or postal code and a town name). In this case, data is dependent on (varies in accordance with) another field in the record. Storing both elements is redundant and wasteful; in addition, it can lead to incomplete data in the database.

In a database that stores both postal code and town names, you can search for one and find the other—given the postal code you can find the town and vice versa. This is often useful, but it works only for those towns and postal codes that are used in addresses in the database. If you order merchandise over the telephone, you will learn that most telemarketers have a separate database of all postal codes for all towns, regardless of which codes and towns are used in their customer database; you provide your postal code and they confirm the town that you are in.

Violating the third normal form can create databases in which people rely on incomplete data. On the other hand, violating the third normal form when the data items are very small (as in postal codes) can sometimes simplify the design of a database project sufficiently that it is worth the risk.

FOURTH NORMAL FORM (SEPARATE MULTIPLE RELATIONS) This rule is very simple to demonstrate using the Appointments database shown previously. If you enter an appointment that consists of a meeting with Jill for 2 PM on Tuesday in your office, and another appointment that consists of a meeting with Joan for 2 PM on Tuesday also in your office, is that a joint meeting with both Jill and Joan or a conflict of two separate meetings?

The fourth normal form requires that there not be two types of relationships within the same database; thus, this must be two separate and conflicting meetings.

This explanation of the fourth normal form is overly simplified; for more details consult a book on database design. For practical purposes, you can avoid running amuck in fourth normal by keeping your databases simple.

FIFTH NORMAL FORM (USE COMMON SENSE) The traditional definition of the fifth normal form has to do with the need to isolate semantically related relationships; it is usually covered in textbooks with a footnote and then ignored. Another way of looking at the fifth normal form is in a broader sense that covers all of the other rules as well: do what makes sense. The way in which you design a database has to do with the data and the use to which it will be put. Issues of efficiency sometimes suggest that you unnormalize data to save processing time and use more disk space. Similarly, issues of security may dictate that you separate logically related fields so that you can enforce necessary procedures.

For all of the normalization rules, do what makes sense. Remember, though, that FileMaker Pro (like all database software) works most efficiently with database projects that are normalized. Also, be careful to do real-life testing before assuming that one database structure is more or less efficient than another. Most actual experiments have shown that the gains achieved by using nonnormalized data are minimal.

World Wide Web Overview

It is less than a decade since the World Wide Web was first proposed and implemented. Just as spreadsheets (particularly VisiCalc) made the first personal computers a mainstream tool, the Web has made the Internet an essential part of late-twentieth-century life. (It is unlikely that the extraordinary spread and use of the Internet would have occurred if people still relied on FTP and Gopher for information search and retrieval.)

Many books have been written about the Web, and you probably have a browser installed on your computer and have used the Web yourself. (If you haven't, you should take some time out very soon to install a browser and get used to using it: this book assumes a basic familiarity with the Web from a user's point of view.)

This section of the book examines the World Wide Web from a high level, much as the previous section examined databases from a similar high level. When you look at databases and the World Wide Web from such a high level, you find a remarkable degree of similarity.

The Web Described

The Web can be described in terms very similar to those used for databases.

The Web Can Manage Large Amounts of Data

From its inception, the Web was designed to manage large amounts of data. You can manage a day's appointments on the back of an envelope; you can probably even manage a week's appointments on both sides of a big envelope. A year's appointments, however, require a different technology.

An important point to note in dealing with large amounts of data is that the issues involved in storage, retrieval, and manipulation do not scale simply from one size to another: there are discontinuities (as in the difference in managing a year's appointments versus those of a day or week). The Web addresses the issues of large scale data management.

See "Databases Handle Large Amounts of Structured Data" on page 15.

Web Data Changes Quickly (Often Unpredictably)

Because the Web is decentralized, its data is subject to constant change. When you place a link on a Web page, there is no guarantee that the destination link is valid (although if the destination is on a page that you also control, that is your responsibility). Anyone who has used search engines such as Yahoo or Alta Vista has encountered dead links and loose ends—links that go nowhere or that go to peculiar places.

See "Database Data Can Change Quickly (Often Unpredictably)" on page 16.

Web Data Needs to Be Selected and Displayed in Different Ways (Sometimes Unpredictable)

One of the reasons for the quick adoption of the Web by corporations is that they have discovered that customers (and potential customers) are very happy to spend a lot of time browsing—as long as the browsing is under their control. A 300-page printed catalog can easily be a nuisance to a customer who is only interested in the 2 pages it contains about horse blankets; on the Web, however, that customer can very happily spend half an hour comparing horse blankets of various kinds. The selection of information—dynamic and under the control of the information user rather than the information provider—constantly changes.

See "Database Data Needs to Be Selected and Displayed in Different Ways (Sometimes Unpredictable)" on page 17.

The Web Has Tools to Manipulate Its Data

The Web is a collection of data and links to data. Its specifications and standards allow for the possibility of various search engines (such as Yahoo, Excite, and Alta Vista), but they are not part of the official Web definition. In practical terms, however, most people consider these selection and manipulation tools part of the Web.

See "Databases Have Tools to Manipulate Their Data" on page 17.

Web Pages Contain Meta-data

Web pages are constructed using HyperText Markup Language (HTML), which contains all sorts of formatting and descriptive information that is enclosed in brackets <such as these>.

Figure 1-5 shows a typical Web page.

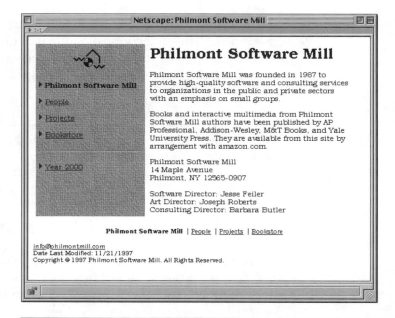

FIGURE 1-5. Philmont Software Mill Web Page

The beginning of the HTML code used to generate that page is shown here:

```
<HTML>
<!--DESCRIPTION: For use with the Standard Site Assistant-->
<!--This file created 1/13/1998 6:17 PM by Home Page
    version 3.0-->
<HEAD>
```

```
<TITLE>Philmont Software Mill</TITLE>
<META NAME=GENERATOR CONTENT="Home Page 3.0">
<X-CLARIS-WINDOW TOP=52 BOTTOM=525 LEFT=68 RIGHT=656>
<X-CLARIS-TAGVIEW MODE=minimal>
</HEAD>
```

Most of the code consists of bracketed formatting instructions which many people would consider a form of meta-data. The italicized code is clearly information about the information contained on the page and is meta-data by anyone's definition.

Note that only the boldfaced text in this code sample is actually shown in Figure 1-5: everything else is formatting or descriptive information. Also note that the italics and boldface type are used for illustrative purposes here and elsewhere in the book: HTML itself does not rely on any such formatting styles.

See "Databases Contain Meta-data" on page 18.

Web Pages Are Often Shared across Time and Space

Finally, it should go without saying that Web pages are often shared across time and space: that is the primary reason for the World Wide Web.

See "Databases Are Often Shared across Time and Space" on page 19.

In short, databases and the World Wide Web represent two different and complementary approaches to the problems of managing large amounts of information and manipulating it effectively—often across the normal boundaries of time and space. The similarities between databases and the Web are not obvious to many people because they were developed by different sorts of people with different backgrounds, but the fundamental similarities are striking.

How the Web Works

The Web itself is based on the Internet protocols and transport mechanism. This section provides an overview of what you need to know. Even if you are an experienced Web user, you may find this section useful since it presents some issues that will become crucial when you publish FileMaker Pro databases on the Web.

Figure 1-6 illustrates what happens when you look at a Web page.

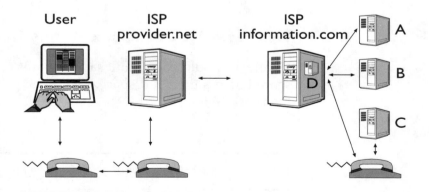

FIGURE 1-6. How the Web Works

Connecting to the Internet

The most basic step is connecting to the Internet. For most people, this involves using a modem attached to their computer to connect to another modem at their Internet service provider (ISP). This is illustrated at the left of Figure 1-6.

Your ISP is your gateway to the Internet. It may be a local company or a large company such as AT&T WorldNet, America Online, or CompuServe. In Figure 1-6, the ISP is identified as provider.net. You have an account with the ISP and you typically pay for the service—either at a flat monthly rate or on a per-hour basis.

Normally you have one modem attached to your computer; your ISP typically has scores (sometimes thousands) of modems connected to its computer for its customers to use because each connected customer requires the use of a modem at the ISP. Standard telephone switching systems are used to place the call.

Variations on this theme are common. For high-volume users, the connection may be a leased telephone line rather than a dial-up connection. In addition, one modem can be shared by several users—often over a local area network (LAN). (Devices called routers often are used to accomplish this.) Furthermore, rather than using the telephone network, cable television lines can be used for connectivity. Lastly, remember that some organizations function as their own ISP.

Once the connection to your ISP is made, you are on the Internet and ready to function. You can assume a direct link between yourself and your ISP (at the left of the diagram), but the telephonic connection is an integral part of the connection.

Connecting to an Internet Address

You request a Web page by typing in an address—such as http://www.*filemaker.com*/index.html. Your ISP connects to the ISP that serves that domain—the part of the address italicized here. It is represented by information.com at the right of Figure 1-6. Conceptually, that ISP is a **domain**—such as filemaker.com. A domain usually corresponds to a single organization such as FileMaker (filemaker.com), Apple (apple.com), Microsoft (microsoft.com), or the British royal family (royal.gov.uk).

INSIDE A DOMAIN Within a domain, there may be many different computers: in the diagram, four are shown. Their addresses are a.information.com, b.information.com, c.information.com, and d.information.com. Each can be addressed individually; furthermore, the domain itself (information.com) can be addressed. In the address in the previous paragraph, www is one of the computers in the filemaker.com domain.

In real life, these computers are given more meaningful names. A computer that is responsible for providing World Wide Web services is often identified as www—as in www.microsoft.com.

Figure 1-6 illustrates some of the variations in configuration that are possible. Computer A and B are linked to the information.com computer directly. Computer C is linked to information.com using a telephone connection—it could be located many miles away from information.com. Lastly, the computer identified as D is in fact not a separate computer but a part of the information.com computer that functions as if it were a separate computer.

The connection between the ISPs (that is, between provider.net and information.com) is their responsibility. Internet routing tables are used to map these names to specific Internet addresses, but none of that is the responsibility either of the user or of the content provider working on computers such as a.information.com or c.information.com.

What happens beyond the connection—inside information.com—is only its business. In fact, you sometimes will connect to an Internet site such as www.apple.com and notice that the actual address you have reached is something like www3.apple.com. In order to handle large numbers of users, some Internet sites use mirrors—duplicate computers with duplicate data; they route users to www1, www2, www3, or whatever their mirror computers are called, so that the load is spread evenly.

WHY THIS MATTERS TO FILEMAKER PRO To publish a File-Maker Pro database on the Web, you need a computer running FileMaker Pro as part of your Web site. That means that you need a computer that runs Mac OS or Windows NT. Many ISPs run Unix computers and cannot run FileMaker Pro.

Refer to Figure 1-6, and you will see how you can easily get around this apparent obstacle. If your ISP runs Unix, you merely need to connect a computer running FileMaker Pro to it using either a direct connection (such as A or B) or a modem connection (such as C). If your ISP does run Mac OS or Windows NT, you can run FileMaker Pro on that computer (as in D). However, many ISPs prefer to keep applications such as FileMaker Pro on separate machines for reasons of stability and security.

Remember that an ISP may be part of your organization; it may even be a file server on your LAN or intranet. Remember also that each computer may be a virtual computer—www.filemaker.com can physically exist on the same computer as sales.filemaker.com and support.filemaker.com. Refer to Part V for more information about these topics.

Connecting to a Web Page

Once you have connected to the Internet and then to a specific site, you download a Web page and view it in your browser. Following the address of the computer in your HTTP request is a file name—index.html in the example used previously.

WHAT IS A WEB PAGE? What your browser actually receives is a string of text characters—the text on the Web page as well as the HTML formatting information. There may be nontextual elements on the page—images, sound, even executable code (such as Java applets)—but they are wrapped in the stream of text characters.

In many cases, Web pages are simply text files: on request, the file is read by the ISP's Web software (at information.com, in the figure) and is transmitted character by character to the receiving ISP and thence to the user's browser. This need not be the case, however. Remember that what happens within the domain to which you connect (information.com, in the diagram) is its business: all that is required is for the ISP to return that string of text characters (with possibly some embedded images, sound, or applets) to the user.

So a computer can generate a Web page programmatically on request rather than reading it from a file. Of course, this means that the computer needs software to format the Web page, but such software—such as FileMaker Pro 4.0—is available. In real life, such dynamically created Web pages often combine template or format information from a file with dynamic information from a database like FileMaker Pro.

WHY THIS MATTERS TO FILEMAKER PRO This, then, is how FileMaker Pro databases can be accessed on the Web. Somewhere within your domain you need a computer running FileMaker Pro. It can be on your ISP (or host or gateway), or it can be on another computer linked to the ISP using one of the methods shown in Figure 1-6.

The request for a Web page containing FileMaker Pro data goes to the appropriate computer; FileMaker Pro generates the data (using the Web Companion software that is included with FileMaker Pro 4.0), formats it dynamically, and creates an HTML page that is returned to the user just as if it had been read from a file.

An alternate mechanism is available and can be used with FileMaker Pro 3.0. In this case, instead of the request being routed to a computer running FileMaker Pro, it is routed to a computer running third-party software that interfaces with FileMaker Pro. The third-party software retrieves the File-Maker Pro data, formats it, and returns the Web page. (For more information, see "Other Web Publishing Tools and File-Maker" on page 494.)

Sessions and Transactions

The architecture described here has two different types of connections. The connection between the user and the ISP—often over a telephone line using modems as shown at the left of Figure 1-6—is a **session**. It is a relationship between two individual modems and is usually billed to a single account. The session may last for some time—it may even be kept open at all times—and it may include all sorts of transactions, such as e-mail, Web browsing, and file transfers.

The request for a Web page described in the previous section is a **transaction**: a request from the user is sent to the appropriate domain, and a response is provided in the form of a Web page consisting of text and possibly embedded nontextual information. The transaction is not designed to be lengthy and consists only of the request and the response. (If no response is received, the user's browser presents an error message.) There is normally no relationship between any transaction and any other.

You will notice when you use a search engine that sometimes the address that you go to will contain more information than the name of a file. It may contain one or more search terms, which are preceded by a question mark. Thus, if you search for "http rfc" in Yahoo, you will see that you are connected to http://search.yahoo.com/bin/search?p=http+rfc. This is the primary mechanism by which additional information is passed to the destination. It will be discussed extensively later (see "Requesting a Resource on the Web" on page 208).

When using a shared resource like a database, people usually think that they have established a connection that is like a session: you often need a password to access a database, and you may initiate many queries. In fact, the normal implementation of database access using FileMaker Pro on the Web is transactional, not session based. Each request contains all of the information needed to let FileMaker Pro accomplish its work. In order to do this, many hidden fields of data are sent back and forth both in the requests and in the responses. (A common such field is the record number of a database record.) This issue will come up many times in this book; it is good to start thinking about the distinction between sessions and transactions now.

*You may see the term **stateless** used to describe systems that do not keep track of information about users between requests. The system—in this case the Web server—does not keep track of the state of any individual user, and each transaction or request is completely self-contained. Because many transactions do require state information, there are a number of ways to work around this issue.*

Servers, Sites, and ISPs

The architecture described in this section can be implemented in many different ways, and each version of the architecture can use its own terminology. To be very precise, here are the distinctions among these terms as they are used in this book:

- An **ISP** is an entity that provides Internet services to clients—either to the public or to members of a private organization such as a school or corporation. Internet services—that is, e-mail, Web, FTP, and other technologies—can be provided over the Internet itself or over an intranet (in which case they can be accessed only by computers connected to that intranet).

- The services that an ISP provides are delivered through **servers**—a Web server, a mail server, etc. Each server consists of both hardware and software. One ISP may have many servers—perhaps one e-mail server, two Web servers, and a Usenet news server. One computer can physically contain two or more servers: in a small organization, a single computer can run e-mail, FTP, and Web servers with no problem. Server is the specific word for the provider of Web services (although you may have a contract with an ISP, you are using their Web server).

• A **site** is a registered location on the Internet (or on an intranet). It is associated with an ISP through address tables (DNS tables) with addresses assigned by Internet organizations. A site can use whatever ISP services are available on the ISP's servers, although the relationship between the organization running the site and the ISP may specify limits and fees for that use. The relationship between the site and its host ISP is maintained through the DNS tables. You can move a site from one ISP to another by applying to the Internet organization that manages addresses in your country (in the United States it is InterNic—http://www.internic.net).

• And just to be complete, the standard term for the browser software that you run on your personal computer is **client**. Sometimes the term is used to refer to the browser software itself; other times it is used to refer to the person using the browser or to the personal computer on which it runs.

FileMaker Pro and the World Wide Web

The specific combination of FileMaker Pro and the World Wide Web opens many exciting possibilities. Basically, they fall into two areas:

1. You can do things that you never did before.

2. You can do things you are doing now much more easily. (For example, for many people, sharing a FileMaker Pro database over the Web is actually easier than sharing it over a LAN.)

This section provides an overview of what you can do and what you need to do it.

What You Can Do

The simplest way to look at the opportunities with FileMaker Pro and the World Wide Web is to start from either end. If you have a database, you can add Web access to it. Note that this means adding access using the technology of the Web—your database can be on the Internet, an intranet, or a LAN.

Likewise, if you already have a Web site, you can add database features to it. Instead of preparing 100 pages of product information for a Web-based product catalog, you can prepare a single template page and then use a database to fill in whatever product information a customer wants to see.

You can use the update capabilities of FileMaker Pro to let people enter data to a database. Even if the only data that they are entering is comments about your Web site, you can easily transform a free-form e-mail survey to a highly structured questionnaire. FileMaker Pro's data validation routines will check that users have provided their e-mail address and answered necessary questions, among other things.

What You Need

In order to use FileMaker Pro databases on the World Wide Web, you need a computer that is running FileMaker Pro. It may be at your ISP itself, it may be a computer linked to it—or it may be at a second ISP that is connected via hypertext links. You can use the same tools and technologies to publish your databases on your LAN or intranet: again, you need a computer running FileMaker Pro or one of the third-party products discussed in "Dealing with CGI Scripts, Other Applications, and FileMaker Pro 3.0 Databases" on page 491.

The FileMaker Pro Examples

There are two sets of examples that are provided with File-Maker Pro. One set (in the Web folder) demonstrates the use of FileMaker Pro databases on the Web. The other set (in the FileMaker Examples folder) demonstrates FileMaker Pro used by itself.

In the FileMaker Examples folder, you will find four sets of examples:

1. An integrated solution that will let you manage most of your office routines.

2. In the Templates folder, you will find databases for home use.

3. Also in Templates, you will find education databases.

4. Finally, in Templates, you will find business databases.

Each database has a different purpose: you may find yourself designing a database project with the complexity of the integrated solution yet based on several education databases. If a database works for you, use it as is. If it is irrelevant, consider what problems it solves: some of them may be of use to you.

In the Web folder, you will find three databases:

1. The Guest Book lets visitors to a site register. This is an example of a database that is updated across the Web (or your LAN or intranet). The data flow is into the database.

2. The Employee Database lets you browse and update databases—the data flows are in both directions.

3. The Shopping Cart database is a special case of a bidirectional database, and it is a real-life example that many people are interested in. It allows people to purchase products over the Web.

Familiarize yourself with the examples. Notice what design techniques you can use for your own purposes; consider what you can do with these databases if you modify them slightly. Finally, make certain that you follow the installation directions and successfully run at least one of the standard examples and one of the Web examples: doing so will guarantee that your FileMaker Pro installation has been successful. *If you install FileMaker Pro and are unable to run the examples, do not assume that things will work themselves out: the reverse is guaranteed.* Use the support resources (manuals, online assistance, the Web, and customer support) to get the examples up and running before you get to work.

Summary

This chapter has provided a very high-level overview of databases and the Web, with particular emphasis on FileMaker Pro. If you are new to the entire area, it may be quite daunting—never fear: the rest of this book is devoted to making the processes described in this chapter possible.

One of the reasons for the rapid adoption of the World Wide Web is that it is so simple—both for people to browse and for people to publish on. If you know someone who was a programmer in the 1970s, sit them down and ask them to describe how they would have implemented any of the examples that ship with FileMaker Pro. If they could have done it, it would have taken enormous efforts—literally years of programming. Today's more powerful computers, coupled with the power of FileMaker Pro, open vast new opportunities.

The next chapter provides a summary of FileMaker Pro. It can serve as a review if you have used FileMaker Pro previously; it can serve as an overview and supplement to the online documentation and manuals if you are new to the product.

Overview of FileMaker Pro

This chapter provides an overview of FileMaker Pro. If you are new to FileMaker Pro, it can help you to get started; if you have used FileMaker Pro in the past, it can serve as a refresher. If you are new to databases in general, you certainly should refer to the FileMaker Pro documentation, online assistance, and the tutorial that ships with FileMaker Pro to help you get started.

The chapter is organized around the major features of FileMaker Pro:

- Databases—how you store data.

- Relations—connecting two or more databases.

- Sorting and searching—how you manipulate data.

- Scripts—automating processes.

- Modes—how you use data on your computer.

- Layouts—how you display data.

Even if you have used FileMaker Pro for years, you should look through this chapter. When you are creating databases for the Web, there are some options and features of FileMaker Pro that—although they have been around for some time—suddenly become very important to deal with. Other aspects of FileMaker Pro (scripts, modes, and layouts, in particular) are less important.

Databases

As discussed in "Database Overview" on page 14, databases contain relatively large amounts of structured data that can be stored, retrieved, and manipulated easily. A FileMaker Pro database contains not only its data, but also the meta-data and structural information that describes the data and helps you manipulate it.

This section describes the data itself.

Records

Within a database, all data is stored in records. Each record is one observation, individual, or item. The structure of each record is like that of every other record in the database, although the values in each record are usually different.

Fields

This section describes the kinds of fields that you can create and what you can do with them, such as the options for automatic entry, validation, and summaries.

Field Definitions

When you create a new FileMaker Pro database, it contains no data and no fields. FileMaker Pro opens the Define Fields dialog box for you to create your first fields; you cannot enter data until you have fields into which to enter it.

You use the Define Fields dialog box (accessed from the File menu's Define submenu) to manipulate the structure of fields in your database. Figure 2-1 shows the Define Fields dialog box from FileMaker Pro 4.0 for the Asset Management database, which is used for all of the figures in this chapter.

Each field in the database is named (in the Field Name column). These are data about the data and as such are not normally displayed; by default each field is usually labeled automatically with its field name, but you often will change those labels.

The second column (Type) describes the type of data stored in each field. The Options column shows additional metadata, including rules for its validation and integrity checking.

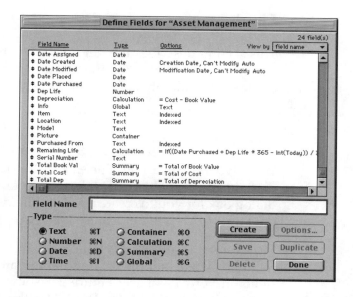

FIGURE 2-1. Define Fields Dialog Box for Asset Management Database

Types of Fields

FileMaker Pro allows you to use various field types. The basic types are shown at the bottom of Figure 2-1. In most cases, you will choose from among the types in the first column—Text, Number, Date, and Time. The data types in the second column (Container, Calculation, Summary, and Global) are discussed later in this chapter (see "Containers" on page 62, "Summaries and Subsummaries" on page 64, and "Calculations, Formulas, and Functions" on page 65 .

CHOOSING A DATA TYPE   As with much of database design, it is not always clear what type a field should be. For example, in the United States a social security number for an individual consists of nine digits that are normally displayed like this:

123-45-6789

The identification number for a business also consists of nine digits, and they are normally displayed like this:

12-3456789

You can store identification numbers as nine-digit numbers, but that will not make the distinction clear. You can store them as strings of characters—including the dashes—and the formatting will be maintained. You can also store them as numbers and use additional information (another field, values of certain digits) to decide how to present the numbers when you display them.

Questions such as this are the bread and butter of database designers. The solutions often come down to a trade-off between the amount of storage space used and the amount of processor time used. (In this example, storing the dashes uses slightly more space; calculating where the dashes should be inserted every time you display a number saves disk space but uses more processing power.)

HOW TO CHOOSE A DATA TYPE   In general, it is best to use the most restrictive data type possible: FileMaker Pro performs error checking to make certain you don't type a W in the middle of a numeric field, for example. Do as much error checking as possible—and have FileMaker Pro do as much of that for you as it can.

So even though you can store everything as text (the least edited field type), you should store numbers as numbers rather than using FileMaker Pro functions to convert text to numbers as needed. Likewise, you should store dates and times using the FileMaker Pro Date and Time data types: that way you do not have to worry about checking if someone has entered an invalid date—FileMaker Pro can do it for you.

Note that numbers, dates, and times are stored in an internal format. How they are displayed is specified in the layouts that you define (see "Layouts" on page 72) as well as on the Web pages that you design to display your database data. In this way you can store a date and display it in European style (day-month-year), U.S. style (month/day/year), or the international standard style (year-month-day). The date that is stored is not affected by its display formats. Similarly, the number of digits used to display a number is a display feature set in the layout, not a characteristic of the stored data.

Data Entry Options

A variety of options are available to you for each data field. Select a field by highlighting it in the Define Fields dialog box (Figure 2-1), and then click the Options button in the lower right of the dialog box.

WHY USE DATA ENTRY OPTIONS?   You may never have used the Filemaker Pro data entry options—after all, they are optional. However, when you start to think about sharing databases and placing them on the World Wide Web, these options take on added significance.

These options allow you to control default values for fields and to specify all manner of validations and edits that can be performed on the data that is entered. A shared database on the World Wide Web will likely be used by many people; even if it is placed on a LAN or intranet, it may have many users (if not the millions who might see it on the Internet). Is it safe to rely on people reading and following instructions? (No.) Are you sure that no one will make an error when entering data? (No—not even you.) By using these data entry options, you can make your database more robust.

ENTRY OPTIONS DIALOG BOX: AUTO ENTER The Entry Options dialog box has two states that are controlled by the pop-up menu at the top. The Auto Enter options are shown in Figure 2-2.

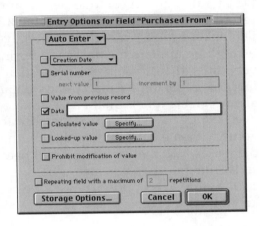

FIGURE 2-2. Define Fields: Entry Options for Auto Enter

When you create a new record in a FileMaker Pro database, normally all fields are blank. This dialog box lets you change that and start with meaningful data. The variety of data is large. From top to bottom in Figure 2-2, your options are as follows:

- Automatic entry. You can automatically have File-Maker Pro enter the creation date, time, or user name for the record. (These values are taken from the operating system values on the computer where FileMaker Pro is running.) Other choices in the pop-up menu let you automatically have FileMaker Pro enter those values for the latest modification of the record. This can be very useful—and very misleading in a shared environment. Computers do not always have the correct date and time; in many environments, people do not properly set their names on their computers. If you are going to use these values for anything more than information, consider using explicit data entry from the user or some form of confirmation.

- Serial numbers. A unique serial number for each record in a database can be a life saver. By having FileMaker Pro assign such a number, you can then go on and manipulate the data by referring to this number rather than to some attribute that might change (such as a person's name). Many database designers always create a field that has a unique serial number even if they have no immediate need for it. If you are going to create a database project with several related databases, you almost always will need some unique serial numbers. Create such a field in each database, set the Auto Enter option to Serial Number, and forget about it until you need it.

- Carry-forward values. You can carry forward a value from the previous record. This is particularly useful as a data entry shortcut. If you carry forward the value from the previous record (a date, perhaps), the user can leave it untouched or change it to reflect a new value for this record. The danger of carrying forward values is that users may get used to ignoring that field and may not notice when they have to change it.

- Specified values. You can fill a field with a given value (the option that is checked in Figure 2-2). Note that this is a static value, not a newly generated serial number or the value from the previous record. You might always set a country field to Canada if most of your data is Canadian, for example.

- Calculated data. You can automatically enter calculated data—perhaps based on other fields in the record. A common calculation is a sales tax amount that is based on a purchase amount. (See "Calculations, Formulas, and Functions" on page 65 to see the kinds of calculations available to you.)

- Looked-up data. The Looked-up value auto entry feature is useful when you are creating a database project that uses related databases. You first set up a relationship between a field in your database and a field in another database (see "Relations" on page 67). Once that relationship has been established, a given field is automatically entered from that database into this one. This almost always violates at least one of the normalization rules discussed in the previous chapter (see "Second Normal Form (Eliminate Redundant Data)" on page 28), but it may be worth it to improve performance.

- Modification. There is an option in this dialog box that prevents users from modifying data. Use this when you are creating a field that will be filled in according to the options you select in this dialog box and which you don't want the user to modify (serial number or creation date, for example). Note that this is the ultimate arbiter of user updates: you can make a field in a layout unmodifiable without checking this option by using access privileges and other techniques (such as not including the field on a layout). That allows the field to be modified sometimes (as, for example, by a supervisor) but not at other times.

- The final option in this dialog box lets you specify that a field will repeat a certain number of times. If you want to allow three telephone numbers for each record, you can create three telephone number fields or create one field which then can repeat three times. Note that this option is the one you check if you want to violate the first normal form (see "First Normal Form (Eliminate Repeating Groups)" on page 24).

You may wonder why FileMaker Pro makes it so easy to violate standard database design principles such as normalization. The answer is—as always—that database design is not a mechanical process and that each case is different. Most experienced database designers would agree that the best choice is to follow the normalization rules. The second best choice is to use these options: they make it clear what you are doing. The worst choice is to violate the design principles on an ad hoc basis. Believe it or not there are databases in the world that contain three telephone number fields— identified as "Telephone," "Extra Telephone," and "Telephone Spare." That is far worse than having a repeating field.

Remember also that the reason for compromising on database design principles is always for efficiency—and you should test performance before deciding that there is a problem. Processors and disk accesses are getting faster and faster by the day. Remember to test in a production-like environment. The speed of the computer and disk on your desktop may be very different from the speed of the computer people access over the Web.

ENTRY OPTIONS DIALOG BOX: VALIDATION   Figure 2-3 shows the other selections in the Entry Options dialog box. These let you specify all sorts of validations that can be performed. Just as with the Auto Entry options, you will find that these are particularly valuable in the shared environment of File-Maker Pro databases on the Web. The validation options are mostly self-explanatory, but a few points should be noted:

- You can specify a calculation to be performed by way of validation. This is similar to the calculation that you can specify to create a value (see "Calculations, Formulas, and Functions" on page 65) except that the result must always be a Boolean—true or false. If the result is false, an error message is displayed.

• You can specify a custom error message to be displayed if validation fails. This can be very helpful if you want to include assistance in the message—the URL of valid teacher names in a university department, for example.

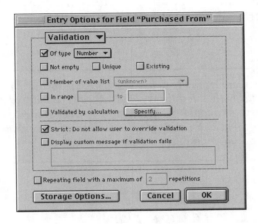

FIGURE 2-3. Define Fields: Entry Options for Validation

• Finally, note that you can allow users to ignore error messages. In an environment of shared databases, it is usual to set the Strict option—not doing so brings into question all of your validation routines. Keeping the Strict option set means that you can assume that every record in your database adheres to the rules that you have described in your validations

STORAGE OPTIONS   The Storage Options dialog box shown in Figure 2-4 is opened from the Entry Options dialog box. This is one of those features that you may have ignored for years, but it can become very important in a shared environment.

FileMaker Pro (like most database systems) uses its own internal devices to store and retrieve records efficiently. If you happen to know that a certain field will be used frequently for sorting or retrieving data (an ID field, for example), you can use the Storage Options dialog box to make certain that FileMaker Pro indexes this field. Indexing a field may make updating marginally slower but usually makes retrieval and sorting significantly faster.

If you are trying to debug a sluggish database, check these settings—both for fields that you think should always be indexed as well as for fields that you think should not be. If you are never going to be sorting or retrieving using a field, for example, turn indexing off so that FileMaker Pro will not ever build an index.

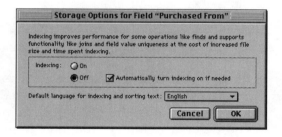

FIGURE 2-4. Define Fields: Storage Options

Containers

Containers are the first of a series of data types that behave differently from the simple and standard data types of text, numbers, dates, and times. They are a special data type that is used to store large data structures such as images and QuickTime movies. The contents of a container are only able to be displayed by FileMaker Pro—you cannot manipulate the contents by indexing them, sorting, or finding. You need to create descriptive fields that can be sorted and manipulated by FileMaker Pro if you want to do this (the name of the image, perhaps a repeating field with the names of five actors in a QuickTime clip, etc.). If you are using images or movies in a database that you will publish on the Web, be very careful to test performance using the slowest connection that your users may use. Note also that Instant Web Publishing (IWP) does not support these objects, although you can have them in databases that IWP uses.

Globals

Globals are an exception to the rule that all data values are stored in fields of records. Globals are fields whose values exist for all records—in other words, there is only one value for each global field in a database (normally there is one value for each record in the database).

Globals are sometimes used to store the results of scripts and calculations; they also can be used to store logos that will need to be displayed in various layouts. Programmers normally avoid the use of globals; they easily lead to sloppy and unmaintainable code. In the case of FileMaker, there is nothing wrong with using globals that contain constant information—such as a logo. However, in a shared database, globals can lead to problems. The value for the global is loaded when the database is opened: if it is subsequently changed by another user, that change may not be reflected immediately in all users of the database. (Changes to normal data fields will be seen.)

Primarily for this reason, you should be very leery of using global fields in databases that are designed to be shared.

Summaries and Subsummaries

There is another—and much safer—way to store data that is relevant to more than one record. Rather than using a global, which provides a single value for the entire database, you can create a summary field, which stores an aggregate value according to the options that you choose from the Define Fields Options dialog box, as shown in Figure 2-5.

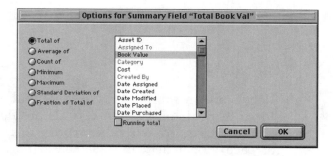

FIGURE 2-5. Summary Field Options

When you create layouts (see "Layouts" on page 72), you will see that you can create layout parts that summarize groups of records in the database. By placing a summary field in the appropriate summary part(s), you can summarize all—or part—of a sorted database's data.

Layouts are used only incidentally for Web-published FileMaker Pro databases; as a result, summary fields may not be the most effective solution for those databases.

Calculations, Formulas, and Functions

You can specify calculations (or formulas) in two cases:

1. You can create a field of type Calculation in the Define Fields dialog box and automatically store a calculated value in it; you specify the calculation in the Auto Entry Data Entry options. You can use other fields in the record as well as numeric constants and functions, in the calculation. You point and click on the fields, operators, and functions, as shown in Figure 2-6.

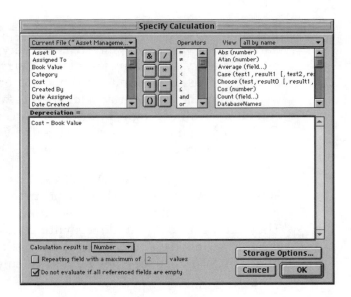

FIGURE 2-6. Specify Calculations Dialog Box

2. You can create a calculation that is used for validation—you do this from the Validation Data Entry Options dialog box. A dialog box almost like that shown in Figure 2-5 opens. The difference is that the

result of the calculation must be a Boolean (true/false or 1/0); if it is true or 1, the validation succeeds.

Note that if you have established a relationship between your database and another one (see "Relations" on page 67), you can use the pop-up menu at the upper left of Figure 2-6 to select fields from related databases.

Value Lists

The final type of data that can be stored in a FileMaker Pro database is a value list. Value lists are very useful in controlling data entry and eliminating keying errors. When you use a value list, users are limited to choosing one of the values in that list for the value of a field. (A typical value list might contain the values Single, Married, Divorced, and Widowed.) Optionally, you can let users update the value list, in which case the added value is shown to other users.

Value lists are quite familiar to Web users—pop-up menus abound on Web pages. They avoid many data entry problems when the number of possible choices is relatively small. They can be used to handle formatting tasks (such as requiring that years be entered with all 4 digits): users rarely even notice that they cannot enter 1 but must enter 2001 when they are choosing from a list.

Anything that you can do to keep the integrity of your database under control is worth doing—particularly in the shared world of the Web.

An alternative to using value lists is to create a small database with one field (such as Marital Status) and to let each record of the database contain the values shown in the previous paragraph. The advantage to this approach is that if you want to use the value list in another database, it is easier to share it when it is itself a small database than when it is a value list.

Relations

Using FileMaker Pro, you can create a relational database project—one in which two or more databases work together. This allows you to construct efficient and logical database structures along the lines discussed in the previous chapter (see "Databases Can Be Related to One Another" on page 20 and "Databases Can Be Normalized" on page 22).

Among the benefits of using multiple databases are the following:

- Data is retrieved only when needed. Rather than retrieving a single 100-field record, you can retrieve a 20-field record and—depending on the layout—one or two other records of similar size. This has benefits for finding and sorting information and has particular performance benefits for Web-based databases.

- You can enforce security constraints on each database, thus achieving different security levels within a single logical "record." (But watch out for security problems with Web publishing—see "Security" on page 409.)

- When changes need to be made in your database project, you can often isolate those changes to a single database, thus decreasing testing time.

Creating a Relationship

Relations between databases are very easy to create in File-Maker Pro. From the Relationships... command (in the Define submenu of the File menu), you open the Define Relationships dialog box as shown in Figure 2-7.

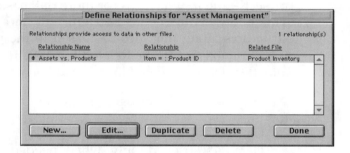

FIGURE 2-7. Define Relationships Dialog Box

Note that each relationship has two partners. One database is the primary or master database. That is the database in which you define the relationship. This is not a reciprocal relationship in many cases, and it does matter which database you choose as the primary database. The FileMaker Pro User's Guide *provides examples of related databases, as do the examples that ship with FileMaker Pro. It may comfort you to know that many people get the relationship backward when they start to create databases. Fortunately, with FileMaker Pro it is very easy to delete a relationship and then recreate it from the other direction.*

When you start, there are no relationships; you click the New… button to create the first one, and you open the dialog box shown in Figure 2-8.

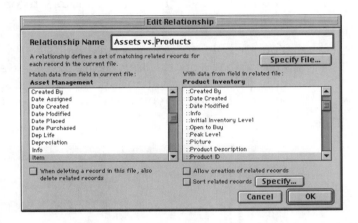

FIGURE 2-8. Edit Relationship Dialog Box

You enter a name for the relationship at the top of the dialog box. Then comes the heart of the relationship: using the Specify File… button, you select the database to which you want to create a relation. You will see the fields in the master database (the one you are working in) at the left; the fields of the related database are shown at the right.

Related fields are always shown with a :: prefix.

In the example shown in Figure 2-8, the Asset Management example database is related to the Product Inventory example database. The relationship is built on the field Item (in Asset Management) and Product ID (in Product Inventory).

This means that FileMaker Pro will use the value in the Item field (in Asset Management) to find a related record with the same value in the Product ID field in Product Inventory. Whenever you have a record from Asset Management, you implicitly have the corresponding record from Product Inventory.

You are able to display related fields by adding them to any layout that you choose. Figure 2-9 shows how a field is dragged into a layout and its contents are selected. First you select the database you want, and then you click on the field.

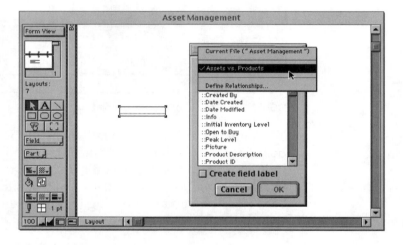

FIGURE 2-9. Adding a Related Field to a Layout

Working with layouts is discussed briefly later in this chapter (see "Lay-outs" on page 72). Layouts are not used extensively in Web publishing, so consult the other FileMaker Pro documentation for details on layouts.

This method of identifying a field to be used may ring a bell with you—it is the same interface that is used in selecting a field to be used in a calculation (see Figure 2-6). In both cases, you can select a related file or define a new relatioinship— opening the dialog box shown in Figure 2-7.

What matters is that once the relationship has been created, you can use the fields from the related files almost as you would the fields in the master file.

Kinds of Relationships

There are two kinds of relationships that you can create: a one-to-one relationship is the sort that has been described here. For a certain value of a common field, there is one related record. A one-to-one relationship might link the postal code in an address file to the same postal code in a file that contains city and state information. The address file only contains the postal code; when an invoice needs to be printed, the relationship can be used to get the city and state.

There are also one-to-many relationships. A customer ID in a customer address file may be related to a customer ID in a billing file. There is one record for each customer's address, but there may be many outstanding invoices. FileMaker Pro provides a structure called a **portal** that allows you to create a view onto the multitude of records that may be related to the master file—in this case, a portal onto all of the outstanding invoices for a given customer.

Look at the Shopping Cart example in the Web folder for a case study. There is a one-to-one relationship called Products from the Orders database to the Customers database. This is used to retrieve the name of the customer for display in the Orders layout. There is a one-to-many rela-

tionship called Ordered Items from the Orders database to the Ordered-Items database; the field that is related is the OrderID field. It is a unique value in the Orders database (using the Data Entry validation options), but it can occur many times in the OrderedItems database—a single order may have many items on it. The checkout.htm file contains the HTML code that lists all of the related items from OrderedItems for a given Order record. How to do this will be explained later, but for now you should run the Shopping Cart example to see how it functions. If you want to look at the database structure and the HTML, feel free—but don't overwhelm yourself.

Layouts

FileMaker Pro lets you create layouts for the entry, display, and manipulation of data. There are two parts to a layout:

1. A layout determines which fields from the database and its related databases the user can use in that layout.

2. The layout contains whatever graphical designs you choose.

For example, Figure 2-10 shows the Asset Management example Form layout, which is used for data entry.

Figure 2-11 shows the List layout, which is used to display several records at a time. Figure 2-12 shows the Report layout, which is similar to the List layout but is designed for printing rather than display on a screen.

If you have used FileMaker Pro in the past, you may not have made the distinction between these two points: it did not really matter a great deal in those cases. Now, however, when you are using FileMaker Pro databases on the Web, the distinction is very important.

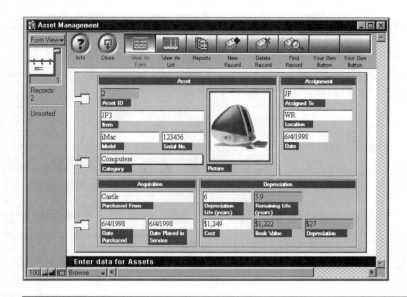

FIGURE 2-10. Asset Management Form View Layout

The graphical elements of the layout for Web-based databases are provided totally by standard Web tools. If you are using IWP, it will take care of the layout for you; if you are using Custom Web Publishing (CWP) with Home Page or with CDML, special HTML tags (CDML) are inserted either automatically or by you to work with HTML in displaying the page. In either case, the FileMaker Pro graphics in the layout are irrelevant to the Web (although graphics in your database's container fields are shown).

The selection of fields in a layout, however, is important for Web-based databases. There is a significant performance benefit to using layouts that contain only the fields that you need for a given layout; accordingly, you may want to design some layouts simply for the Web—do not worry about what they look like in FileMaker Pro, just use them to select the fields that you care about.

Make certain that the fields are included only once in the layout. You can display a field twice in a layout—perhaps using different formatting rules. FileMaker Pro uses the formatting that you have set for a field in the layout; if it appears twice, you may use the wrong format.

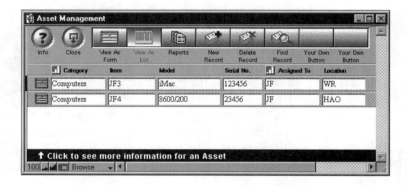

FIGURE 2-11. Asset Management List View Layout

Layouts for the Web

If you use IWP, you can choose four layouts for your site. IWP will take care of the graphics; your choice of layouts is provided only to determine which fields will apear in each layout.

The model provided by IWP is worth considering even if you are designing your own site and plan to use Custom Web Publishing. The four layouts for IWP are as follows:

1. Form layout—this is designed to show a single record in detail; it also is used for data entry. Its layout is similar in spirit to the Form layout shown in Figure 2-10.

2. Table layout—this is designed to let users browse through several records at a time. Its format is similar to the List layout for Asset Management shown in Figure 2-11.

3. Search layout—this is the layout that people can use to search your database. Note how the choice of fields in a layout matters: only the fields you provide in this layout can be searched on.

4. Sort layout—this layout lets people sort the database.

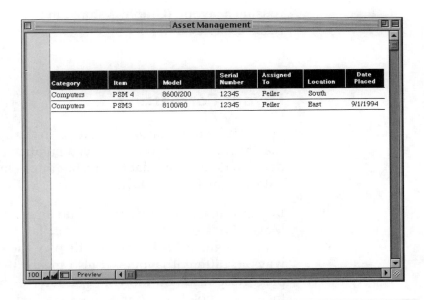

FIGURE 2-12. Asset Management Report Layout

For reasons of efficiency, you may choose to force the fields in the Search and Sort layouts to be indexed, using the Storage Options dialog box shown in Figure 2-4.

You can use the same layout in several ways: the simplest possible database for the Web has one layout that is used for all IWP displays as well as for use with FileMaker Pro on a single computer. Graphical elements in a layout are ignored on the Web: they can be there or not, as is the case if you are reusing a layout. (Graphics stored in the database's container fields are relevant.)

Layout Formatting

Fields in layouts can be formatted in various ways (refer to the FileMaker Pro online documentation and manuals for details). Remember that this formatting is independent of the data storage in the database.

In particular, numbers, dates, and times are stored in File-Maker Pro's own formats; their display in a layout is up to you. This means that you can display the fields in different ways in different layouts. It also means that when you display those fields on the Web you have a chance to reformat them. Do not tear your hair out when layout formatting information disappears on the Web—it was never there in the first place.

Sorting and Searching

FileMaker Pro—like any database—is designed to manage data efficiently, and that includes sorting and searching. As noted previously, you can optimize these routines by indexing fields (although indexing fields normally somewhat slows up data entry).

Many people rush to sort and resort databases. Before you do so, stop and think if what you really want to do is to search the database and select certain records. Do you really need an alphabetized list of your students to find Gustav Mahler's telephone number? If you want to find all the potters in your Creativity in the Penitentiary class, you do not have to sort all of the records by medium (clay): you can select all of the records where the medium is clay.

This is detailed in the FileMaker Pro documentation, and a little experimentation with the examples will show you the power of searching and finding data (rather than sorting). In the past, you may not have worried very much about this distinction, and on a single computer it is often not a serious distinction. In a shared environment (such as the Web), it is a very important design consideration. Sorting a database takes significant computer resources. Some database designers go so far as to recommend that you never sort a database: after all, the data manager is designed to do the searching and finding that you would do manually after sorting the database.

As you design databases for the Web, you will develop a sixth sense of what operations are likely to be expensive (in the sense that they hog the computer's resources and degrade performance for others).

There is a very real worry that an unsorted database is somehow unclean or messy. Learning to rely on the FileMaker Pro software to keep track of everything is something that comes gradually. If you are worried about having an unsorted database, you are not alone: but you are on the right track. If you do need to sort the database periodically, it is best done by moving the database off the Web and sorting it on a local machine before you put it back. For more details, see "Sorting" on page 473.

Scripts

FileMaker Pro provides an extensive scripting language. You can attach scripts to graphical elements and to logical events. The scripts can do a variety of chores, such as opening other databases, setting display and layout options, and even sorting the database.

If you are converting existing databases to the Web or if you are experienced at creating databases without the Web, your scripts may mingle the graphical interface with logical events. For example, you may have a script attached to a button that sorts the database and then chooses a List layout in which to view it.

Bearing in mind that layouts on the Web are used only for lists of fields to be dealt with, you should separate any existing scripts into interface scripts and functional scripts. Thus, a script that sorts the database or searches for particular values should not also manipulate layouts. (The fact that scripts can run other scripts makes this easy to do: you can separate one script into two and create a third script that runs the two of them.)

One type of script should be examined very carefully. You may have a script that automatically runs when a database is opened (or closed). It may position the database to a certain record, select a given mode and layout, and otherwise prepare it for the next use. Do not waste time having that script run every time the database is opened on the Web. Separate it so that only the positioning (which will matter on the Web) is done and the user interface manipulation (such as layout selection) is not.

Modes

The final aspect of FileMaker Pro that you need to know about is its modes. These allow you to browse records, entering and modifying data; find and search for data (these are synonymous terms); preview reports that are designed to be printed on paper; and create and manage your layouts.

None of these modes matters on the Web. IWP implements the equivalent of four modes—table (list) views, form views, search views, and sort views. As noted previously, if you use CWP, you will probably implement similar modes yourself as well as a few others. The reason for the similarity is very simple: there is only so much you can do with the data in a database. You can look at it, enter/modify it, select a subset, and resort it.

Of course, the further you get from presenting a database to the user, the further away from those basic functions you get. If you look at the File-Maker Pro Web examples, the Employee Database certainly falls into this paradigm. The Guest Book and Shopping Cart, however, do not clearly reveal their database roots. Increasingly, you will find applications for FileMaker Pro databases on the World Wide Web that do not appear to be traditional database applications.

Summary

This chapter has provided an overview of the FileMaker Pro features that are most important to you when you publish on the Web. Basic functionality is provided by the core File-Maker Pro software; the interface for Web users is quite different from that available to people using FileMaker Pro directly—and you can modify that interface as you see fit.

Having looked at FileMaker Pro, it is time to turn to Home Page—the companion Web authoring tool from FileMaker, Inc.

Home Page Overview

The Internet consists of a set of standards (called **protocols**) that are published in draft form, discussed, modified, and finally adopted for general use. Interested parties, including the public, users, publishers, software designers, and hardware developers, are able to participate in this process, which continues all the time. Each protocol is described in a Request for Comments (RFC) that is numbered; these can be found on the Web in a number of locations. They are the basic references for all Internet standards.[1]

Each Internet protocol has a version number associated with it: as the Internet evolves, enhancements are constantly needed. In some cases, this collegial process is not fast enough, and vendors—particularly developers of Web browsers—typically have implemented proposed modifica-

---

1. One source for RFCs is http://www.internic.net.

tions in their products before they have been through the discussion phase. This is why in some areas one browser can do something that another one cannot: they have implemented not-yet-adopted standards.

This chapter provides a very brief overview of the Web protocols followed by a quick look at Home Page—the easiest tool for creating and managing Web sites with FileMaker Pro databases.

The Web Protocols

The two basic protocols for the World Wide Web are

1. **HTTP** (HyperText Transmission Protocol)—the protocol that is used to communicate between the user's browser and a Web site.

2. **HTML** (HyperText Markup Language)—the protocol that is used to format Web pages.

HTTP

HTTP is the mechanism by which you request a Web page and have it returned to you from a server. You use HTTP when you type in an address such as http://www.filemaker.com and press the Enter key.

HTTP contains specifications for all aspects of the communication, including issues involving firewalls, proxies, gateways, and tunnels—all of which are mechanisms that may be employed between the client and the server for purposes of security and performance improvement. (If you need to worry about them, your ISP or network manager will tell you.)

There is really only one thing that you need to remember about HTTP: it is stateless. That is, each request for a Web page is followed by a single response, and that is the end of it. As noted previously, any state information (for example, the list of items that you are in the process of purchasing at a commercial Web site) must be maintained using some technique other than the connection. The standard techniques for maintaining such state information are listed below.

- You can transfer information in the HTTP request, as discussed in "Sessions and Transactions" on page 43.

- You can store information in a cookie—information that the client browser is requested to maintain. Since cookies represent data on an individual's computer that can be read by a remote computer, browsers normally allow users to turn off cookie storage. Thus, you cannot rely on being able to store cookies in all cases. (In a controlled environment, such as a corporate intranet, cookies may be prohibited—or required, as the case may be.)

- You can store information on the server—in a File-Maker Pro database, for example. In this case, a unique key to the data is likely to be passed back and forth in HTTP requests, and the data is retrieved as needed.

As a result, it is substantially easier to structure a system in which a single request contains all the data needed to process a transaction as opposed to one in which several different Web pages and forms need to be accessed in order to complete the transaction. Of course, sometimes there is no alternative (in the Shopping Cart example, as in most online commerce sites, you want the customer to access many, many pages and buy many, many items).

The current version of HTTP is 1.1; it is described in RFC 2068, dated January 1997. It replaces HTTP 1.0, described in RFC 1945.

HTML

HTML is the publishing language of the Web. It is a Standard Generalized Markup Language (SGML)—a way of combining text and presentation information in a single text-based file.

Logical Specifications

What HTML provides is a way of logically specifying how a document should look. This notion of logical specification is distinct from a physical specification. A physical specification is exact—for example, this paragraph is set in Palatino type, with a font size of 11 points (the character height) and a line space of 13 points. That is an unambiguous specification. The logical specification that HTML provides interacts with the options that you set in your browser. You can usually choose the default typefaces that are used for proportional and fixed-width fonts. Thus, the Web page author does not specify a font or a size: what is specified is the type of font and the relative size—the user's browser choices determine the results.

This idea of logical specification extends to all aspects of Web pages. Users can resize windows, and so lines are often of varying lengths depending on user (not designer) choices. Tables of data often depend on the size of the window in which they are displayed, so once again the user (not designer) controls a page's appearance.

Elements and Tags

The formatting information in HTML is contained in elements. Elements are interspersed with the content of a Web page and are surrounded by tags that are themselves surrounded by < and >, as, for example, in

```
<TITLE>
Web Example
</TITLE>
```

<TITLE> is the starting tag of the TITLE element; </TITLE> is the ending tag of the TITLE element. The content of this particular TITLE element is "Web Example."

Three points are worth noting about this little example:

- Spacing does not matter except within the content. The three lines shown about could equally well be typed as a single line.

- Capitalization of the tags is irrelevant—<TITLE>, <Title>, and <title> are the same tag. Capitalization does matter for content—Web Example is different from WEB EXAMPLE. In this book, tags are capitalized for clarity.

- Tags usually come in pairs, delimiting the start and end of a logical entity; the second tag is optional in many cases. The second of a tag pair starts with /. Tags are surrounded by the special characters < and >.

Tags can be nested: you can have two paragraphs within a column of a table—and all of those elements must be delimited by tags. If you look at even a moderately involved Web page, you will be impressed by the complication of the HTML.

Most browsers allow you to view the HTML source of a Web page you are viewing. If you have not done so, it is instructive to look at a few "simple" pages.

As new features are added to HTML and as more sophisticated Web sites are demanded, it is clear that HTML itself is becoming too complicated for most people to work with.

The Future of HTML

There are two approaches to this problem:

1. When you use Home Page, you work with a graphical user interface and do not worry about the underlying HTML that is generated. When you do need to modify the HTML for some FileMaker Pro functions, you can do so by knowing exactly where to look—and ignoring everything else.

2. Combining content and formatting information in a single file is a large part of the problem. Increasingly, people are removing the formatting information to separate files. HTML now supports the notion of **style sheets,** which explicitly move formatting to style sheet files. The implementation of FileMaker Pro on the Web relies on **format files**—a similar approach to breaking down the problem into manageable parts.

The current version of HTML is 4.0. HTML 3.2 is still widely used.

Home Page

Home Page 3.0 marks a significant step in the evolution of Web authoring tools. The first generation of such tools simply provided a WYSIWYG (what-you-see-is-what-you-get) way of creating and editing Web pages. In those days (1995–96), Web pages were simple affairs, and HTML 1.0 was a pretty simple language itself.

With rapid adoption of the Web, designers quickly pushed HTML to and beyond its limits. Tables appeared on Web pages, as did forms, frames, and style sheets. The new features in HTML 2.0 and HTML 3.0 posed a challenge to all Web page designers. Home Page, however, solves many of the problems. Its interface is simple and intuitive, leaning heavily on word processing and page layout concepts that are widely known. Whereas there was not a great deal of difference between writing a Web page in HTML 1.0 and using Home Page 1.0, by the time of Home Page 2.0 and HTML 3.0, the difference was significant. Today, it is safe to say that most Web pages are designed using graphical tools like Home Page rather than by writing HTML code.

Because of the rapid development of the Web, many of the most experienced Web designers have grown up with the Web—and with HTML. Many of them look with disdain at graphical tools like Home Page. Similarly, the most experienced programmers in the 1970s and 1980s grew up with primitive languages like Assembler, and they looked down their noses at new-fangled and inefficient tools such as databases and graphical user interfaces. Home Page simply is the easiest way to create and maintain a Web site, and its integration with FileMaker Pro makes it one of the two best choices for use in developing a FileMaker Pro Web site (the other choice is Instant Web Publishing). However, if you prefer to write HTML code, Part III of this book is for you.

The Home Page online documentation and manuals are extensive; the examples and templates provide many design choices for you to copy and learn from. In this chapter, you will find an overview of the points to look out for if you are using Home Page with FileMaker Pro. As with the previous chapter, it is not a summary of the product: it is a guide to the features that matter in this context.

Home Page Environment

With Version 3.0, Home Page provides site management tools that are rapidly becoming essential to anyone who publishes on the Web. There are tools to validate links and to organize the files on your site. As people around the world are discovering, maintaining a Web site is a lot of work.

One way to cut down on that work is not to modify the data on the Web site. As you will see throughout this book, if you can isolate variable information and store it in a database, you can rely on FileMaker Pro to format it as needed. Any data that changes—from daily news items to staff contacts to products, etc.—can be stored in a database, which is much easier to maintain than a Web site. Leave your Web pages for the unchanging information (which may turn out to be little more than your site's name and the basic graphics and navigation tools that appear on every Web page).

Site Management

While not forcing you to do so, Home Page encourages you to create a directory or folder on your computer that mirrors the directory on your Web server. You can open that site in a window that is shown in Figure 3-1.

Note the Images folder: this is a convenient way to group all of your site's graphics into one location. Home Page provides a Consolidate feature that will collect graphics from wherever they may happen to be on your hard disk (or network) and copy them if necessary to the site's Images folder. This prevents problems that arise from having missing graphics.

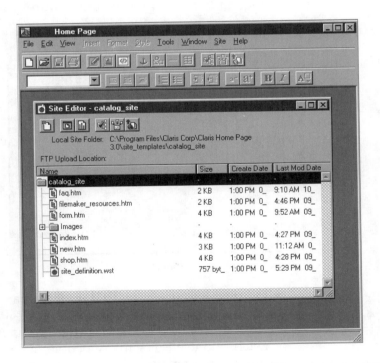

FIGURE 3-1. Site Editor Window

You can have folders within folders—a site within a site, but most people find it more convenient to treat each section of a site as a separate site.

Integrated Uploading

As you can see from Figure 3-2, Home Page keeps track of the files on your site—on your disk as well as uploaded to your Web site. You can let Home Page decide which files to upload and when. Certainly anyone who has forgotten a changed file will appreciate this feature.

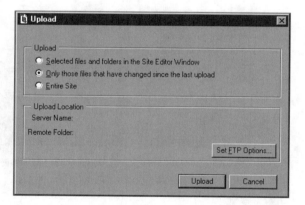

FIGURE 3-2. Upload Window

In Figure 3-3 you see the FTP options that you can set from the Upload window of Figure 3-2. Home Page incorporates the FTP functionality of such programs as Archie, Anarchie, or Fetch into itself. For many people maintaining Web sites, the only time they use FTP is to transfer files to and from the Web: this just lets you get rid of one more piece of software.

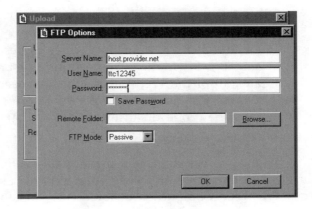

FIGURE 3-3. FTP Options

FileMaker Pro Tools in Home Page

Home Page provides two sets of tools for you to use in creating Web sites that involve FileMaker Pro databases. You can use the FileMaker Pro assistant, which will build the entire site for you automatically (once built, it can be modified as you see fit), or you can use the FileMaker Pro Reference Library for online assistance in coding the pages manually.

Remember that you can use Instant Web Publishing (IWP) to provide access to your FileMaker Pro database; if you do so, you do not need Home Page at all.

FileMaker Pro Assistant

The FileMaker Pro assistant (which is described in detail in "Using the FileMaker Connection Assistant" on page 363), creates all of the Web pages that you need to manipulate a FileMaker Pro database. It lets you store them in a folder—either a new one or an existing one that contains site files already.

To use the assistant, you must have the FileMaker Pro database that you want to use open; it must also have FileMaker Pro Web Companion enabled (see "Instant Web Publishing Environment Steps" on page 104—you use this aspect of Instant Web Publishing even if you are ultimately not going to use IWP).

In this chapter, the To Do example from the FileMaker Pro Education examples is used. It is shown in Figure 3-4 as it looks in FileMaker Pro.

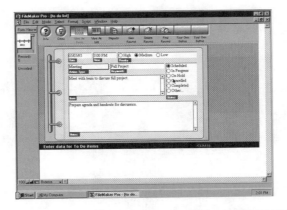

FIGURE 3-4. To Do Example

You choose New... from the Home Page File menu, and then click the Use Assistant button as shown in Figure 3-5.

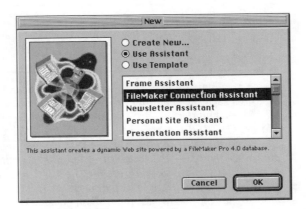

FIGURE 3-5. Using the FileMaker Connection Assistant

You then connect to the FileMaker database as shown in Figure 3-6.

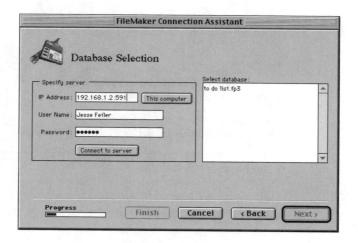

FIGURE 3-6. Selecting a Database

Note that if you are using one computer (as opposed to running the database on a separate computer on a network), you can use the button to select the computer you are working on. Home Page will fill in the IP address (192.168.1.2 in Figure 3-6); however, Web Companion may use a special port on that computer. If the Web Companion configuration uses a port other than 80—the standard—you must type it in after the address preceded by a colon, as in Figure 3-6. Port 591 has been registered as a standard, and it is likely to be the correct port if 80 is not used. There are more details on this in "Summary" on page 121; for now, just remember that if you click This Computer and do not see any databases in the scrolling list at the right of the window, try appending :591 to the IP Address field.

The assistant will then step you through the processes of choosing a layout, specifying how (if at all) searches and sorts can be done, and how the data should be displayed. It will generate the entire site for you.

Even if you decide not to use the assistant, it is very helpful to run through it at least once. You will see the possibilities available to you. Also, if you generate a site from your database (or from one of the examples), you can refer to the HTML code that has been generated to see how to do things.

FileMaker Pro Reference Library

The other way that Home Page helps you is by providing libraries of code that you can insert into your Web pages. This code includes CDML (Claris Dynamic Markup Language) tags that you use to manipulate FileMaker Pro databases. Part III of this book is devoted to CDML.

Summary

Home Page provides a simple and elegant way to create and manage Web sites. It also provides powerful tools to help you integrate FileMaker Pro databases into these sites.

This part of the book has provided an overview of the basics—databases, FileMaker Pro, and Home Page. The next part of the book deals with Instant Web Publishing—the tools that are built into FileMaker Pro that enable you to publish databases without writing any HTML code or developing any special Web pages. (As noted previously in this chapter, you need to turn Instant Web Publishing on to use the FileMaker Connection Assistant in Home Page.)

FileMaker Pro databases on the Web have limitless possibilities, ranging from electronic commerce to Web pages that are modified merely by changing data (rather than changing HTML) to workgroup databases. With Instant Web Publishing, those opportunities are present in just a few hours.

Instant Web Publishing

Instant Web Publishing

This part of the book covers Instant Web Publishing. First, the user experience and interface are described—anyone who uses a FileMaker Pro database that has been published on the Web with Instant Web Publishing needs to understand how to use that database. Next, a chapter describes how you can publish your database. The third chapter helps you configure your database server to support Instant Web Publishing.

Note that while the chapters become increasingly specialized (from general users to database publishers to system administrators), the sequence in which you need to carry out these steps is the reverse of the chapters: you start by preparing the server, then you publish the database, and finally people use it.

The final chapter in this part helps guide you through troubleshooting your database Web site.

Instant Web Publishing is just that—the ability to take a File-Maker Pro database and make it accessible over the Web quickly by selecting a few options. It requires no Web authoring tools and no HTML coding. It does require a few setup steps—most of which you need to do once to enable any Internet publishing from FileMaker Pro; thereafter, only a handful of steps need to be repeated for each database that you publish.

This chapter provides an overview of the process followed by a complete description of the Instant Web Publishing user experience.

It Really Is Instant: A Step-by-Step Example

This is an overview of the Instant Web Publishing process. In this chapter, the Event Schedule example from the FileMaker Pro examples is used to demonstrate the process. You can follow these steps using any of the examples—or any of your own databases.

The Event Schedule example is shown in Figure 4-1. This is the Form view layout; when you open the example another layout may be selected and the data that you see may be different.

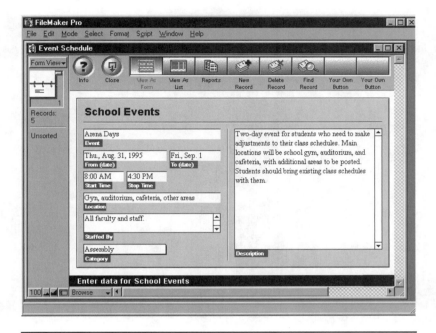

FIGURE 4-1. Event Schedule Example

The FileMaker Pro examples that ship in the Web folder use other Web publishing techniques. Instant Web Publishing is about publishing databases that have not had any special preparation for the Web; experiment with the regular (i.e., non–Web folder) examples.

FileMaker Pro Commands and Functionality

In this and every FileMaker Pro database, there are two sets of commands available to users. Figure 4-2 shows the standard FileMaker Pro commands and functions.

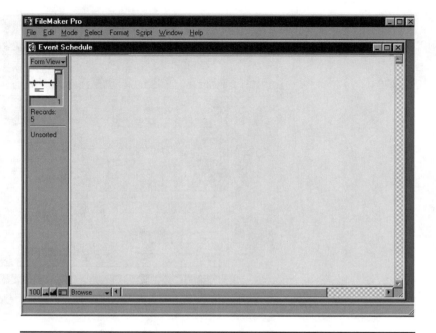

FIGURE 4-2. Event Schedule Example

Standard FileMaker Pro Commands

At the top of the window are the menus and menu commands that are available to users. At the left of the window is the status area, in which are commands that let users select layouts and see the status of the database records. The book control lets you navigate forward and backward by clicking on the upper or lower page. The bookmark at the right shows the relative position of the current record in the file: you can also drag it up or down for fast positioning of the display. (When the display consists of page images, as in Preview mode, the book and bookmark are used to navigate back and forth in the pages rather than in individual records.)

The commands in the menu bar as well as the elements in the status area may change depending on the mode the user is using and the access options that have been set for the database. Furthermore, the status area control at the bottom of the window lets users display or hide the status area as they see fit. (It can also be displayed or hidden by using scripts.)

Database Solution Commands

The custom commands, functions, and controls for the Event Schedule example are shown in Figure 4-3.

FIGURE 4-3. Event Schedule Example

Commands and functions often are combined into FileMaker Pro scripts and are associated with interface elements that are unique to a database solution. In this case, buttons are drawn into the Form view layout and are given solution-specific meanings.

Instant Web Publishing Commands

Once you appreciate the distinction between the FileMaker Pro commands—those that are available to every database and database solution without any effort on your part—and the solution-specific commands—those that you (or the database designer) must implement and design—Instant Web Publishing becomes quite clear.

Instant Web Publishing replaces the first set of commands: the FileMaker Pro commands. If you want custom commands—commands that are customized either in the specific tasks that they perform or in the way in which they are presented in the interface—you must use Custom Web Publishing.

You can create custom commands in scripts that are part of the database, but—with the exception of scripts that run automatically such as when a database is opened or closed—there is no way to execute scripts in Instant Web Publishing. You have no buttons to which you can attach scripts, and the Script menu is not part of Instant Web Publishing.

Just as many people do with FileMaker Pro itself, you can start with the standard commands—or with Instant Web Publishing. Experiment on yourself and with users to see what else is needed, and then customize your database solution—with buttons and interface elements for the FileMaker Pro users, and with Custom Web Publishing for your Internet users.

Instant Web Publishing Environment Steps

There are two sets of steps to using Instant Web Publishing. The first set need only be done once for your computer—and often only once for a local area network (LAN) or intranet that you are using.

1. Set up Internet protocols on your LAN, intranet, or individual computer.

2. Enable and configure FileMaker Pro Web Companion.

For further information, see "Using FileMaker Pro Web Companion" on page 141, which covers all of these points.

Instant Web Publishing Database Steps

Once you have established your environment, these are the steps that you follow to publish an individual database:

1. Create or select a database to publish.

2. Create layouts and associate them with FileMaker Pro Web Companion functions.

3. Set database-specific FileMaker Pro Web Companion parameters.

For further information, see "Preparing FileMaker Pro Databases for Instant Web Publishing" on page 123, which covers all of these points.

The User's Perspective

When you connect to a FileMaker Pro database over the Internet (or via a LAN or intranet), you are able to see and manipulate the database data much as you would if you were using FileMaker Pro directly. This section shows the primary elements of Instant Web Publishing from the user's point of view.

The primary interface features of Instant Web Publishing are

- Home page—normally provided by FileMaker Pro Web Companion

- Table view

- Form view

- Search/Find/Select view

- Sort view

- FileMaker Pro Web Companion help

Once the setup is complete, there is no difference between connecting to a FileMaker Pro database over the Internet, a LAN, an intranet, or using FileMaker Pro's special connection on a single machine with no Internet connection. The setup procedures are described in "Using FileMaker Pro Web Companion" on page 141. In this chapter and elsewhere in the book (unless otherwise noted), all of these connection methods are dealt with as one. Thus, "connecting to a FileMaker Pro database via the Internet" could mean actually using the Internet, a LAN, an intranet, or the single-machine connection.

The Home Page

When someone connects to a computer running FileMaker Pro Web Companion, they see a home page such as that shown in Figure 4-4.

This figure shows the default home page in Microsoft Internet Explorer running on Windows; it looks almost identical whether the browser is Internet Explorer, Netscape Navigator, OmniWeb, or another product. Furthermore, the browser functions the same whether it is on Windows, Mac OS, Unix, or any other operating system.

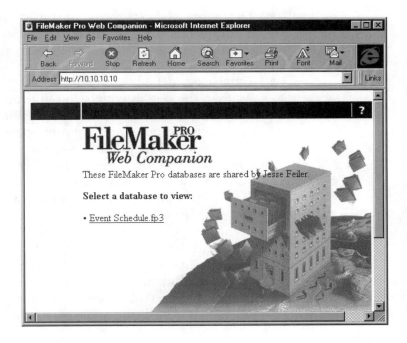

FIGURE 4-4. FileMaker Pro Web Companion Home Page

When you configure FileMaker Pro Web Companion, you can select this default home page or another page that you design and place in a specific location (FileMaker Pro's Web folder). (See "Setting a Default Home Page" on page 146 for more information.)

The default home page shows all of the FileMaker Pro databases that are currently open for sharing on the computer where FileMaker Pro is running. Users can click on any database to open when using Instant Web Publishing. The only databases that are not listed on this page are the following:

- Databases that have not been enabled for Web sharing. (See "Database Preparation" on page 130.)

- Databases whose names (not considering the suffix—if any) end with an underscore. Samples of such names are privatedb_ and privatedb_.fmp.

- Databases opened by FileMaker Pro on other computers than the one to which you are connecting via the Internet. (Thus, if you are running FileMaker Pro on your own computer and are connecting to a computer that is also running FileMaker Pro, the databases on your own computer are not listed on this home page unless they have been opened by the copy of FileMaker Pro that is running on the computer to which you are connecting.)

- Databases not currently opened by FileMaker Pro. A database file that is enabled for Web sharing, has an appropriate name (no underscore), and that is on the FileMaker Pro Web Companion computer must still be opened to be made available.

The home page is set for FileMaker Pro Web Companion, not for each database. Therefore, it may be set up by your Webmaster or by someone at your ISP.

The Browser Window

When you click on a database from the home page, you see it in a browser window such as that shown in Figure 4-5. (The browser windows come in two versions: one for computers with Java installed and one for computers that are not able to run Java.)

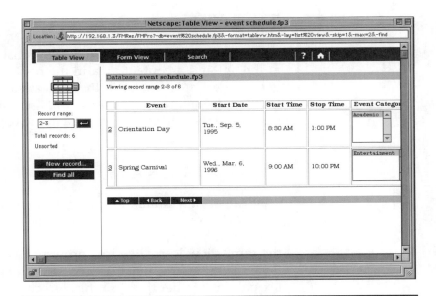

FIGURE 4-5. Database Browser Window: Table View with Java

Across the top is a command bar with tabs letting you move between the Table and Form views, access the Search command, and go to the FileMaker Pro Web Companion help and home pages. (These tabs are shown in Figure 4-5 from left to right.)

At the bottom of each browser window are tabs allowing you to go to the top of the current display as well as to the previous or next page. Depending on the data that is displayed, any of these tabs may be blank (there is no back button on the first page of a display, for example).

All Instant Web Publishing pages adhere to this general format. Between the command bars at the top and bottom of each page, the contents vary depending on the specific view.

Table View

The Table view (shown in Figure 4-5) consists of a status area at the left and a content area in the rest of the window. The general design is similar to that of a standard FileMaker Pro window (compare Figure 4-5 with Figure 4-1): there is a status area at the left and a data area in the rest of the window.

Table View Status Area

The Table view status area lets you navigate through the database records. In Figure 4-5, you see what it looks like in a browser that supports Java. In Figure 4-6, you can see what the same view looks like in a browser that does not support Java: the same functionality is present, but it is achieved with textual links rather than graphical icons.

RECORD RANGE   The Record Range icon (in Figure 4-5) or the Next/Previous/Top/Bottom buttons (in Figure 4-6, non-Java browsers) let you move through the database. You can navigate to specific records by typing in a record number in the Record Range box and pressing the Enter or Return key.

SORT...   When you set up a database for Instant Web Publishing, you can allow users to sort the data as they see fit (other options are available—see "Preparing for Sorting" on page 137). Figures 4-5 and 4-6 show a database for which user-controlled sorting is not enabled; the same database is shown in Figure 4-7 as it appears when the user can sort the data.

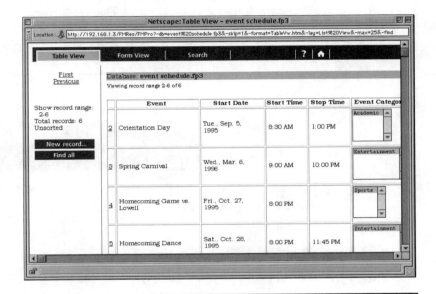

FIGURE 4-6. Database Browser Window: Table View without Java

NEW RECORD   The New Record button lets you enter a new record into the database; it immediately switches you to a Form view page that is empty except for default values that you specified in the Define Fields window. (See "Data Entry Options" on page 56.)

The New Record button will not be present if updates over the Web are not allowed. (See "New Record…" on page 115 for an example of adding a record to the database.)

Note that the New Record button behaves differently from the New Record menu command in FileMaker Pro. In FileMaker Pro, the New Record command (whether used from the menu bar, via a keyboard equivalent, or in a script) creates a new record in the database. The data that you enter is then placed into that record. If you enter no data, the record—blank or with default data—still exists. The New Record button on the Web pages takes you to the Form view page (see "Form View" on page 113), where you can enter data. The record is not added to the database until you click Save on the Form view page.

FIGURE 4-7. Database Browser Window with Sort Button

FIND ALL The Table view displays the currrently selected records in the database (you select them using the Search tab at the top of the page). If you want to see all of the records in the database (thereby discarding the selection you chose in the Search window), click the Find All button. This is the same as the Find All command in the FileMaker Pro menu bar.

Table View Data Area

Most of the Table view display is taken up by the data. Each row represents a single record in the database. At the left of each row is a record number that is underlined—clicking on it opens that record in the Form view (which typically is more detailed than the Table view). (For more information see "Form View" on page 113.)

You control which fields are displayed in the Table view (as you do for all of the Instant Web Publishing views). You create a layout in FileMaker Pro and associate it with the Table view when you configure FileMaker Pro Web Companion (see "Preparing FileMaker Pro Databases for Instant Web Publishing" on page 123). The format that is used is that chosen in the FileMaker Pro layout; the order of the fields is the order that you have chosen in the Define Fields window (see "Field Definitions" on page 53).

Form View

You open a Form view either by clicking the Form View button at the top of a page or by clicking the New Record or Edit Record buttons on pages where they exist, or by clicking the record number at the left of each record's data in the Table view.

The Form view is shown in Figure 4-8 for a browser that supports Java and in Figure 4-9 for a browser that does not support Java. Like the Table view, it has a status area and a data area.

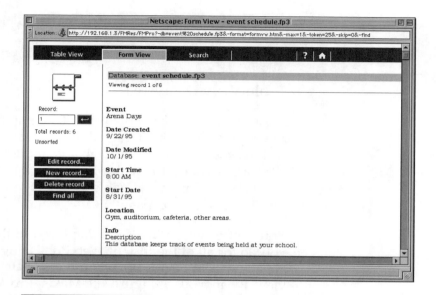

FIGURE 4-8. Database Browser Window: Form View with Java

Form View Status Area

The Form view status area is at the left of each Form view page. It is similar to the status area of the Table view as well as of standard FileMaker Pro layouts.

BOOK ICON   At the top of the Form view status area is a book icon—the same control that is present in FileMaker Pro. Its behavior is the same as that in FileMaker Pro. As with the Record Range control in the Table view, this is created using Java; Figure 4-9 shows the textual equivalents used to provide this functionality in a browser that does not support Java.

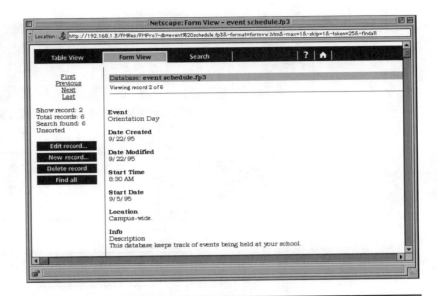

FIGURE 4-9. Database Browser Window: Form View with No Java

EDIT RECORD... The Edit Record... button displays the Form View with editable fields, as shown in Figure 4-10.

NEW RECORD... The New Record... button also opens the data entry view shown in Figure 4-10. As noted previously, the behavior in Instant Web Publishing differs from that in FileMaker Pro: with Instant Web Publishing, the record is only created when you click Save, whereas with FileMaker Pro the record is created as soon as you choose the New Record command.

You can watch the behavior of Instant Web Publishing and FileMaker Pro if you run FileMaker Pro on the same machine as your Web browser, as shown in Figure 4-11.

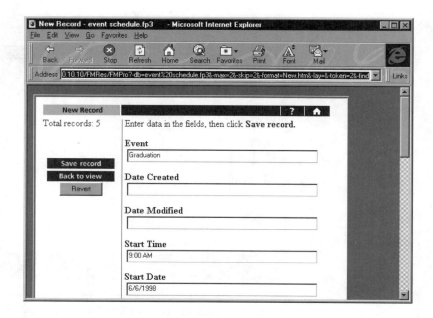

FIGURE 4-10. Adding a Record in a Web Browser

The FileMaker Pro database (which is shown at the right of Figure 4-11) represents what actually is happening. The information in the Web browser is updated on demand—its demand. Thus, the number of records in the database, their sort status, etc., are correct and up to date in the FileMaker Pro window; they are only updated in the browsers of connected network users the next time those browsers are refreshed.

If you think about it for a moment, you can see that this is essential. If the statistics were updated constantly, the displays in Web browsers would be jumping around, and users would have a tough time trying to get their keystrokes in between the screen changes.

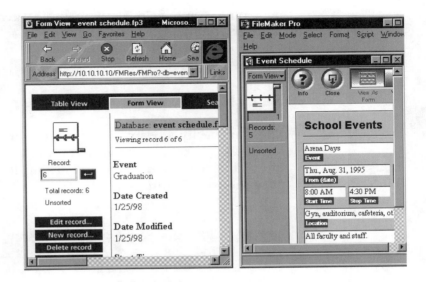

FIGURE 4-11. Result of Adding a Record in a Web Browser

DELETE RECORD The Delete Record button in Form view deletes the currently displayed record (as you would expect). Since browser displays may not reflect the current status of the database, it is possible to delete a record that someone else is viewing—and that they may be about to save (thereby undoing your delete). (See "Transaction Processing" on page 457 for more details.)

Form View Data Area

This differs from the Table view data area in that only one record's data is shown. When you set up a database for Instant Web Publishing, you can specify different fields to be seen in Table views and Form views. Typically, Form views are more complete than Table views, but even Form views may omit some fields (automatically generated sequence numbers, timestamps, etc.).

Search

You can specify a Search view when you set up a database for Instant Web Publishing. If you do, the Search tab at the top of the window is shown. Clicking it opens the search page shown in Figure 4-12.

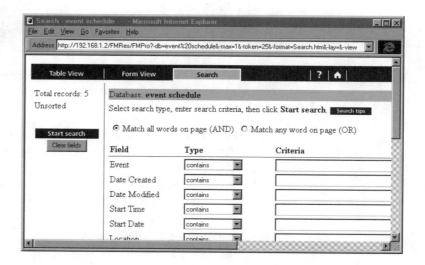

FIGURE 4-12. Starting a Search

Searching, finding, and selecting are synonyms for the same basic database procedure.

The fields that you can search on are specified when you set up your database for Instant Web Publishing; the type of comparison is determined by the kind of field that you have set in the database's Define Fields window.

START SEARCH When you click the Start Search button, the search is performed in the FileMaker Pro database, and the results are presented in a Table view as shown in Figure 4-13.

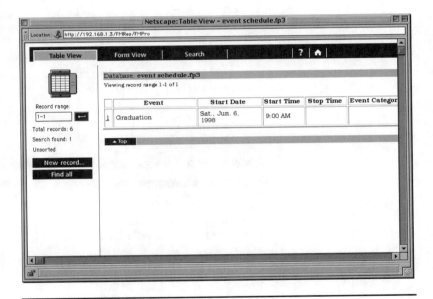

FIGURE 4-13. Results of Search

Sort

If you set up your database to allow users to sort it, they can click the Sort... button in Table view (as shown in Figure 4-7) to open the page shown in Figure 4-14. This allows them to specify the sorting mechanism in much the same way that they can specify the searching procedures described previously.

Remember that sorting a database is often a prelude to manually searching it; sorting is one of the more expensive operations in FileMaker Pro. Whenever you can encourage users (and yourself!) to use the searching routines rather than sorting the database, you will improve performance for all users.

Sort View Status Area

In the status area of the Sort view are three buttons that control the sort processing; to the right are the interface elements that let users specify the sort.

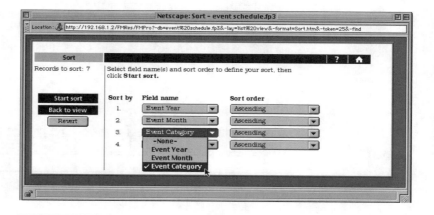

FIGURE 4-14. Sort Page

START SORT This button carries out the sort and returns you to the Table view. It may slightly mislead you into thinking that you will have an opportunity to stop the sort in midstream: you don't. Starting the sort fires it off and it continues until it finishes.

BACK TO VIEW When the sort is complete, you are automatically returned to the Table view. However, if you want to return without having completed the sort, you can use this button.

REVERT The Revert button reverts the settings at the right of the Sort page to their previous values. *It does not revert the database to its unsorted condition.*

Sort View Data Area

You specify the sort using the fields and controls at the right of the window. This is the same interface as that of the Search view; however, you can set up the database to use different fields in the Search and Sort views.

Summary

This chapter has provided an overview of the Instant Web Publishing user experience. You can use it as your Internet-enabled database system, or you can develop your own interface, as described in Part III of this book. Even if you decide to develop your own interface, you should study the functionality of Instant Web Publishing: these are the tools and features that users want from a database.

In the next chapter, you will see how to set up your File-Maker Pro database for Instant Web Publishing.

Preparing FileMaker Pro Databases for Instant Web Publishing

There is little work to setting up a database for use with Instant Web Publishing. Almost all of the features and functions described in the previous chapter are installed for you automatically by Instant Web Publishing.

This chapter shows you how to prepare your database for Instant Web Publishing.

Preparing the Database for the Web

There are two sets of preparations you need to undertake in order to publish a FileMaker Pro database with Instant Web Publishing. Logical preparations are the steps that you follow with regard to the database structure and security. Physical preparations are the changes that you make to the database to allow it to be shared over the Web.

Logical Preparations

A database that is published using Instant Web Publishing will be displayed in the standard formats shown in the previous chapter. You can select the fields that are shown in the Table and Form views, and you can specify the fields that can be used for searching and sorting, but you do not control what the display looks like in terms of graphics and design. (Field formatting is the only graphical attribute that is used from your layouts.)

In the Table view, each record is shown in a single row (see "Table View" on page 110); in the Form view, a single record is shown with the fields arranged vertically (see "Form View" on page 113). From this fact, several consequences arise that have to do with relationships.

As noted previously (see "Relations" on page 67), you can define two types of relationships between databases:

1. A one-to-one relationship means that one record in database A is related to a single record in database B. For example, database A might contain employee address information, and database A might contain employee payroll information. There is a single record in each database for each employee.

2. A one-to-many relationship means that one record in database A is related to any number of records (sometimes none) in database B. Such a structure might be used when database A consists of employee addresses and database B consists of employee evaluations. For

each employee, there is one address but there can be any number of employee evaluations on file.

Portals

FileMaker Pro allows you to establish one-to-many relationships between two databases. You display the data of one-to-many relationships in a **portal**, where the portal contains the records from the "many" database that are related to the "one" database record currently being browsed. Figure 5-1 shows the Contacts database from the Integrated Solution example that ships with FileMaker Pro.

There are two portals in this database; each contains records from a related database in which multiple records can exist for this contact. You can spot the portals because they have vertical scroll bars and contain structured data elements in similarly formatted rows (they are the Phone, URL, Email portal in the upper right and the Action History portal in the lower right). The General Comments field in the lower left is a simple text field, not a portal: it does have a vertical scroll bar, but it does not have structured data elements in similarly formatted rows.

You can look at all of the Contacts database's relations by choosing the Define Relations command from the File menu; Figure 5-2 shows the results.

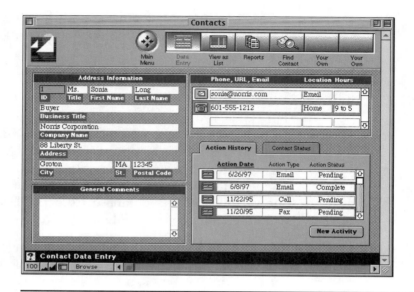

FIGURE 5-1. Contacts Database with Two Portals

The triplet of Activity Log | Date, Activity Log | Type, and Activity Log | Status is used for the three headings in the Activity History portal in the lower right. When you click on the appropriate tab, the contents of the portal change to use a different layout that uses another relationship. This is an example of making FileMaker Pro do the work that you otherwise might do in a script.

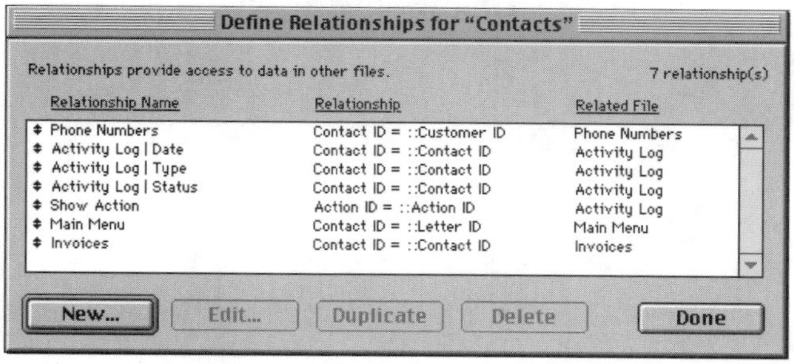

FIGURE 5-2. Relationships for Contacts Database

Given a database structure such as this, try to imagine how you could possibly squeeze the data onto a single line as the Table view must do. It is difficult to incorporate a one-to-many relationship in a single line without making for a very complex format. Displaying a database (such as this one) with two sets of one-to-many relationships is not easy. One of the points of a tabular display is to allow people to compare data by looking down columns: if the columns are variable and complex, such comparisons are difficult.

This is why data from portals can cause problems when displayed using Instant Web Publishing. If your database has portals, you have three choices:

1. Experiment with Instant Web Publishing and see what the result looks like. If it is too complex and complicated to easily read (remember that you probably know the data better than your users do, so it will always be easier for you to read it), try to simplify it by using a layout with fewer fields.

2. Use Custom Web Publishing (as described in the next two parts of the book) to display the related records. This is one of the most common reasons for using Custom Web Publishing, and examples abound for this. Home Page's FileMaker Pro database assistant is remarkably adept at automatically creating Web pages that support portal data.

3. Modify your database to remove the one-to-many relationship. This almost always involves unnormalizing the database (which is the reason for creating one-to-many relationships in the first place). If you must do so, refer to "First Normal Form (Eliminate Repeating Groups)" on page 24 and follow the directions in reverse (that is, do not create a database that adheres to first normal form).

Related Fields

Related fields from another database where the relationship is one to one can easily be displayed by Instant Web Publishing. There is no ambiguity and there are no formatting problems. There is, however, a potential security problem.

When you define a relationship in FileMaker Pro, if a database allows you to relate to it, your database essentially takes on security responsibilities. Subsequent changes to the related database's security status will not affect those relationships. In other words, don't plan on adding security at some later time: you can always remove security, but adding it may be tricky.

When it comes to related fields, remember that the database that is creating the relationship (the one in which you define the relationship with the Define Relations command from the file menu) is responsible for the security of both its data and that in its related fields from another database.

Furthermore, note that a database that is opened as part of a relationship is listed on the FileMaker Pro home page (see "The Home Page" on page 106) if it is shared and can be opened from there.

Security

Most people create a database project on a single computer, and they typically use either no security or a password that allows them unrestricted access to the databases. (If you don't do this, it can be difficult to create, test, and debug the databases.) Unfortunately, this is precisely the environment that leads to inadvertent security breaches in related databases.

Publishing a database—whether on the Internet, an intranet or LAN, or on a public access kiosk—can inadvertently publish all sorts of information that you would prefer not to have visible. A chapter later in this book ("Security" on page 409) deals with the issue at length. For now, you can use the following rules of thumb, which will be refined later:

- If the data you are publishing—in the database and any other databases related to it—is public information, worry only about security with respect to updates. In other words, make certain that the data cannot be changed inappropriately, but don't worry about its publication. (Some people might find it amusing to change all of the telephone numbers in the directory that you publish if you allow them to update the data.)

- If the data is in any way sensitive, do not publish it in any manner without preparing—and verifying—a security scheme. This involves publication over networks as well as the "publication" that ensues when you let someone use the computer on your desk or when a friend borrows your laptop for a weekend.

- Unless you have carefully planned and tested your security implementation, assume that every field of every record of every database that is involved with Web publication is visible. As noted previously, a relation to one field of a database exposes that entire database via the FileMaker Pro home page. Remember that database design includes security, and that the most logical and efficient database structure (fully normalized, for example) is often modified to be less logical and less efficient while isolating certain data fields for security reasons.

- Remember that data and software for which you are responsible can get you in a lot of trouble. You may not take security seriously, but some people do—and they tend to be people who can inconvenience you (to say the least). Remember that the gangster Al Capone was finally brought down on a tax evasion charge—not on gangsterism. Although the law is widely flouted, it is illegal in the United States to export software that implements a form of encryption known as strong encryption. That form of encryption is widely used in Internet software—including browsers such as Microsoft Internet Explorer and Netscape Navigator. Taking a laptop computer with such software installed out of the United States is a violation of law (actually, it is an act of treason, for reasons that are too complicated to explain).

This section is not designed to scare you away from publishing databases on the Web; it is only intended to remind you that you are playing in a different league when you publish your databases, and you must remember to pay attention to some things that previously may not have mattered.

Database Preparation

Having prepared your database with regard to its structure and security, you are ready to physically prepare it to be shared over the Web. From the File menu, choose the Sharing… command, as shown in Figure 5-3.

FIGURE 5-3. Sharing... Command

This will open the File Sharing Setup window shown in Figure 5-4.

If the Sharing... command is disabled, that is because you do not have authority to export data from the database. Use a password that does give you such authority: for further information consult the FileMaker Pro documentation.

In the Companion Sharing section at the bottom of the window, click Web Companion. If it is not visible or is disabled (you cannot check the box), read "Setting Up FileMaker Pro Web Companion" on page 143.

FIGURE 5-4. File Sharing Setup

The Single User and Multi-User buttons at the top of this window are used to control sharing among multiple users of FileMaker Pro. When you share a database via FileMaker Pro Web Companion, it is normally not a multi-user environment: there is one "user"—FileMaker Pro Web Companion. It services requests from users on the Internet or your local network.

Layouts for the Web

Your next step is to prepare and configure the layouts that Instant Web Publishing will use. You can set them by clicking the Set Up Views button at the bottom of the File Sharing Setup window (Figure 5-4), by double-clicking the FileMaker Pro Web Companion entry in the Companion Name view at the bottom of that window, or by choosing Web Companion from the Preferences/Document menu.

For each of the layouts that Instant Web Publishing will use, you need to supply a layout. This layout can be a default layout consisting of all fields (created automatically by File-Maker Pro) or it can be a new layout that you create with the relevant fields for Table or Form view, searching, and sorting. You can reuse layouts as you want; therefore, you can have anywhere from zero to four layouts when you use Instant Web Publishing.

As noted previously, the graphical elements of a layout (including text styles of data) are ignored for Instant Web Publishing. All that matters are the fields that have been selected and the field formats that you have set for them.

Setting the Table View Layout

Once you have opened the View Setup window by any of the means previously described, you can set the layout for each view. The Table view setup is shown in Figure 5-5.

The default value of the pop-up menu (highlighted in Figure 5-5) simply selects all of the fields from the database for that view. You need not create any layout at all to use this default.

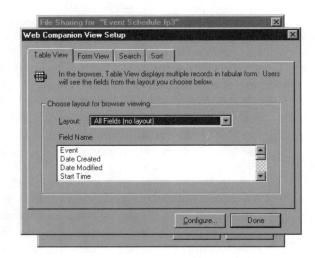

FIGURE 5-5. Web Companion View Setup (Table)

Setting the Form View Layout

The Form view setup is shown in Figure 5-6. It functions just as the Table view does. In this figure, however, you can see how the layouts that you have created in the database are available for your choice in this window.

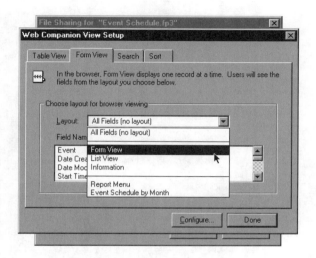

FIGURE 5-6. Web Companion View Setup (Form)

The layouts shown here are those from the Event Schedule sample that has been used previously. Note that those layouts include some prepared for printing as well as layouts that are designed purely for interface features—they have no data. Thus, the Report Menu layout, which is shown in Figure 5-7, contains no fields that would be usable by Instant Web Publishing. Note also that you associate database layouts with Instant Web Publishing views only with this window: you could select the database layout "Form View" for the Instant Web Publishing Table view if you wanted to.

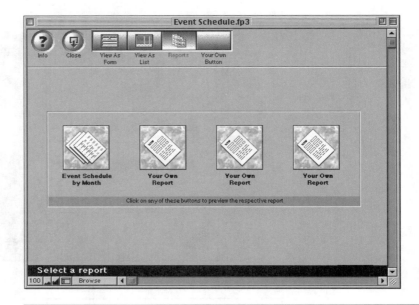

FIGURE 5-7. Report Layout from Event Schedule Database

Setting the Search View Layout

The Search tab in the Web Companion View Setup window functions exactly the same way: the same rules apply.

Preparing for Sorting

The Sort tab in the Web Companion View Setup window functions differently from the other three. When you click it, you open the window shown in Figure 5-8.

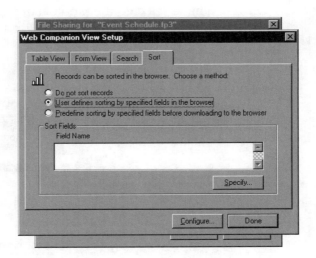

FIGURE 5-8. Web Companion View Setup (Sort)

There are two stages to setting up sorting for Instant Web Publishing. In the first, you select which of the three sort options you want:

1. No sorting.

2. Users can sort on fields that you specify according to options that they choose (such as whether to sort in ascending or descending order).

3. You can specify not only the fields but also the details of the sort; if you do so, the database is sorted when-

ever a user looks at it in Table view (the view that shows more than one record at a time). Remember that sorting is an expensive operation and that specifying an automatic sort to be performed many times can be injurious to your database's performance. Encourage searching rather than sorting.

Once you have selected the kind of sorting to be allowed, you click the Specify button to open the window shown in Figure 5-9.

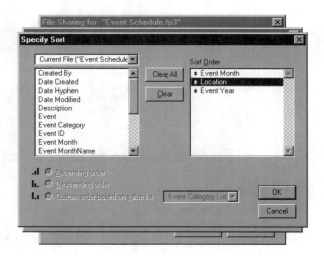

FIGURE 5-9. Web Companion View Setup (Sort Specification)

This is a familiar window to users of FileMaker Pro: it is the standard window in which you specify any sort. As shown in Figure 5-9, the window appears as it does when the second sort option is selected (allowing users to specify the direction of the sort). If the third option is selected (you specify the fields and the direction of the sort), the buttons at the bottom of this window are enabled.

Summary

In the previous chapter you saw how Instant Web Publishing appears to users; this chapter has presented a step-by-step guide to implementing the features and functionality presented previously.

Both chapters, though, rely on FileMaker Pro Web Companion being installed and configured. This needs to be done only once for your FileMaker Pro server: in fact, you may never need to do it yourself. Your Webmaster or network administrator may do it for you, and you may find everything set up so that you can skip the next chapter.

However, if you are the Webmaster or network administrator (and possibly everything else as well), the next chapter is for you.

Using FileMaker Pro Web Companion

FileMaker Pro Web Companion needs to be configured only once for the Web server to which people will connect to access your database. It may have been configured by your network administrator or Webmaster: if so, you can skip this chapter. Alternatively, you may publish your FileMaker Pro database on the Web by using a third-party product such as Lasso or Cuesta: these substitute for FileMaker Pro Web Companion.

This chapter describes what FileMaker Pro Web Companion does and how to configure it for use over a network as well as on a single computer (which is usually used as a testing mechanism).

What FileMaker Pro Web Companion Does

When you connect to an Internet site, the protocol that you are using (HTTP—the Web; FTP—file transfer; SMTP, POP, or IMAP—e-mail) determines the **port number** that you contact. An Internet service provider normally runs several programs to handle Internet requests—a Web server, a mail server, an FTP server, etc. Each of these is said to listen at a specific port; messages coming to that port on that Internet site are handled by the appropriate server. (For more information, refer back to "Connecting to an Internet Address" on page 40.)

Each Internet protocol has a default port number: for the Web (HTTP), that port is 80. As a result, when you connect to FileMaker's site (www.filemaker.com), you do not have to add the port number to the address (www.filemaker.com:80)—it is done for you automatically. (Note that port numbers are separated from Internet addresses by a colon, not a period.)

This mechanism allows several servers to handle the same protocol on a single machine, and it will become important when you configure FileMaker Pro Web Companion (see "Ports" on page 148).

Requests for Web pages are routed over the Internet to the Internet address of the computer on which your version of Web Companion is running. FileMaker Pro Web Companion is a server that listens at the specified port; when it receives a request, it processes it and returns the appropriate page to the user. Typically, Web Companion constructs that page dynamically; it may be the default FileMaker Pro home page, it may be the results of a search, or it may be a complicated page assembled from FileMaker Pro and created using Custom Web Publishing. Whatever it is, it is Web Companion's job to fulfill the request.

For Web Companion to do its work, FileMaker Pro must be running on the same computer. You do not run Web Companion explicitly, nor do users access it directly. Their access to it is by sending an HTTP query to the Internet address of the machine on which Web Companion is running.

Setting Up Your Internet Connection

Before you start, your computer needs to have TCP/IP installed on it. Most computers now come with TCP/IP installed: you need it to access Internet services such as e-mail and the Web. The easiest way to set up TCP/IP is to install a Web browser: often they come with automated installation scripts. (Note that TCP/IP is the protocol involved; your form of connection to the Internet—dial-up, local network, etc.—is a separate issue. TCP/IP can work with many forms of connections.)

Make sure that a Web browser works on your computer before attempting to configure Web Companion.

Setting Up FileMaker Pro Web Companion

There are two steps to setting up FileMaker Pro Web Companion:

1. You configure FileMaker Pro to use FileMaker Pro Web Companion.

2. Next, you set the parameters to customize FileMaker Pro Web Companion.

Remember that this is done only on the machine from which you will publish databases: you do not have to do this on computers that will merely access FileMaker Pro databases over the Web.

Enabling FileMaker Pro Web Companion

Use the Preferences/Application command as shown in Figure 6-1 to open the window shown in Figure 6-2. Click the Plug-Ins tab.

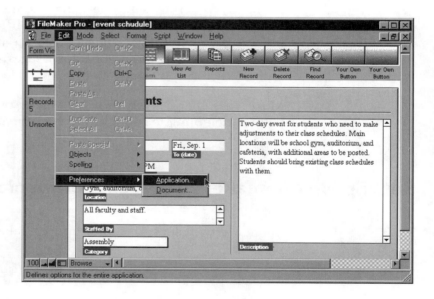

FIGURE 6-1. FileMaker Pro Preferences Menu

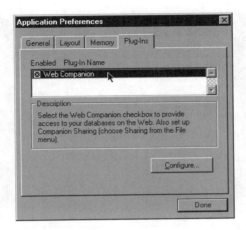

FIGURE 6-2. Application Preferences (Plug-ins)

Web Companion should be listed in this window: if it is not, FileMaker Pro has not been properly installed. If it is grayed out and you cannot check the box to enable it, TCP/IP is not installed properly.

Click the Configure button to configure Web Companion.

Configuring FileMaker Pro Web Companion

The Web Companion Configuration window is shown in Figure 6-3.

All that you need to do is to click the box that enables Instant Web Publishing. However, if you want, you can customize FileMaker Pro Web Companion in a number of ways. (Remember that this customization refers to this computer and all of its FileMaker Pro databases: you are not customizing an individual database.)

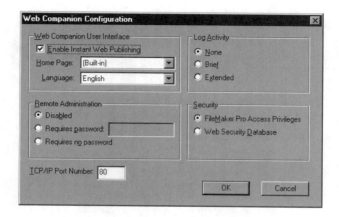

FIGURE 6-3. FileMaker Pro Web Companion Configuration

Setting a Default Home Page

When someone connects to FileMaker Pro Web Companion via the Internet, they are presented with a home page. When Instant Web Publishing is enabled, that page is generated by Web Companion and consists of all open FileMaker Pro databases. You can click on the database that you want to browse.

As noted previously, databases whose names end with an underscore are excluded from this list; databases that are opened as part of a relationship are included (provided that they have been configured for sharing). This default home page, which is built dynamically by Web Companion, can inadvertently provide access to databases you may not want to publish. For that reason, you may want to substitute your own home page that lists only the databases you do want to publish. (To see how to do this, see "Controlling Your Database with HTML" on page 207.)

Another reason for creating your own home page is so that the primary logo is that of your organization rather than that of FileMaker Pro. Or, you may want to include additional information on the page that helps your users.

Whatever your reason, if you do want to create your own home page, place it in the Web folder inside the folder where FileMaker Pro is located. (The **Web folder** is created when you install FileMaker Pro. It is the folder where Web Companion looks for all of the files that it needs.)

The links on your home page can be used to open databases published with Instant Web Publishing. For the syntax of these links, see "FileMaker Pro Web Companion Requests" on page 218.

Languages

The language pop-up menu lets you select the language that FileMaker Pro will use in creating its dynamic page and in its help pages.

Logs

You can select the type of log—if any—that you want Web Companion to maintain. Logs are discussed in greater detail in "Logs" on page 427. You need not make any changes to the default values in order to get started with Instant Web Publishing.

Security

Security features that you can set up in the FileMaker Pro Web Companion include general security and password control. These issues are discussed further in "FileMaker Pro Security Features" on page 414 and "Remote Administration" on page 426. Again, you need not make any choices here to get Instant Web Publishing up and running.

Ports

The final entry on the Web Companion Configuration dialog box may need your attention. As noted previously, each Internet server application listens at a given port number. You address the specified computer with an Internet address and either implicitly or explicitly direct your message to the appropriate port.

Port 80 is the default port for HTTP. When you request a Web page, the address starts with "http," and the default port number is 80. If the computer has another application running that manages Web pages, it will probably have port 80 in use. You must assign another port number to FileMaker Pro Web Companion so that the two sets of messages (requests for Web pages and requests for database access) do not conflict.

You can use any port number that you want, but port 591 has been registered with the Internet Assigned Numbers Authority; it should be your first try if 80 proves to be a conflict. Even if there is no other Web application running on your server, you may want to configure Web Companion to use port 591 so that if a Web application is added to the configuration it will not cause a conflict. Although it is technically possible, it is impractical in most cases to use a port number other than 80 for the default Web server application.

If you are trying to connect to a FileMaker Pro Web Companion site and you cannot do so, try adding :591 after the address.

Using FileMaker Pro Web Companion without a Network

There are two ways to use FileMaker Pro Web Companion on a single machine—that is, to use one computer both as the server (Web Companion) and as the client (accessing the database via a browser):

1. If your computer has an IP address, you can use the IP address of that machine as the URL to which to connect.

2. If your computer does not have an IP address, you can configure the special IP address 10.10.10.10 for FileMaker Pro Web Companion to use.

Using an Existing IP Address

When a computer is connected to the Internet, it has an IP address—a combination of four sets of numbers (such as 196.162.1.4). If your computer is always connected to the Internet—either directly or through a router on a local network—it has such an address that remains constant.

If your computer is connected over a dial-up phone line, the IP address may change with each connection. Typically, the first two or three sets of numbers are the same (representing the Internet service provider's address), and the last set of numbers varies as you connect to different modems. This is the type of connection that most dial-up users have; the technical term is SLIP or PPP.

A third case exists when you connect to the Internet over a local network. A device called a **router** is used to connect the network to the Internet; each computer on the local network has an IP address that may be based on the router's address.

Thus, with a dial-up connection to an Internet service provider whose Internet address is 255.231.1.0, each person connecting receives an address such as 255.231.1.1, 255.231.1.2, and so on. In cases where the router connects once for all of the computers on the local network, each person connecting over that network receives an address such as 192.168.1.2 or 192.168.1.3—where the base address (192.168.1.1) is the address of the router on the local network.

In the first case (a static IP address), you specify the IP address for your computer in the Network control panel (Windows) or the TCP/IP control panel (Mac OS). In the second case (PPP or SLIP), you specify the Internet service provider's IP address, and your computer's IP address is dynamically assigned each time you dial in. In the third case (called DHCP), you specify the address of your network's router, and it assigns your computer's IP address each time you connect.

Why This Matters

You must know how the machine with FileMaker Pro Web Companion on it is set up. If it uses a static connection, you can connect to that IP address at any time and be connected to Web Companion (provided that it is running). For a dynamic IP address (either on a dial-up connection or on a LAN that uses DHCP), you can connect using the IP address that has been assigned when that compter connected to the network. Thus, the address that works today may not work tomorrow. This is bearable for testing (you can always look to see what the address is that you need), but it does not work well for production environments.

For this reason, it is preferable to run Web Companion on a computer whose IP address is known and predictable. In practice, this means either a computer that is always connected to the Internet or one that is connected via a dial-up connection for which the Internet service provider offers the option of a static IP address—a guarantee that you will always get the same address. (Note that not all ISPs do not offer this service and that it normally costs extra.)

Using a Special IP Address

You can use a special IP address (10.10.10.10) to bypass all of this. You set the IP address of the computer on which File-Maker Pro Web Companion is running to 10.10.10.10, and you can connect to it over your local network. This can make testing easier for you. Unfortunately, it means that that computer needs to be reset if it is to be used for normal Web access.

A common use of the special IP address is to test using one machine. For dial-up connections, an IP address is only assigned when the computer is connected to the Internet. Using the special IP address, that computer has an IP address when it is not connected to the Internet—and you can connect to it by typing 10.10.10.10 into your browser's URL field.

Details on setting up a special IP address are contained in a Read Me file that is located on the CD-ROM that contains FileMaker Pro. Be aware that there are normally two Read Me files on that CD-ROM: one is at the root level of the CD-

ROM and contains marketing and descriptive information. A second one is located in the same folder as FileMaker Pro itself and contains errata, technical information, and these instructions.

If you decide to set up a computer with the special IP address, keep a careful record of the parameters that you have changed so that you can change them back later. Otherwise, you may cripple that computer for later Internet access.

Domain Names and IP Addresses for FileMaker Pro Web Companion

Domain names—such as www.filemaker.com—are associated with a specific IP address by the domain name authority in each country. (That association is part of the registration process for the domain name.) After a domain name is registered, people can type in a meaningful URL (like www.filemaker.com) instead of a quartet of digits (the true IP address).

When you connect to a site, a default Web page is displayed—often index.html. If you are using FileMaker Pro Web Companion to manage your site's home page, it can generate a default home page or use a custom home page that you have specified, as described previously. In this way, anyone who connects to your site will automatically be connected to Web Companion.

In most cases, this is not the best structure. Usually it is best to continue to provide your own home page (index.html or whatever your ISP requires). On that home page, include a link to the FileMaker Pro Web Companion home page.

If Web Companion is running on another computer (as is the case if your primary site is on a Unix machine and a different computer runs FileMaker Pro Web Companion and File-Maker Pro), link to the other computer using either its domain name or IP address. In this case, the default port of 80 is often sufficient, since the computer that runs FileMaker Pro and Web Companion does not support other Web services and there is no conflict between port numbers.

In either case, the user experience is the same: on your home page, users will find details of who you are, contact information, etc. Then they will find a link that takes them to File-Maker Pro Web Companion's home page and from there to all open FileMaker Pro databases. (If you have several File-Maker Pro servers, you might have several links—in a school or college they might be to the Personnel Department, Student Admissions, Calendar, etc.)

As with all Web sites, assume that locations of pages will change. If at all possible, place links to your FileMaker Pro database(s) in one place—such as on your home page—rather than scattering them throughout your site. In that way, when the address of your FileMaker Pro computer changes (and it will), you have only one link to change. All the other links on your site will point back to the database link on your home page and it is just that one link that will be out of date.

Summary

Setting up FileMaker Pro Web Companion is not complicated; however, like any task that is done only occasionally, it is easy to forget a step or two.

To ensure that Web Companion has been properly configured, launch FileMaker Pro and open one of the sample databases in the Web folder installed with FileMaker Pro. Try to connect to it using the appropriate IP address for that computer (either from a browser on that computer or another one). If you cannot, stop here and backtrack to get Web Companion installed properly. Then work with your own databases. FileMaker Pro Web Companion needs to be properly installed for any FileMaker Pro publishing to succeed.

The final chapter in this part covers basic troubleshooting.

Testing and Troubleshooting Instant Web Publishing

When it comes to testing and troubleshooting your Instant Web Publishing site, you need to take into account both the issues of database testing and of Web site testing. This chapter provides an overview of the steps to take.

The main points in this chapter are

- Why test

- What to test

- How to test

- Solving problems in public

Why Test

Some people think that when they have followed the steps in the previous chapters and managed to access their FileMaker Pro database via a Web browser their work is through. It is only beginning.

Whether your responsibility is primarily for the database operations, the data itself, the Web site, or some combination, you have to test that everything is working properly. Although there are a few isolated cases in which database publication is done primarily for one person's convenience (so that he or she can access a private database from several different locations), most Web publication is done so that a number of people can access a single database. By its very nature, the publication of your Web database is a public act: your work is on display. For that reason alone, you should make certain that everything works as promised.

Beyond that, remember that by publishing a database, you are taking responsibility for the work of others. If they are able to update the database, an accident in which updates are lost does not just waste your time—it wastes the time of your colleagues (and possibly customers and clients!).

What to Test

Every aspect of the project needs to be tested. You can break the testing down into manageable phases:

- Test the database itself.

- Test the Web design.

- Test the operations.

Testing the Database Itself

Before you worry about the Web aspects of your database project, test the layouts, field edits and validations, relations, and so forth. Is all the data stored that is needed? Can all the data be retrieved appropriately?

You do not have to test the database layouts that may have been created for a non-Web version of the database project (since they are not used in Web publishing). Similarly, you do not need to test reports, scripts, and other interface elements that are not used.

Make certain that the database you are publishing on the Web is clean and correct before you worry about the Web features.

Testing the Web Design

Next, test the Web design itself. This is very easy with Instant Web Publishing—the primary thing you need to test is that there is a way to get to the FileMaker Pro Web Companion home page (default or custom) from the appropriate locations on your Web site. You should also test that the appropriate fields are shown in the Table and Form views, and that searching and sorting use the correct fields. Pay particular attention to security issues for databases whose fields are related. In the Table view, consider the pros and cons of every field that you include in that layout—the more fields you display, the harder it is to read the output and the more time it takes to process requests. Strike an appropriate balance between efficiency and complexity.

With Custom Web Publishing, this type of testing also entails testing that the custom-written Web pages and format pages do in fact properly display the data and that they function as promised.

Testing the Operations

Perhaps the most complicated part of testing your database is testing the support and maintenance operations that are described in Part V starting on page 407. It is easy to think that backups will just happen—they don't. It is tempting to think that disks and servers won't crash—they do.

What will you do if your database becomes corrupted due either to a hardware failure or to accidental (or malicious) misuse? What happens if FileMaker Pro and Web Companion are not running when your Web site is accessible? How do you let people know where the problem lies? You are often judged not by how well your database functions when everything goes well but by how it functions when there are problems. (Remember how frustrated you can become when you cannot connect to a site on the Web.)

How to Test

Books have been written about testing systems—lengthy books, and many of them. Depending on the data that you are publishing and the environment in which you are publishing it, you may want to delve very deeply into this issue. Books on client/server architecture and on distributed databases as well as on mainframe systems contain testing strategies and techniques that are applicable to the general case of publishing databases on the Web.

This section covers several specific and critical testing tips.

Use Different Computers

Although it can be very convenient to develop and test a Web site on a single computer, be very careful about doing any but the most cursory testing in such an environment. Graphics and links that function perfectly in such a case may in fact fail when they are moved to the normal server. This happens when the graphic or link accidentally points to a specific file on your own computer. It all works well, but when the files are moved to your Web server, the pages will still be looking for a file on your computer—which is nowhere to be found.

For the same reason, be careful about testing—even over a network—with a connection to the machine on which you have developed a Web site. The safest way to test is to move everything to a different computer from the one you developed on and connect to that computer over a TCP/IP network.

Home Page has tools to verify links and to consolidate image files so that you can reduce the likelihood of these problems.

Filenames

Different operating systems use different naming conventions and different formats for filenames. A suffix of .html or .htm is usually applied to the files that a Web server will use. On some computers, only a three-character suffix is allowed. Therefore, if your files will be moved at any time to such a machine, limit your suffixes to three characters.

This may not be possible if you have to move files among machines that alternately require the .html and .htm suffixes. Always try to find a naming convention that minimizes renaming.

Although most modern operating systems allow spaces within filenames, it is wisest to eliminate spaces and any special characters. Thus, although it make sense to name a directory "Kids Pages," there will be less confusion in the long run if you name the directory "kidspages." ("kids_pages" is a common type of compromise, but even it can cause problems because the underscore character can be missed if you look at it quickly.)

Types of Graphics

The safest types of graphics to use are GIF files and JPEG files. Avoid graphics formats that are optimized for print (TIFF) and that are not fully supported on all platforms (such as Mac OS PICT files). Again, test on as many platforms and with as many browsers as possible.

URLs and Capitalization

Some file systems distinguish between capitals and lower-case letters in filenames; others do not. Thus, for some computers KidsPages is a different file than kidspages. It is wisest not to rely on such subtle differences—particularly because they may disappear when you move files to another environment.

Remember that the Internet and the World Wide Web are composed of many different computers running many different operating systems. Unix—which is one of the operating systems that does distinguish between capitals and lowercase letters—is frequently used for Web servers, which may interact with computers running FileMaker Pro under Windows and Mac OS.

Use Different Browsers

Although HTML is a standard, there are many versions of HTML and many interpretations of the standard. The browser that you use may have some idiosyncracies to it that make your Web pages function properly, whereas they fail in other browsers.

To prevent this problem, stick to standard HTML code and avoid tricks. (You do not have to write any HTML with Instant Web Publishing, but you may have it as part of your Web site.) To test whether you have strayed from the straight and narrow, test the Web site—all of its pages—with the browsers that most of your users might have. It does not matter if your organization is standardized on one browser—perhaps Internet Explorer. Increasingly, people are accessing Web sites from their homes and from out-of-office locations (that is, after all, one of the advantages of the Web). The browser that you use at home may be Netscape Navigator, and the browser that your customer uses might be Netscape Communicator.

Designing a Web site that must be used with a specific browser—or a specific version of a browser—is very dangerous. Anyone who has to access several Web sites will quickly become frustrated as they have to switch browsers. The Web has gained popularity because it is an open standard. Test to make certain that your site is open to all browsers.

The question of browser versions is more difficult. One strategy is to make certain that the current version of a browser is supported, as well as the immediately previous version. If you have access to a prerelease (or beta) version of that browser, you can test that it works, too—that is one of the reasons for distribution of beta versions. Additional features of your Web site (such as Java) may need further testing. This quickly becomes a daunting task. People are starting to consider a technology's capacity for incorporating change when they consider whether to use it.

Use Different Networks

The ways of connecting to the Internet (and intranets) vary. Test using dial-up connections with slow modems as well as using the fastest direct connections that you can find. What is lightning fast with a direct connection may be painfully slow over a modem.

Test Concurrency

The hardest testing for any multiuser database system is testing for concurrent users: what happens if user A is viewing a record while user B is updating it at the same time that user C is sorting the database?

Thinking about concurrency testing is a valuable step in planning your database project. Get in the habit of thinking in terms of multiple users as you design your databases.

Test Failures

It is not enough to put error messages in your database (such as in the data validation edits). Test what happens when the errors are triggered—do the right messages appear?

Test also what happens when users make incorrect entries. Do you catch all invalid input? You will probably find a number of places where you are missing data validation edits. It may make no sense to enter a record in a student database with a blank name for the student's name—but someone will do so (perhaps by inadvertently hitting the Return key).

Don't just test that things work: try to break the system.

Stress Testing

When you publish your database, you may find many more people using it at one time than ever happened before. Using as many people and browsers as you can find, try to see what happens to performance as you add users.

You will probably find an uneven curve of performance: additional users slightly degrade performance until some threshold is reached, at which point all hell breaks loose. Beyond such a threshold, performance may deteriorate so badly that people start to disconnect from your site in the middle of updates, leaving possibly incomplete data around. Before you know it, a performance problem can turn into a data corruption problem.

You may not have the resources to do this sort of stress testing: part of monitoring your database performance should include looking at performance statistics and gathering this type of information from the actual logs of use. (See "Logs" on page 427.)

Save Records

Finally, save records of your testing—particularly of performance testing. You need baseline statistics to know how your database site is performing so that you can monitor changes as they occur.

Solving Problems in Public

This is the last and most important point to consider. When you publish your database (or any pages on your Web site), you are committing to solving problems in public. When you use a FileMaker Pro database on a computer on your desktop, you know if your computer crashes, and you know how things are going.

When you publish that database on the Web, your first clue that something is wrong may be a phone call from an irate user (or your boss). Have a very clear plan available—with options as needed—so that you can react quickly to problems.

A typical plan might include the following steps:

- Immediate steps to take on suspicion of a problem to minimize damage until the scope of the problem is known. (You might limit all access or shut down the FileMaker Pro server.)

- Subsequent steps to restore functionality (use if the problem appears to be one that can be solved while the database is running).

- An alternate set of Web pages that allow read-only access to a database that may have problems. (This is an ideal use of Instant Web Publishing—even in an environment that normally uses Custom Web Publishing.)

- Steps to notify people who may have been affected (or may yet be affected) by the data.

- A final—and essential—step to notify people that all is well.

Summary

Both databases and Web sites require significant testing, in large part because they usually involve a number of people spread over several locations. This chapter has presented some of the points to consider in laying out and maintaining a test plan.

Do not automatically think that a test plan is the final step of a project: in fact, many experienced system designers develop the test plan in conjunction with the initial design of a system. Thinking about what needs to be tested and what may go wrong can often help you design a more robust and complete system.

Instant Web Publishing provides a simple way to publish your FileMaker Pro databases. However, it often is the case that you need more sophisticated functionality and graphics than are available with Instant Web Publishing. The next part of this book examines the most flexible form of Custom Web Publishing—Custom Web Publishing using HTML and the CDML tags that are specific to FileMaker Pro.

Custom Web Publishing with CDML

Custom Web Publishing

Custom Web Publishing (CWP) lets you move beyond the standard templates of Instant Web Publishing to customize the appearance and functionality of your Web pages. Beyond customization, Custom Web Publishing lets you accomplish things that simply cannot be done with Instant Web Publishing—most important, the use of one-to-many relationships that are shown in portals in FileMaker Pro.

This chapter describes the sorts of things you can do with Custom Web Publishing. It concludes with a short section on setting up Custom Web Publishing.

The User's Perspective

With Instant Web Publishing, there are six standard elements of the user's perspective (for more information, see "The User's Perspective" on page 105):

1. The home page—which can be generated automatically or specially designed—shows the databases that are available for use on the computer where FileMaker Pro is running.

2. The Instant Web Publishing pages have standard elements for navigation and information display.

3. The Table view manages multiple records from the database with multiple fields from each record displayed.

4. The Form view shows the fields of a single record and may allow for data entry and revision.

5. The Search view lets users specify a search that may result in a number of records being found; the results of the search are shown in the Table view.

6. Finally, the Sort view lets users sort the database in predefined or dynamic ways.

These are the basic functions of any database project; you can implement them in Custom Web Publishing if you want. The most likely modifications that you will make are to the basic design elements (item 2 in the preceding list) and to the functionality that is available in items 3 through 6.

The examples in this chapter—drawn from examples that ship in the Web folder of FileMaker Pro—demonstrate how Custom Web Publishing can be used.

The Home Page

The home page shown in Figure 8-1 is part of the demonstration in the Web folder. Conceptually, it is similar to the home page shown previously (see "The Home Page" on page 106), but it is not built dynamically. The links to open each of these databases are different from the links generated by a default Instant Web Publishing home page.

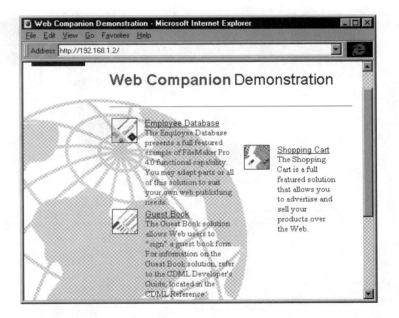

FIGURE 8-1. Custom Web Publishing Home Page

If you use a customized home page, you can mix links to Custom Web Publishing databases and to Instant Web Publishing databases—for details, see "FileMaker Pro Web Companion Requests" on page 218.

A Data Entry Form

Instant Web Publishing creates Form views that have a similar look to them (although you specify which fields are shown). When you create your own Web site, you may want to create form views with your own graphics and style. Figure 8-2 shows a data entry form from the Guest Book example in the Web folder.

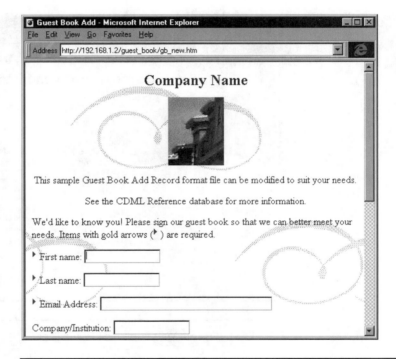

FIGURE 8-2. Guest Book Data Entry Form

Among the customized features shown on this page are

• A customized logo and design.

- Instructions integrated into the data.

Other features that you might want to add to a data entry form include

- Links to other pages with reference information and assistance.

- Values for pop-up lists that reflect database values (for example, the guest book might include a pop-up list that is retrieved dynamically from database values, as shown in Figure 8-3).

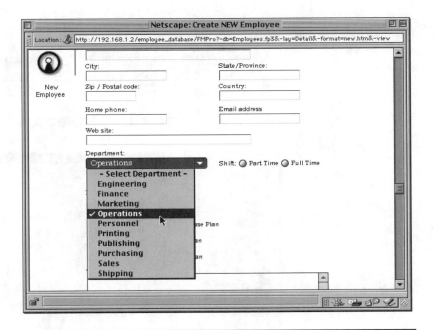

FIGURE 8-3. Dynamic Value List (in Employee Database Example)

A Tabular Data View

Data retrieved from the database can be shown in a tabular data view that is like the Table view of Instant Web Publishing. As shown in Figure 8-4, such a view can contain more information than in the standard Instant Web Publishing view.

The following are among the customized features of this view.

- A changing image in the lower left that lets users view specials and order them with a single click (implemented in the navspecial.html file).

FIGURE 8-4. Tabular Data View

- For further details about an individual item, you can click on its name (in Instant Web Publishing, you click on the record number at the left of each row).

- The Buy It icons at the right of the page let users add an item to their shopping cart, which entails automatically creating a record (see "Generating Data with CWP" on page 178).

- Although this window clearly shows the results of a database search (for specials), it is not generated by a special search screen (such as the Search screen in Instant Web Publishing); rather, it is generated by clicking on a Specials button and executing a prepared search (for all items marked as specials). This is a subtle difference, but one that makes a tremendous difference to the user, who need not worry about the innards of the database.

Creating a Shopping Cart

The Shopping Cart example implements one of the most basic designs for commerce over the Web. The elements of such a system are as follows:

- A customer database

- A product database

- An orders database

Customer Database

This is a database of customers, along with their addresses, billing information, etc. In the Shopping Cart example, this is Customers.fp3. One of the screens that is implemented in the Shopping Cart example is shown in Figure 8-5. Note that this screen allows existing customers to retrieve their own customer record (a search function) and new customers to create a new record. Such dual-function screens are a hallmark of Custom Web Publishing.

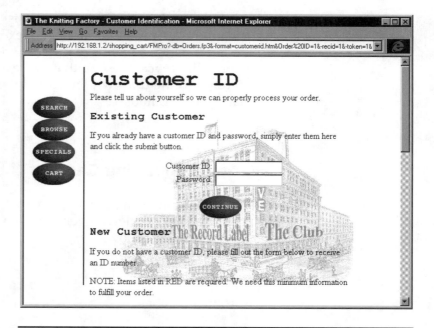

FIGURE 8-5. Customer ID Page

Shopping Cart Orders

This is a dynamically built database containing the order a customer is building (this is the shopping cart). In the Shopping Cart example, this is the Orders.fp3 database and the related OrderedItems.fp3 database. The shopping cart view is shown in Figure 8-6 using a Web browser and in Figure 8-7 using FileMaker Pro itself.

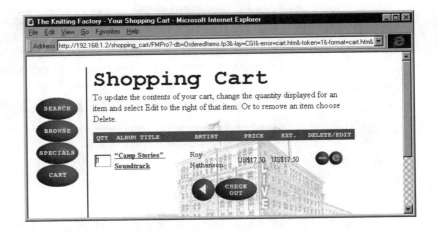

FIGURE 8-6. Shopping Cart Contents

The Orders database contains a related database (Ordered-Items.fp3) with which it has a one-to-many relationship. The OrderedItems database is shown in the portal that is outlined by the dotted line in Figure 8-7.

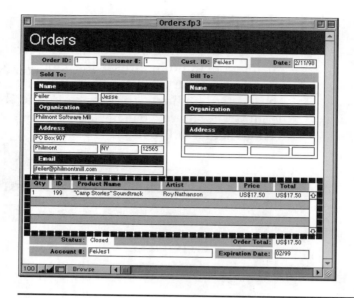

FIGURE 8-7. Orders Database in FileMaker Pro

Products Database

This is a database of products, prices, and descriptions. In the Shopping Cart example, this is the Products.fp3 database. It has a related database, Tracks.fp3. Each product is a recording; there is a one-to-many relationship between each recording and the Tracks.fp3 database, which contains the names and sound files of various tracks. (This structure is parallel to the one-to-many relationship between orders and ordered items.)

Generating Data with CWP

When you click the Buy It icon for an item (as shown in Figure 8-4), you add it to your shopping cart. In FileMaker terms, you add a record to the OrderedItems database that relates to an Order record for your current order (the shopping cart). All of this is fine if you are used to thinking in database terms, but users are accustomed to thinking of orders and invoices. Thus, the information shown in Figure 8-7 is displayed for users using the Custom Web Publishing format shown in Figure 8-8.

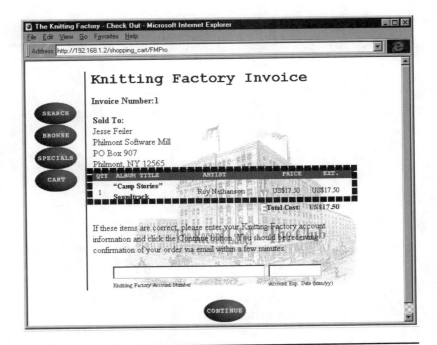

FIGURE 8-8. Shopping Cart Invoice

Note that although only one item has been ordered, the portal that can contain multiple items exists explicitly in the File-Maker Pro layout shown in Figure 8-7; its functionality is provided in the area marked by the dotted outline in Figure 8-8. (See "Looping" on page 241 for more details.)

Sending E-mail with CWP

The final feature of Custom Web Publishing that is widely used is the ability to carry out several actions with the click of a button. In this case, when the user completes an order, various database updates are completed and a summary of the transaction is sent via e-mail as shown in Figure 8-9.

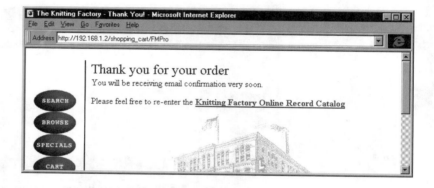

FIGURE 8-9. E-mail Confirmation of Order

A wide variety of operations can be performed automatically in this way, including packaged searches (such as for all specials of the day), updates of databases, and almost anything that you can think of that FileMaker can do with its scripting mechanism.

Setting Up Custom Web Publishing

For its setup, Custom Web Publishing relies on the installation and configuration of FileMaker Pro Web Companion, just as Instant Web Publishing does. There are two steps that must be taken beyond the steps described in "File-Maker Pro Web Companion" on page 141:

1. Although Instant Web Publishing may be enabled, access to your Custom Web Publishing databases must be either through a customized home page (i.e., not the default) or via a link that you create directly to the page. The links that are created in the default Instant Web Publishing home page will not correctly open Custom Web Publishing databases. See "FileMaker Pro Web Companion Requests" on page 218.

2. The databases and Web pages should be in the Web folder that is located inside the FileMaker Pro folder on the computer that is your Web database server. For the sake of convenience, place each database and its associated Web pages, images, notes, etc., into its own folder—as the examples in the Web folder are organized when you install FileMaker Pro.

Summary

This chapter has summarized one typical application that uses Custom Web Publishing. The model given here is very simple and is the structure that is used in most commercial systems. There are some nuances that you may want to deal with (such as what happens if someone leaves a shopping cart unattended for hours, how to manage out-of-stock conditions, payment for transactions, etc.); many of them are handled later in this book. Rest assured, though, that this example is not the sort of simplification you deal with when you write a program that prints out "Hello World." You can use this database project yourself in real life.

The remaining chapters in this part examine the basics of HTML, the details of CDML (the FileMaker Pro extensions to HTML), integration of standard HTML with your FileMaker Pro databases, and issues relating to forms and JavaScript.

This is the heart of the technology involved with FileMaker Pro and the World Wide Web. If you use Instant Web Publishing or Custom Web Publishing with Home Page, you will be using this technology without having to deal with many of its details. In those cases, this part of the book can provide a background reference; if, on the other hand, you prefer to code HTML directly without using the graphical interface of Home Page, you need to explicitly use the syntax and tools described in this part of the book.

\<P>HTML\</P>

HTML—HyperText Markup Language—is the language used for Web pages. You use HTML to publish FileMaker Pro databases on the Web, but depending on your publishing method you may have little or nothing to do with actually writing HTML.

There are two cases in which you do need to concern yourself with HTML:

1. If you need to automatically manipulate FileMaker Pro databases (such as by creating a link that when clicked will add a record, find selected records, etc.), you need to write an HTML request that performs that act.

   If you are setting up a database using Instant Web Publishing and allowing manipulation only by direct user intervention—clicking on the Sort button, for example—you do not need to worry. However, almost all custom solutions with their customized buttons require this minimal amount of HTML coding.

2. If you want to create your own interface pages, rather than relying on the default pages of Instant Web Publishing, you must use HTML to create those pages. However, if you use Custom Web Publishing with Home Page, Home Page generates all of the HTML for you and you may never need to look at it. Nevertheless, since the HTML is stored after Home Page creates it, you can modify it if you want (the HTML used in Instant Web Publishing is created dynamically and you can neither observe nor modify it).

This chapter provides a summary of HTML's structure and a step-by-step walk-through of one of the HTML pages that ships as part of the Shopping Cart example.

Although many books have been written on HTML, this brief summary of HTML may well be enough for you to do much of your work: rarely do HTML programmers and designers start from a blank piece of paper (or blank screen). You usually start from an existing HTML document—from an example, from Home Page, or from another project. The development of most HTML (as of most computer programs) consists largely of modifying and extending existing code. In short, you probably don't need to know how to develop a Web site from scratch; instead, you need to be able to understand how an existing site is designed and implemented so that you can build on the existing work.

HTML Overview

HTML is one of several Structured Generalized Markup Languages (SGMLs). Originally, these languages were designed to integrate content and formatting information into a single text-based document. The formatting information (used to "mark up" the document, as copy editors would say) was enclosed in distinctive characters—typically < and >.

There are other ways of formatting text-based documents:

- The formatting information can be kept separate from the document's content. In such a structure, the formatting information (fonts, paragraph spacing, etc.) is kept—often in binary form—in one part of a file; each piece of formatting information is keyed to one or more parts of the document itself—often using character position numbers.

- Formatting information can be integrated into the text but kept in binary or other nontextual formats.

Word processing programs often use the first of these methods. The use of binary (nontextual) formatting information means that the documents are not easily read by humans. This lack of readability can be an advantage for proprietary formats.

Markup Information

As markup languages have evolved, the information that is provided has been of several kinds:

- Formatting information—including fonts, indentations, headings, etc.—has been present from the start.

- Structural information—often having no visible representation—has been added.

- Meta information—information about the document (author, etc.)—is needed to categorize and organize documents.

The ratio of markup information to content in documents is becoming greater and greater. The original notion of adding a few formatting codes to the text of a document has mushroomed; as a result, one of the primary benefits of SGMLs— the ability to easily read the content and the markup information—has been lost.

Managing Markup Information

For this and other reasons, the trend in SGMLs is to break a single document into many parts. This is done in various ways:

- Formatting information is gradually being moved to style sheets. The details of formatting information— font sizes, colors, etc.—are placed in files that can be referenced from basic HTML documents. This allows the detailed formatting information in the style sheets to be reused; it also allows alternate formatting to be used based on user choices of style sheets. It also makes the basic HTML document much shorter and clearer.

- A relatively new SGML called XML (Extensible Markup Language) has been developed that focuses on content, structure, and data rather than presentation aspects of documents. Elements can be defined by users and can reflect the data that is involved. Thus, whereas standard HTML has elements such as paragraphs and tables, a user of XML can define an element such as name or city.

- Images, applets, and scripts are placed in separate files. They can be included using standard HTML syntax; HTML and CDML files can be included with FileMaker Pro syntax (FMP-Include).

- On demand, FileMaker Pro Web Companion merges HTML and CDML tags with databases and constructs dynamic Web pages. The HTML components themselves may contain style sheets, images, applets, and scripts. Thus, the page that is downloaded to a browser may come from many different locations.

When developing a FileMaker Pro Web site, the use and reuse of images, applets, and scripts is an easy way to keep your files easily readable and understandable. In addition, it makes it easier to keep your site consistent and up to date since changes to a single graphical element that may appear on several pages can be made in a single file that is included several times.

The actual presentation of information in a user's browser is a combination of separate strands of content, structural information, styles, and data (such as database information, as distinct from the surrounding content, which might be logos, informational text, etc.). This combination is made in two locations: at the Web server that assembles the Web page and at the browser that displays the page. Style information (including preferred fonts) may be part of the user's environment, whereas content and data are almost always assembled by the Web server.

It is important to keep this model of the dynamic combination of strands in mind: not only is it what is happening, but it also can make it easier to track down problems (that peculiar font may have been someone's browser choice, not the

Web page author's aberration) and can make multiperson projects easier to manage.

Elements

HTML documents consist of elements. An element consists of content that is surrounded by starting and ending tags. Together the three components (starting tag, content, and ending tag) are referred to as a single element.

Thus, a paragraph in HTML consists of text such as the following:

```
<P>
This is a paragraph.
</P>
```

Some elements are not allowed to have content—for example, a line break element specifies a line break but contains no content. (What would the content be?) These elements contain no ending tag. The line break, for example, is simply inserted in one place in the HTML document.

Other elements have optional content. (The BODY element is one such element.) Elements with optional content do have ending tags—how else would a browser know where the end of the optional content is?

Elements can be contained within one another—a paragraph may be placed within a column or table, for example. However, not all elements can be placed within all other elements.

Except within content, capitalization, spacing, and text styles have no meaning in HTML. If you are using a text-based browser (or the HTML edit mode of Home Page), the HTML code is often formatted using color and indentations to make it easier to read. If you are modifying existing HTML code, one of the first things you may want to do is to make the elements clear by lining up starting tags (such as <P>) with ending tags (such as </P>). Having done so, you will see that the structure of an HTML page becomes clear; modifying an existing page (which is what a great deal of HTML authoring is all about) then becomes a matter of focusing on one or two specific elements that need changes or additions.

Tags

Tags delineate the start and (optionally) end of HTML elements. They are embedded in brackets (< and >.) Capitalization does not matter, but spaces between multicharacter tags should be eliminated (e.g., the break tag, <BR>, should not be written <B R>).

Attributes

HTML elements may have attributes in addition to content. (Some elements that are not allowed to have content may have attributes, and vice versa). Attributes are such items as margins, fonts, filenames, and colors that should be associated with the given element. Attributes are of the form

```
attributename=attribute value
```

Attributes are separated by spaces. Thus, the HTML code

```
<IMG SRC="images/header.gif" ALT="4.0"
    WIDTH=99 HEIGHT=67 BORDER=0 ALIGN=top>
```

consists of the following:

- An IMG (image) element. The IMG element is defined as having no content and no ending tag.

- A SRC (source) attribute, which specifies the file in which this image is located. (This is not the element's content—content is placed physically within the tag; a reference to a file is an attribute.)

- An ALT (alternate) attribute, which is a text string that browsers can display instead of the image if the user has opted not to view graphics.

- WIDTH and HEIGHT attributes, each of which specifies a dimension of the image.

- A BORDER attribute, specifying the width of the border to be placed around the image.

- An ALIGN attribute, indicating how the image is to be aligned with surrounding text.

HTML Documents and Their Editors

HTML documents are text documents—they contain no binary information. Special characters are coded using numerical character references and character entity references.

Characters—whether typed directly or specified with references—may occur as part of quoted strings. All characters that are not part of quoted strings are HTML syntax (such as <P>, <BODY>, and the actual text of a Web page). Thus, numeric character references and character entity references ultimately are enclosed in quotation marks—but they may adjoin standard characters, as in the character string

```
Copyright © 1998 Philmont Software Mill
```

which is typed as an HTML string thusly:

```
"Copyright &copy; 1998 Philmont Software Mill"
```

Numeric Character References

Characters have numeric equivalents. Although it is easiest to describe the letter *A* by typing A, many characters—particularly in non-Roman alphabets—cannot be described by typing a single key. In such cases, it is necessary to use the numeric equivalent. These numeric equivalents are typically expressed in hexadecimal or decimal notation. In hexadecimal, each Roman character consists of two digits, each of which can have the value 0–F (in the sequence 0,1,2,3,4,5,6,7,8,9,A,B,C,D,E,F). In decimal, each Roman character consists of one digit with the value 0–255. Unicode and double-byte characters use four hexadecimal digits and corresponding decimal values.

A numeric character reference for the character å is å in hexadecimal and å in decimal. The difference is the presence (or absence) of the # immediately following the &#. Capitalization has no effect on numeric character references. &xe5; is the same as &XE5;.

Character Entity References

Certain commonly used characters can be described by symbolic references. For example, the copyright symbol ©, which cannot be typed with a single keystroke, can be described using the character entity reference ©, which is much easier to remember than its numeric character reference (© or ©).

Hexadecimal Values

It is sometimes necessary to type numeric values that cannot be expressed in binary digits; this is often the case in describing a color, which may be specified as three hexadecimal values. To do so, the value is typed in quotation marks, starting with a # and with two hexadecimal digits per value, as in the following example:

```
BGCOLOR="#ABCDEF"
```

The three hexadecimal values specified here are AB, CD, and EF.

Creating and Editing HTML Documents with Graphical Editors

It would seem that since HTML documents consist entirely of text characters, a simple text editor would be the best tool to use to create and edit them. In fact, there are three primary reasons why a graphical editor such as Home Page is preferable:

1. With special characters, documents quickly become very hard to read; a graphical editor can convert the special characters described in the previous section into their values (and their colors).

2. The HTML elements can be hard to locate—particularly when embedded within one another. The visual elements are easily seen.

3. Most important, the end result of the process is not an HTML document (the input to the user's browser) but the graphical depiction of the HTML document (the output from the user's browser). A "perfect" HTML document may not look like you want it to.

Creating and Editing HTML Documents with Text-Based Editors

Nevertheless, there are many reasons for using text-based HTML editors. These include familiarity with them, a preference for manipulating the HTML code directly, and the need for people with different software environments to collaborate on a single Web page. Home Page provides both graphical and text editing features.

An HTML Example

The easiest way to get a general understanding of HTML is to look at the code that underlies a simple page. For example, the home page of the Shopping Cart example is shown in Figure 9-1.

There are four major elements in the page:

1. The background image

2. The Knitting Factory image

3. The Enter button

4. The FileMaker Pro logo at the bottom

Clicking either the Knitting Factory image or the Enter button creates a new record in the Orders.fp3 database. (It is not uncommon for the behavior of buttons such as OK, Enter, and Start to be duplicated by logos and background images: basically, the theory is that a click anywhere on the page should have some default action.)

FIGURE 9-1. Default.Html Page

There are two sources of movement on this page. The File-Maker Pro logo at the bottom is an animated GIF—an image that automatically refreshes itself in various ways, simulating movement. In this case, the FileMaker Pro logo rises from the globe. The second source of movement is the Enter button: as the mouse is moved over the button, it changes color. This is done with a JavaScript (which is shown in "Enhancing the Interface with Scripts" starting on page 328).

The source code for this page is shown and annotated in this section. The JavaScript section is omitted (but is shown in the chapter on "Using Scripts" starting on page 311).

Note that this is a walk-through of real HTML code. It is neither the simplest nor the most complicated such code around. The purpose of the walk-through is to give you a sense of what HTML looks like and what it does.

The HTML Source Code

All HTML files consist of the element <HTML>, as shown at **1̄**. Note that the file does not *start* with an HTML element, it *is* an HTML element. The starting tag is at **1̄**, and the ending tag is at **1̄8̄**. All other elements are contained within the HTML element.

Comments start with <!-- and end with -->. Often, they are generated automatically by your editor (as at **2̄**). As with all computer code, more comments are better than fewer. When you look back at the code weeks (or months) from now, you may not remember what you had in mind.

```
1̄<HTML>
2̄<!--This file created 2/16/1998 12:37 PM by Claris Home
    Page version 3.0-->
```

HEAD Element

The HEAD element starts at **3̄** and ends at **6̄**. An HTML head contains information about the document itself. The TITLE element (**4̄**) is used by browsers to title their windows (see Figure 9-1) as well as to identify bookmarks and histories. The next elements in this section are generated by Home Page; you need not worry about them and you do not need to enter them if you are constructing an HTML file by hand.

The final section of the HEAD element is the definition of the JavaScript used to animate the Enter button. This element is shown at **5** and is described in "Enhancing the Interface with Scripts" on page 328.

The HEAD element is technically optional, but it should be contained in all HTML elements, if only to specify the TITLE element. Only one HEAD element is allowed inside an HTML element.

```
3<HEAD>
    4<TITLE>Welcome to the Knitting Factory</TITLE>
    <META NAME=GENERATOR CONTENT="Home Page 3.0">
    <X-CLARIS-WINDOW TOP=42 BOTTOM=613 LEFT=4 RIGHT=534>
    <X-CLARIS-TAGVIEW MODE=minimal>
    <!--This is the main entry point for the Knitting
        Factory shopping cart solution.  This page simply
        contains 4 images. When two of the images are
        clicked, they'll create a new record and take you to
        the search page.
    -->

    5<SCRIPT LANGUAGE="JavaScript">
    <!--Hide from older browsers
        ...
        (For the code that has been removed here, see
        "Enhancing the Interface with Scripts" on page 328)
    //End hiding-->
    </SCRIPT>
6</HEAD>
```

BODY Element

After the HEAD element, HTML elements contain a single BODY element, which starts at **7** and ends at **17**. The starting BODY tag (**7**) contains two attributes—the background color for the body and the background image for the body. These attributes are commonly used for BODY tags to provide a default look to a Web site or page.

The color—as with all colors—is specified as three hexadecimal values, each represented by two hexadecimal digits. Using a graphical editor makes all of this transparent to you: you select a color from a color wheel or other color picker, and the software figures out what the actual numbers are.

The background image is a GIF (Graphics Interchange Format), one of the standard file formats for Web images. (The other commonly used format is JPEG.) For the sake of convenience, most Web site designers place all of their images into a single folder—usually called Images. Thus, this file is headerbg.gif, located in the folder images, which is assumed to be in the same location as the page itself. Figure 9-2 shows the file and folder layout of the Shopping Cart example inside the Web folder of FileMaker Pro.

FIGURE 9-2. Shopping Cart File and Folder Structure

```
7<BODY BGCOLOR="#6666CC" BACKGROUND="images/headerbg.gif">
```

The CENTER element, which starts at **8** and ends at **16**, contains the balance of the elements—in fact, all of the visible content of the page. It simply specifies that all elements should be centered on the page.

Tables

Starting at **9**, a series of elements are used to define an HTML table; these elements and their tags are italicized throughout the file. The TABLE element contains two rows (the TR elements), each of which contains a single cell (the TD—table data cell—elements). The first row contains the Knitting Factory logo and the Enter button; the second contains the FileMaker Pro logo at the bottom of the page.

Tables are used in two general ways in HTML:

1. Tables can be used to display tabular data: this is the purpose for which they were designed. New versions of HTML make it possible for browsers to display table data dynamically, rendering the rest of the page while database accesses continue.

2. Because tables provide a way of structuring pages into grids of rows and columns, they can be used—as they are here—simply to position elements on a page. Automated HTML generators (like Home Page) rely heavily on tables to let you create good-looking pages.

If you are using a graphical editor like Home Page, the table elements will be created automatically as you draw your page. If you are creating an HTML page manually, you are likely to use tables far less. For now, you can safely skip over the italicized portions of this code and focus on the content.

```
 8 <CENTER>

 9 <TABLE BORDER=0 CELLSPACING=0 CELLPADDING=10 WIDTH="100%">
   <TR>
   <TD ALIGN=center VALIGN=top BGCOLOR="#FFFFFF">

10 <P>
11 <A
12    HREF="FMPro?-db=Orders.fp3&-format=search.htm&-new"
        onmouseover="return setimg('enter',true)"
        onmouseout="return setimg('enter',false)">
13    <IMG SRC="images/kf.gif" ALT="The Knitting Factory"
        WIDTH=341 HEIGHT=250 BORDER=0 ALIGN=bottom>
14 </A>

15 <BR>

   <A
      HREF="FMPro?-db=Orders.fp3&-format=search.htm&-new"
        onmouseover="return setimg('enter',true)"
        onmouseout="return setimg('enter',false)">
      <IMG SRC="images/enter1.gif" ALT="Enter"
        WIDTH=75 HEIGHT=41 BORDER=0 ALIGN=bottom
        name=enter>
   </A>
   </P>

   </TD>
   </TR>

   <TR>
   <TD ALIGN=center VALIGN=top>
   <P><NOBR>
      <IMG SRC="images/BannerAnim.gif"
        ALT="Powered by FileMaker Pro"
        WIDTH=230 HEIGHT=90 BORDER=0 ALIGN=top>
      <IMG SRC="images/header.gif" ALT="4.0"
        WIDTH=99 HEIGHT=67 BORDER=0 ALIGN=top>
   </NOBR>
   </P>

   </TD>
   </TR>
   </TABLE>
```

16 </CENTER>
17 </BODY>
18 </HTML>

Paragraphs

HTML documents are divided into paragraphs; these paragraphs correspond in a general sense to paragraphs in any document, but they can include more than just words (and need not contain any words). Paragraphs in an HTML document can contain images and links. In general, all information in an HTML document is contained in one paragraph or another. Even when tables are used to organize information, the contents of each table data cell are one or more paragraphs.

Text that is to be placed in a paragraph is simply typed into the paragraph between the starting tag (<P>) and the ending tag (</P>). Other HTML elements (images, formatting elements, etc.) are placed within the paragraph element as well; the delimiters < and > allow browsers to keep HTML elements separate from text.

Carriage returns are normally stripped out by browsers; when it is necessary to insert a blank line, the Break element (<BR>) is inserted as at **15**; this causes the two images in the first paragraph to be displayed one below the other. In other cases, it is necessary to not allow browsers to insert a return; at the end of the file, the no break (<NOBR>) element prevents the "FileMaker" graphic and the "4.0" graphic from being separated.

When it is necessary to use the < or > symbols as text (that is, not as delimiters for HTML tags), use the character entity references < (less than, <) and > (greater than, >) instead of the symbols.

The first paragraph in this case starts at $\overline{10}$. Although no attributes are specified for this paragraph, it is common to specify formatting attributes at the paragraph level.

Anchors

Anchor elements are delimited by the <A> and </A> tags, as shown at $\overline{11}$ and $\overline{14}$. Anchors are often named (using the NAME attribute); when an anchor is named, it can be used as part of a URL to go to a specific part of an HTML document. If the anchor that starts at 11 were named

$\overline{11}$ `<A name="shopping-cart-anchor" >`

then you could open this document and cause the browser to position this anchor on the screen by typing in the following:

`default.htm#shopping-cart-anchor`

The name of this file is default.htm; if you are connecting to it over a network or by using TCP/IP on a single machine, the full address would be something like

`http://www.yourdomain.com/shopping_cart/default.html#shop-ping-cart-anchor`

or

`http://10.10.10.10/shopping_cart/default.html#shopping-cart-anchor`

In addition to being used to locate sections of a document, anchors are also used to specify links to other documents or to other anchors within the same document. A named anchor is typically used as the destination of a link *from* somewhere else; an anchor with a link in it is the source of a link *to* somewhere else.

Hypertext References (Links)

In order to specify a link to another document or anchor, the HREF attribute is placed inside an anchor, as at $\overline{\textbf{12}}$. The entire anchor (everything from the <A> to the </A>) is "hot"—that is, clicking on any of the contents of the anchor element causes you to jump to the hypertext reference. An HREF attribute normally is a URL, and it may contain any of the optional features of a URL—an anchor, data following the ? character, and so forth.

In the case given here, the HREF attributes produce valid URLs that are not the locations of static HTML files but which provide a way of sending data (the characters following the ?) to FileMaker Pro Web Companion—FMPro. This is discussed in more detail in "Using CDML" starting on page 233. Ignore for now the onmouseover and onmouseout lines; these are discussed in "Scripts and HTML" starting on page 312.

Note that HREF is an attribute of the anchor element—the end of the <A> tag is the > symbol that appears at the end of $\overline{\textbf{12}}$.

Images

The entire contents of an anchor are "hot." In this case, the contents of the anchor consist of an image—the graphic of the Knitting Factory, which is located in the file images/ kf.gif (the file kf.gif in the images folder). An image is placed in an HTML document with the IMG element, as shown at **13**. IMG must contain the name of the file; it may also contain an alternate text representation (for browsers where graphics are not enabled) as well as specifications about the size of the graphic.

Note that images need not be in local files: it is not uncommon to reference an image that exists on a totally different Web site. This is often the case with corporate logos.

Images commonly used on the Web are of two kinds:

1. JPEG—Joint Photographic Experts Group

2. GIF—Graphics Interchange Format

These formats allow images to be compressed and then expanded so that storage space and transmission time are saved. The formats are accepted by various Web browsers, Web authoring tools, and standard graphics software. As the name suggests, JPEG was designed for photographs and other images of that nature. These are characterized by many colors (or shades of gray) and by a lack of sharp lines (faces, trees, and snapshots of birthday parties come to mind). The JPEG format uses the characteristics of such images as well as information about how people perceive images and colors to eliminate picture data that the brain can easily interpolate.

GIF was designed to handle the sorts of images that you create with computers: text, blocks of color, etc. Its compression algorithms work well with nonrealistic images, for which JPEG is less than optimal.

JPEG is a "lossy" format—each time the JPEG image is saved, it is compressed again. Repeatedly saving a JPEG image results in a loss of quality. If you use JPEG images, be certain to keep the original around.

Home Page keeps track of image types and automatically converts other image types to GIFs.

The Basics

From this simple HTML example, these basic points emerge:

- HTML files consist of a single HTML element.

- The HTML element contains a HEAD element and a BODY element.

- Although the HEAD element is technically optional, it should be present and should contain—at the very least—a TITLE element and a comment describing the purpose of the file.

- Everything displayed on the Web page is entered in the BODY element. All information—text and graphics—is displayed in one or more paragraphs (P elements). Paragraphs are drawn on the Web page from top to bottom.

- A paragraph can contain text that is typed directly into the HTML file. It can also contain an image, which is referred to by an IMG SRC element that specifies the size and location of the image (normally in a disk file).

- All or part of the contents of a paragraph may be placed in an anchor (A). An anchor may have a name—in which case it may be used as the destination of a link (as in http://www.yourdomain.com/yourpage.html#anchorname). It may also contain a link to another Web resource; such links are specified by the anchor's HREF attribute. An anchor may have only one name and only one link, but need not have either.

- The placement of paragraphs one below the other on the Web page can be altered by using tables. Tables can have rows and columns of varying sizes. For each table row element (TR), you can specify one or more data cells (TD)—one for each column in that row. Within the table data cell, you may place one or more paragraph elements, thus changing the strict top-to-bottom placement of paragraphs in a nontable format.

There is a lot more to HTML than this, but you can go very far (and understand a lot of existing HTML code) if you master these basics. Further points to remember about HTML include the following:

- HTML elements may have contents (as a paragraph does) and an ending tag (such as /P) in addition to their starting tag (such as P). The starting tag is always required.

- When trying to understand an existing HTML file, remember that spaces and blank lines do not matter. Start by lining up starting and ending tags so that the structure of the file is clear to you. (Many text and graphical HTML editors do this automatically; they also often use color to highlight tags.)

Learning More HTML

All browsers let you look at the raw HTML source code for a page you are viewing. When you see an effect that you particularly like (or don't like), look at the HTML to see how it has been done.

Summary

This chapter has provided an introduction to HTML—what it is and how it works. The easiest way to learn HTML is to read the HTML code for Web pages that you visit. Remember that most people do not write HTML code from scratch: your mission will usually be to modify or extend existing HTML code. In that case, you need to be able to find your way around the code and to figure out what it is doing.

In the next chapter, you will see how FileMaker Pro extends HTML and adds custom tags to HTML elements.

Controlling Your Database with HTML

This chapter describes how you formulate requests that manipulate FileMaker Pro databases: these requests can add, delete, or edit records; display them; sort the database; or do any other operations that you want. All of this processing is filtered through FileMaker Pro Web Companion. Your job is to send properly formatted requests to Web Companion so that it can do its work.

This chapter describes the standards behind all requests for Web resources. (If you are familiar with the subtleties of HTTP GET and POST methods, you can skim over this section.) It then describes the format files that you create for Web Companion to use in fulfilling these requests; it continues with a description of each of the requests that you can send. It concludes with some tips on creating such requests—even if you are not familiar with HTML.

These requests are most often used with Custom Web Publishing—which is why this chapter is located in this part of the book. However, you can use these requests with Instant Web Publishing as well, as you will see later in this chapter.

Requesting a Resource on the Web

When you type an address into a browser or create a link (technically, an HREF attribute of an anchor) on a Web page, you probably think only of the URL you are typing. When the command is executed, a message is sent; that message has two parts—the header and an optional body.

The specification of HTTP states that there actually are at least three parts to the message header that is sent. HTTP defines a request-line that contains these three parts:

1. A method that describes what the Web server is supposed to do about the URL.

2. The URL itself.

3. The version of HTTP to which this message conforms. (This allows for updates to Web servers to be independent of updates to clients: each knows the most recent version to which the other will respond.)

In addition to the message header (the request-line), the message may contain a message body.

All HTTP requests must receive a response (even if it is an error stating that the address is wrong, the server is busy, etc.). If no response is received, the browser that sent the request gives the user an error indicating that no response was received. The Web page that you see in your browser is technically the response to the request that you have specified by typing in a URL.

This terminology of request and response is very specific. The words are common English-language words, and they are used as people use them in ordinary conversation. Try to get into the habit of using this terminology correctly. If you are sloppy—such as referring to a URL as the address of a Web page—you will confuse yourself and others, particularly when you start dealing with dynamic HTML (which is what FileMaker Pro Web Companion uses).

Methods

The most frequently used HTTP method is GET: it requests that the Web server get the resource (usually a Web page) described in the URL. Note the careful phrasing here: it allows for the Web server to generate an HTML message that is not a static page. GET is the method that is assumed when you type in a URL or create a link (with HREF).

Another frequently used HTTP method is POST: it is designed specifically to transfer data to the resource named in the URL. That data can be specified using MIME encoding, which means that you can transfer pictures, sounds, and so forth to the resource. The POST method is used with forms, which are described in "Using Forms" starting on page 289.

Other methods are defined, but these are the two that you deal with when you are using FileMaker Pro and FileMaker Pro Web Companion.

URLs

A URL for the Web (HTTP) is specified as having six parts:

1. It starts with the **scheme** followed by a colon and two slashes (http:// for the Web).

2. Next, the **host name** is specified either as four digits separated by periods (such as 192.168.1.3) or by a domain name (such as www.filemaker.com). If the host is omitted, it is assumed to be the same computer on which the request is being made.

3. Optionally, a colon and a **port number** can be provided. Each scheme has a default port (for HTTP it is 80) to which it automatically connects. (Ports are discussed in "Setting Up FileMaker Pro Web Companion" on page 143.)

4. A **slash** follows the specification of the host and port. If the local computer is assumed by having a blank host name and if the default port is used, the URL looks like this at this point: `http:///`. For a URL without a port, it looks like this: `http://www.filemaker.com/`, and for a URL with a port, it looks like this: `http://www.filemaker.com:80/`.

5. Next, the **path component** is supplied. This is the name of the resource to which the request is directed. Often, it is a Web page with a name that ends in .htm or .html. Thus, the path might be weeklydata.html. If the file is located within a directory on the host computer, that directory (and others) are specified and separated by slashes, as in projectA/webfiles/weeklydata.html.

    In other cases, the path specifies an application to which the request is directed; the application is responsible for replying to the request. FileMaker Pro Web Companion's path is FMPro: all requests to File-Maker Pro Web Companion are addressed using the host name and the optional port number, as well as the subdirectory of the Web folder in which your format files are placed (if you use subdirectories). Thus, a request to Web Companion can be any one of the following forms:

```
http://www.yourdomain.com/FMPro
http://www.yourdomain.com:80/FMPro
http://www.yourdomain.com:80/shopping_cart/FMPro
http://192.168.1.3/FMPro
http://192.168.1.3:80/FMPro
http://192.168.1.3:80/employee_database/FMPro
```

6. If the request contains **data** to be sent to Web Companion as part of the header, that data (called the **searchpart** or **query**) follows the path and is preceded by a question mark. The data format is described in the following section.

A Note on Paths

Rather than addressing a specific file—such as index.html—you often ask FileMaker Pro Web Companion to refer to a format file; this information can be sent as part of the data you send in the final part of the request. That file should be located in the Web folder that is inside the FileMaker Pro folder. If it is located within a subdirectory (subfolder), that subdirectory should be part of the path; FMPro ends the path, as in the examples above.

Note that subdirectories are specified starting from the File-Maker Pro Web folder, not from the root directory of the computer.

Sending Data as Part of a Request

The simplest HTTP requests simply specify the location of a resource that will provide a response—which usually is a Web page. (With FileMaker Pro Web Companion, that location is always FMPro.) In order to tell the resource what you want it to do, you must pass additional information as part of the request.

This is a common need. When you connect to a search engine (such as www.yahoo.com or www.excite.com), you can use it to search for information. If you watch your browser, you will see that when you click on the Search button a URL is constructed that includes your search term. The general syntax for passing information as part of requests is specified as part of HTTP; each search engine uses its own modification of the general syntax, as does FileMaker Pro Web Companion.

There are two ways to pass information as part of a request:

1. You can pass the information in the URL as a search-part.

2. You can pass the information in the message body.

Searchparts and Queries

You can include a searchpart in the URL that is part of the request. The searchpart contains text data, each element of which is identified by a descriptive name. The format is

```
descriptorname=textvalue
```

Some elements have no data; their format is

```
descriptorname
```

If more than one element is provided, the elements are separated by ampersands (&). The name of each descriptor is specified by the resource that you are addressing. Thus, File-Maker Pro Web Companion's descriptors are described in this chapter; the descriptors used by Yahoo are its own.

The data sent in a searchpart must be text data, adhering to Internet standards. The numbers and letters of the alphabet are the most basic text elements; other symbols are represented as described in "Numeric Character References" on page 191.

When you use the GET method (to retrieve a page from a Web location), data is always sent in the searchpart.

"Searchpart" and "query" are interchangeable; "searchpart" is used in the URL specfication, and "query" is used in the HTTP specification.

Sending Data in the Message Body

Sending data in the searchpart of the URL has three possible disadvantages:

1. Since it is part of the URL, the data that is being sent may be visible in a browser's location display. (You can verify this by looking at the URL that is generated when you click the Search button in a search engine.) This can pose security issues.

2. Only text data can be sent in a searchpart.

3. Large amounts of data can be unwieldy in a searchpart. Although the searchpart and the URL are designed to be read by machines, some browsers have

difficulty with long requests, even though they should not.

The POST method is designed to send relatively large amounts of data to a Web resource; the response is often a Web page indicating that the data has been processed. Accordingly, the POST method relies on a message body to pass data. None of the three disadvantages of searchparts exists in a message body:

1. The message body is never shown in a browser's location display.

2. The message body is used for various purposes; browsers and other Web software are used to dealing with multiple-part, multiple-type messages (such as messages that contain text, sound, video, and custom data types—often all in one message).

3. Message bodies are typically long; unexpected problems with browsers usually do not occur with long messages.

Third-Party Tools

If you use a third-party tool to access FileMaker Pro (such as Lasso or Tango), you send a request to the tool using that tool's syntax. The principles of operation are exactly those are described here.

What It Means to You

Whether you use the GET method and the searchpart or the POST method and the message body, you have a simple way of passing information to FileMaker Pro Web Companion. In the balance of this book, the following conventions are used.

SENDING A REQUEST TO FILEMAKER PRO WEB COMPANION   This means sending a GET or POST request to FileMaker Pro Web Companion. It may be on a remote computer or on your own computer. In any event, the result is the generation of a request with a URL whose path is FMPro. This phrase implies all of these possibilities (and their combinations).

PASSING VARIABLES TO FILEMAKER PRO WEB COMPANION   This means sending one or more named data elements to File-Maker Pro Web Companion. They may be sent using a searchpart and the GET method or by using the message body and a POST method. When sent as part of the search-part, the syntax is as described previously in this chapter (see "Searchparts and Queries" on page 212); the syntax for the message body is described in a later chapter (see "Using Forms" starting on page 289).

WHERE IS FILEMAKER PRO WEB COMPANION RUNNING?   File-Maker Pro Web Companion may be running on the same computer that you are using and may be addressed using the special 10.10.10.10 IP address (see "Using FileMaker Pro Web Companion without a Network" on page 149) or by the standard IP address of your computer. It also may be running on another machine that is itself addressed either by an IP address or by a domain name. It is always identified as FMPro. Rather than repeating these variations, messages to FileMaker Pro Web Companion are shown without the scheme, host name, and optional port. Thus, instead of providing a complete URL such as

```
http://192.168.1.2/FMPro
```

or

```
http://www.yourdomain.com/FMPro
```

the convention

```
.../FMPro
```

is used to imply whatever path you take to reach FileMaker Pro Web Companion. Note that a URL in a file on the computer where Web Companion is running can reference Web Companion by omitting the host name. Thus,

```
FMPro
```

is always valid syntax for referring to FileMaker Pro Web Companion from an HTML file on the same machine as Web Companion. Self-contained database projects often use this syntax; when you move the entire project—database and HTML files—to another folder or another computer, you do not have to change IP addresses or domain names. See the FileMaker Pro examples for illustrations of this naming convention.

.../FMPro is used to imply any of these versions of the syntax.

Format Files

Format files are input to FileMaker Pro Web Companion. They contain HTML as well as CDML (Claris Dynamic Markup Language—the FileMaker-specific syntax defined for FileMaker Pro Web Companion). A browser cannot interpret CDML, but Web Companion can—it uses it to create HTML that is then sent back to a browser.

The CDML syntax that is found inside format files consists of tags that are enclosed in square brackets ([and]). If you open a format file in a Web browser, you will see these tags, as shown in Figure 10-1. (This is the same format file that was used to construct the HTML shown previously in "Shopping Cart Contents" on page 177.)

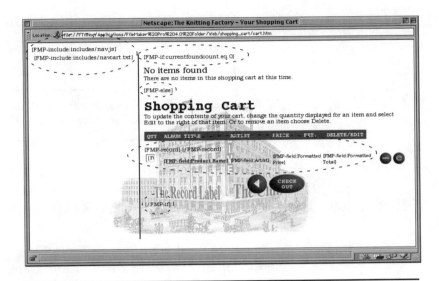

FIGURE 10-1. Shopping Cart Contents (CDML)

Instead of opening a format file directly, you pass its name to FileMaker Pro Web Companion when you ask Web Companion to do something (add a record, search, etc.).

The syntax for the file to be used in the case of good results is

```
-format=goodfile.htm
```

In the case of an error, it is

```
-error=errorfile.html
```

If you do not supply a filename for the -error variable, Web Companion will use its default display.

The names of the files should be qualified with respect to the HTML file from which the request is issued. In practice, simply use the name of the file without any path information and place the file in the same folder as the HTML file. See the examples in the FileMaker Pro Web folder for models. (The suffix .htm or .html is determined by your Web server's standards. Ask your Webmaster, network administrator, or ISP which style is required for use.)

The details of CDML and the contents of format files are discussed in the next chapter, "Using CDML," starting on page 233.

FileMaker Pro Web Companion Requests

You need to be able to construct a full-fledged FileMaker Pro Web Companion request if you are going to do any automatic manipulation of databases (that is, any manipulation from a link or button rather than from a user's click on a default Instant Web Publishing home page).

An Instant Web Publishing Request

In fact, you have seen the syntax of such requests before: Instant Web Publishing generates them automatically on its default home pages. If you click on a database in the default home page shown in Figure 4-4 on page 107, you generate a request that takes you to the Instant Web Publishing page shown in Figure 4-5 on page 109 or Figure 4-6 on page 111.

At the top of those windows, you can see the syntax that formed the request. It is

```
http://192.168.1.2/FMRes/FMPro?
        -DB=Event Schedule.fp3&
        -Format=tablevw.htm&
        -Lay=list view&
        -Token=25&
```

```
-Error=Err.htm&
-Findall
```

For clarity, the single line has been split into several lines here. Also, the blank spaces within the names of the databases, which are always replaced with their numeric equivalent—%20, have been restored to normal blank spaces. Note also that the special FMRes path is used for Instant Web Publishing—you normally use a path to the subdirectory of your Web folder (inside the FileMaker Pro folder) in which your files reside.

This particular request is deciphered here as an example. All of the variables are defined later in this section.

- -DB specifies the database to be used. Whether you use Instant Web Publishing or Custom Web Publishing, the database must be open. If the database has been set up for use with FileMaker Pro Web Companion (see "Preparing the Database for the Web" on page 123), Web Companion will automatically recognize it when it is opened. It uses the database's name—not its fully qualified name with directory and folder. Thus, this variable consists only of the name.

- -Format identifies the format file to be used to format the response in the case of success. That format file often contains CDML to display data.

- -Lay specifies the layout to use. This is the name of a standard FileMaker Pro layout. It is used primarily to determine which fields should be used; little of the layout's formatting information is used. If you are using Instant Web Publishing, your setup identifies the layouts to use. In Custom Web Publishing, you can vary the layouts as you wish.

- -Token is a variable that you can use for any purpose that you want. Its value is passed into the request; the format file can retrieve whatever value that is.

- -Error is the name of the format file to be used by Web Companion in constructing a response in the case of failure.

- -Findall is the action that Web Companion is to take. This variable has no value: its name specifies the action to be taken.

Thus, this request says, "Find all records in Event Schedule.fp3; retrieve the fields specified in layout list view. In the case of success, display the data using the format file tablevw.htm; in the case of failure, display a message using Err.htm. Limit the retrieval to the first 25 records."

A Custom Web Publishing Request

A similar request is shown in Figure 8-3 on page 173. It is

```
http://192.168.1.2/employee_database/FMPro?
        -DB=Employees.fp3&
        -Lay=Detail&
        -Format=new.htm&
        -view
```

This specifies a request that is sent to FileMaker Pro Web Companion with the path employee_database (assumed, as always, to be within the Web directory inside the FileMaker Pro directory). The database to be used is Employees.fp3; the layout is Detail, and the format file is new.htm. The database and format file are within the employee_database directory. In this case, rather than the Findall action specified in the previous example, this request asks that the view action be performed.

All FileMaker Pro Web Companion requests are basically similar to these. They are constructed from actions and variables such as those shown here. Each request has one (and only one) action. Each request has a number of variables; the variables are usually determined by the action.

Actions

These are the things that you can command a FileMaker Pro database to do over the Web. The format of the request can be either a GET or POST request. In Table 10-1, the FileMaker Pro Web Companion actions are shown. Each of them requires certain variables to be included in the request. These are shown in Table 10-1 and their details are described in Table 10-2.

Additional variables may be provided for many actions. For example, a -Format variable can be provided for any action, and an -Error variable can also be provided. (They are required for the actions that result in data displays.) These let you specify format files for Web Companion to use on completion of its actions. If they are not provided, the Web Companion uses its default formatting.

Note that *field name* (used in the third column of Table 10-1) is not a variable: it is a placeholder for the name of a field in the FileMaker Pro database. Thus, if you have a field called "serialnumber," the request could include the syntax

```
-DB=mydatabase.fp3&-RecID=1&serialnumber=1234
```

In a number of the actions shown in Table 10-1, *field name* specifies a specific field to use (to edit, use in a search command, etc.). In many cases, a single request can have a number of field names in it, reflecting a number of fields to edit, several items for a search, and so forth.

Similarly, the -RecID variable specifies a record number (assigned by FileMaker Pro) on which to act.

Action	Description	Variables Required
-Delete	Delete record.	-DB, -RecID
-Dup	Duplicate record.	-DB, -RecID, -Format
-Edit	Edit field(s) in a record.	-DB, -RecID, *field name(s)*
-Find	Find record based on the value of one or more fields.	-DB, -Format, *field name(s)* (For more than one *field name*, -LOP is available to let you specify the logical operator to use in combining the fields.)
-FindAll	Find all records.	-DB, -Format
-FindAny	Find any record (often used to be able to access a global field that is the same for all records).	-DB, -Format
-Img	Display image in a given field of a certain record.	-DB, -RecID, *field name*
-New	New record. (Note that one or more *field name* variables may be provided; any such values are placed in the corresponding fields.)	-DB
-View	Simply process the format file; data for a search or data entry will be entered by the user. No record data is displayed.	-DB, -Format

TABLE 10-1. Request Actions

Variables

Table 10-2 shows the variables that you can use in requests together with the actions from Table 10-1.

Variable	Description
-DB	Database name. Must be opened by FileMaker Pro; do not include path, just use the name—schedule.fp3, for example.
-Error	Error response. HTML format file to be shown if an error occurs during action processing. (Compare with -Format.)
-Format	HTML format file to be shown if no error occurs during action processing. (Compare with -Error.)
-Lay	Layout name. The name of the FileMaker Pro layout to be used; its primary purpose is to describe the fields that are to be used in this request. If omitted, the first layout for the database is used—this is almost always inefficient.
-LOP	Logical operator AND or OR to be used in combining multiple field names for a -Find command. See "Logical Operators for Finding Data" on page 225 for more details.
-Mail...	Mail variables are shown in Table 10-5. on page 228.
-Max	Max records. The maximum number of records to find with the -Find command.
-Op	Operator to be used in evaluating a single field name condition (such as equals, less than, etc.). See "Logical Operators for Finding Data" on page 225 for more details.
-RecID	Record ID. The number of the record to act on.

TABLE 10-2. Request Variables

Variable	Description
-Script	Perform script. This variable can be added to any operation (such as -Find); if it is present, the script indicated here will be executed after the operation.
-Script.PreFind	Perform script before find. This variable specifies a script to be executed before any finding and sorting that is done as part of an action.
-Script.PreSort	Perform script before sort. This variable specifies a script to be executed before any sorting that is done as part of an action. (Compared with -Script.PreFind, this variable executes after a find and before a sort; -Script.PreFind executes before both the find and sort.)
-Skip	Skip records before displaying. This is the command that implements the functionality in the status area bookmark. Use in conjunction with -Max to, for example, display the 10 records starting at record 200, as in -Skip=200&-Max=10.
-SortField	Sort field. The value of this variable is a field name to be used in sorting. You may have several occurrences of -SortField in your request; if so, they are used to refine the sort (as in sorting by last name, then by first name).
-SortOrder	Sort order. The direction (ascending, descending, or custom) of the sort; -SortOrder applies to the -Sort-Field that immediately follows it. See Table 10-4 for details of the values.
-Token	Token. This is a variable whose meaning is defined in your format file. If you want to pass some information from the request into the format file, use -Token. Typical uses are passwords, status indicators, and other information that is not part of the database but rather is part of the transaction. The -Token variable helps you to implement transactions that get around HTML's stateless architecture.

TABLE 10-2. Request Variables (Continued)

Logical Operators for Finding Data

You can use the -LOP, -Op and field name variables to build complex queries for data. The process duplicates the process that you use in FileMaker Pro; it may seem more complex because you are used to the graphical interface, but the operations are exactly the same.

Figure 10-2 shows how you use FileMaker Pro to find data.

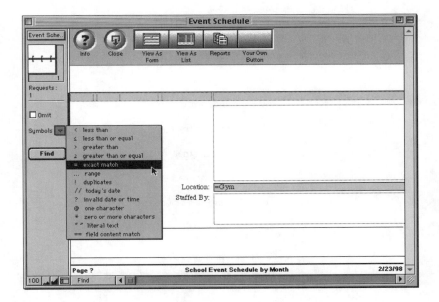

FIGURE 10-2. Specifying a Find in FileMaker Pro

You enter values to search for in fields on the layout. You can use the Symbols pop-up menu (as shown in Figure 10-2) to insert logical operators that are used to compare the value you type with the values in the database.

It works exactly the same way when you formulate a request to FileMaker Pro Web Companion. As part of the request, you specify one or more field names together with values. For example, the syntax for Figure 10-2 would be

```
Location=Gym
```

Instead of choosing an operator from the Symbols menu, you specify it using the -Op variable and the values shown in Table 10-3.

Short	Long
eq	equals
cn	contains
bw	begins with
ew	ends with
gt	greater than
gte	greater than or equals
lt	less than
lte	less than or equals
neq	not equals

TABLE 10-3. Operators for Comparisons (-Op Values)

You can use either the short or long syntax; thus, the two lines below are equivalent:

```
-Op=eq
-Op=equals
```

If you do not specify an -Op variable, "begins with" is used by default. The -Op variable must immediately precede the field name on which it should operate.

Sorting Order

Similarly, you can use the -SortOrder variable to specify how -SortField variables should be sorted. (Sorting is done during the Find actions if sorting variables are present.) The syntax and meanings are shown in Table 10-4.

Short	Long	Meaning
Ascend	Ascending	Sort a to z, −10 to 10.
Descend	Descending	Sort z to a, 10 to −10.
Custom		Sort using the value list associated with the field on the layout. (You must have specified a layout for this to work.)
Custom=Value List Name		Sort using the value list named.

TABLE 10-4. Values for -SortOrder

What Is RecID?

The record ID identifies the record in the database that is to be acted on by an action such as -Delete, -Dup, or -Edit. This is not the number that appears in the status area of a File-Maker Pro database—that is called the record number. In a multiuser environment, record numbers can change easily—particularly if you allow users to sort the database. What is record 27 one moment may be record 38 the next. (This is yet another argument for not sorting databases.) Furthermore, the record number varies depending on the records selected in a Find command. Record IDs, however, remain untouched by sorting and finding. They are assigned when records are created, and are never changed after that.

The standard way to use record identifiers is to create a hidden field in your format file that displays retrieved data; place the record identifier into that field. When you then allow a user to click a Delete button, retrieve that identifier from the hidden field and pass it into the -Delete request. (See "A Form Example" on page 293 and "Hidden Controls" on page 302 for examples of this technique.)

Mail Requests

You can submit requests to send e-mail to confirm orders (as in the Shopping Cart example) or to relay information in a secure manner. (Rather than let someone see the data, they can locate what they are looking for and you can e-mail it to a known address regardless of who actually made the request.)

Table 10-5 shows the variables that can be set for mail. An example is given in "An E-mail Example" on page 307.

Variable	Description
-MailSub	Subject for mail.
-MailTo	To address for mail.
-MailFrom	E-mail address of sender.
-MailBCC	E-mail address of blind carbon copy recipient(s). Separate multiple recipients by commas.
-MailCC	E-mail address of carbon copy recipient(s). Separate multiple recipients by commas.
-MailFormat	Text file to be used for mail message; CDML replacement tags may appear in the file to automatically customize it.

TABLE 10-5. CDML Variables for Mail

Variable	Description
-MailFrom	E-mail address of sender.
-MailHost	The name of the SMTP host that will be used to send the mail. Note: this is the server's SMTP host—the one available to the computer on which FileMaker Pro Web Companion is running.

TABLE 10-5. CDML Variables for Mail (Continued)

Integrating FileMaker Pro with a Web Site

Based simply on the information in this chapter, you can go very far in integrating FileMaker Pro databases with your Web site. The requests described here are used both for Instant Web Publishing and Custom Web Publishing: using the commands shown in the tables in this chapter, you can manipulate databases and format files to your heart's content.

Requests to Instant Web Publishing

The functions of format files have been described here; their syntax is described in the following chapter. However, even without writing a single format file, you can do everything described here—if you use Instant Web Publishing. There are six format files available for your use:

1. TableVw.htm is the format file for the table (multi-record) display.

2. FormVw.htm is the format file for the form (single-record) display.

3. New.htm is the format file for data entry to new records; it is similar to FormVw.htm, but its data fields are editable.

4. Edit.htm is the format file for editing existing records. It is very similar to New.htm.

5. Search.htm is the format file that is used to specify and start a search.

6. Sort.htm is the format file to specify and start a sort.

Note that these files are not real: when FileMaker Pro Web Companion encounters these names, it generates the appropriate format files dynamically. However, you can use these names as if the files were actual files.

You can see the requests that are generated as you use Instant Web Publishing. Copy them and paste them into your Web pages, modifying them as you see fit.

What you cannot do (without creating format files) is programmatically manipulate the data from the database. In other words, you can create requests that open records, create records, and so forth, but the user will have to type in the information. If you want to be able to generate the text "Thank you, Anni" based on a customer ID number (such as 562334), you need to use CDML to extract the name "Anni" from a record found by searching on the customer ID 562334.

Notwithstanding this limitation, you can attach HTML requests to Web pages (both text and graphical elements) so that your FileMaker Pro databases can be manipulated easily. Furthermore, if two people are working together, one person can create format files and another person can work on Web page design. This is frequently the case when the Web site design is managed by a graphic design team and the format files are developed by database specialists.

Format File Specification

Remember that all requests must adhere to the syntax described in this chapter. Thus, no matter what the designer of the format file does behind the scenes, the following information can be provided to potential users of the format file:

- Use this file with these actions…

- Use this error file with this format file…

- If used, the -Token variable means…

Merging Web Sites

FileMaker Pro must be running on the computer to which you address the FMPro request. As noted previously, this might not be the computer on which your Web site resides. (That computer might be a Unix computer, for example, and the FileMaker Pro database might be running on a Windows NT or Mac OS computer.)

If this is the case, make certain that the host name or IP address is included in the URL for FMPro. Instead of asking users to type in an unfamiliar and complicated address, you can provide a button to click on and open the FileMaker Pro database. Few people will notice that they have jumped to another computer. If you want to make this even more transparent, you can use format files that contain HTML elements that are identical to the graphical elements on your primary Web site. (You can also include references in order to dynamically import graphics from one site to another; this can result in poor performance, and many people copy the graphics.)

Summary

This chapter has provided the details of formulating HTTP requests to FileMaker Pro Web Companion. You can use these requests with the Instant Web Publishing formats; you can also use your own formats, as described in the next chapter.

Using CDML

Custom Web Publishing revolves around CDML—Claris Dynamic Markup Language. CDML differs from HTML in that it is designed to be processed by FileMaker Web Companion as it constructs dynamic Web pages. (HTML is designed to be transferred across the network and to be processed by browsers on client machines.) The end result of the interaction between FileMaker Web Companion and CDML is HTML that is downloaded to your browser.

This chapter deals with the basics of this process.

If you use Custom Web Publishing with Home Page, the CDML files are created automatically for you. You can examine them and see how they work: this can be a good learning experience. You may want to take the CDML generated by Home Page and modify it for your purposes. As noted previously, it is much easier to modify existing (and working!) syntax than to start from scratch. Even easier is to take code from the File-Maker Pro examples. In that case you can actually see what it does by running the example, then you can study and modify it for your own purposes.

CDML Elements

CDML is comparable to HTML in a number of ways. It consists of elements, each of which can consist of a starting tag, content, and an ending tag. As with HTML, the content and ending tag are not required in all cases. Although HTML tags are delimited by < and >, CDML tags are delimited by [and]. As you will see, their content often consists of HTML elements.

CDML elements fall into the following categories:

- Replacement

- Looping

- If elements

- File manipulation

- Links

- Range elements

- Tags for finding and sorting

- Lists

- Cookies and headers

Parameters

Some CDML elements allow you to specify options, such as a format to be used. Logically, these parameters are similar to the attributes of HTML elements, but they use a simplified syntax.

Parameters for CDML elements follow the starting tag name, separated from it by a colon (:). If more than one parameter is given, the parameters are separated by commas. The following examples demonstrate this syntax:

```
[FMP-CurrentDatabase:HTML]
[FMP-Field:ColorChoice, URL]
```

The italicized words are parameters. The order of parameters is important (since they are not named in the syntax); in almost all cases, parameters are optional.

Replacement

In static (traditional) HTML, everything that is to be presented as part of a Web page is in a file. The text is typed in, references are typed in, and images are inserted by providing references to the locations (usually files) where they can be found. A certain degree of dynamism can be provided by changing the image files—on many sites, scripts or other automated processes replace the contents of such files with a changing video or still image of a street. But the HTML itself remains constant.

As soon as you deal with dynamic pages, you need the ability to put place-holding elements into the HTML that will be replaced on demand with their actual values. This is essentially what CDML does. The format files contain many

CDML elements that are read by Web Companion and replaced with dynamic values as needed.

The replacement elements let you insert such mundane variable information as the date and time into your Web pages; they also let you deal with the heart of much database publishing—inserting data from a database into your Web page. You use them by simply typing them into your format file. Thus, you can type

```
Today is [FMP-CurrentDate].
```

and expect a browser to display

```
Today is Saturday, January 1, 2000.
```

CDML replacement elements are divided into environmental and database elements.

Environmental Elements

Environmental elements let you access information such as the date, time, and name of the user. None of this information has anything to do with FileMaker Pro or its databases.

You can use environmental information in several ways:

- You can incorporate information such as the date and time into customized HTML to greet individuals and place the time on Web pages that are displayed.

- You can store environmental information in hidden fields on the Web page. These fields can then be used to update database records with logs of visits. You can use this environmental information as part of a security system; such a mechanism might allow access for individuals only from certain IP addresses. For more information, see "Using Address Information for Security" on page 429.

- You can use these elements in a format file to generate customized e-mail, using the syntax shown in "Mail Requests" on page 228.

Parameters for Replacement Element Formats

For some replacement elements, you can specify a format by using a parameter. For example, [FMP-CurrentDate] has three possible values for its format parameter:

```
[FMP-CurrentDate:short] returns 1/1/2000.
[FMP-CurrentDate:abbrev] returns Sat, Jan 1, 2000.
[FMP-CurrentDate:long] returns Saturday, January 1, 2000.
```

The default is short.

Note that the actual formatting of dates and times is governed by the options set in the control panel for the computer on which Web Companion is running—not the user's computer. The sequence of month, day, and year and separators (/ rather than .), as well as the use of four- versus two-digit years, are user options on most operating systems.

Environmental elements are shown in Table 11-1.

CDML	Description
[FMP-ClientAddress]	This is the host name for the user (www.file-maker.com, for example). Not all connections use a domain name: if none is available, the IP address (four numbers separated by dots) is returned.
[FMP-ClientIP]	This is the quartet of numbers specifying the user's address.
[FMP-ClientPass-word]	The HTTP password in use on the browser.
[FMP-ClientType]	Every browser sends an identifying text string in every HTTP request that it makes. That string normally identifies the browser, its version, and its operating system (OS). This element returns that string.
[FMP-ClientUser-Name]	The HTTP user name in use on the browser.
[FMP-CurrentDate]	The date on the Web Companion computer; it is returned using the OS defaults set on that computer. The optional formats :short, :abbrev, and :long may be added to this element—for example, [FMP-CurrentDate:abbrev].
[FMP-CurrentDay]	Returns the day of the week on the Web Companion computer. Optional formats are :short (default) and :long.
[FMP-CurrentTime]	Returns the time on the host computer where Web Companion is running, using the options set in that OS (such as 12- or 24-hour clocks). Optional formats are :short (default) and :long.
[FMP-CurrentToken]	This is the value of the -Token variable that may have been passed in as part of the request. This is one way you communicate between the outside world (such as standard HTML) and format files; the -Token variable is legal in any HTML reference.

TABLE 11-1. Environmental Elements

Database Elements

Database elements let you access information about the current state of the FileMaker Pro database—its name, the current record ID, and so forth. Current elements let you access many of the variables that you set in requests. Thus, the -DB variable in a request is used to set the database name that you can interrogate using the [FMP-CurrentDatabase] element.

The most frequently used of these elements is the [FMP-Field] element. You use it to insert data from a database field into a CDML file. Thus, the code

```
Current price is [FMP-Field: preis]
```

inserts the value of the field preis in the current database record into the text, creating a string such as

```
Current price is 5.40.
```

This little illustration demonstrates that field names in a database can be quite distinct from the portrayal of information from that database. "Preis" is the German word for "price."

In addition to placing database information into text to be displayed, you can place the information into either visible or hidden fields in a form. Then, when the form is submitted, that data is passed along to the same or another database record. Since HTML is stateless, it is this process—repeated over and over—that lets you automatically retrieve and store information. As you explore the possibilities, you will see that such techniques make it possible for you to hide the database totally from users, letting them function only on its information.

Database elements are shown in Table 11-2.

Encodings for Database Elements

A number of database elements accept a parameter that specifies the encoding to use on the text value that replaces the CDML element. If this parameter is allowed, the entries in the table show the values that are permitted for that variable. (Not all elements take the encoding parameter, and not all elements that do take it accept all possible values.)

The possible values for the encoding parameter are as follows:

- Raw—do nothing.

- HTML—use standard HTML encoding, adding elements for bold, italics, and so on.

- Break—HTML encoding with soft carriage returns (line wraps) replaced by the <BR> element of HTML.

- Display—translate to the language specified in the Web Companion configuration.

- URL—use URL encoding, which, among other things, converts spaces to %20.

CDML	Function
[FMP-CurrentAction]	The most recent action from the values in "Actions" on page 221. Encodings: HTML (default) and Display.
[FMP-CurrentData-base]	Value of -DB in the most recent action.
[FMP-CurrentError]	FileMaker Pro error number of most recent error. It is the number returned by the Status(CurrentError) function.
[FMP-CurrentFormat]	Value of -Format in the most recent action.
[FMP-CurrentLayout]	Value of -Lay in the most recent action.
[FMP-CurrentSkip]	Value of -Skip in the most recent action.
[FMP-CurrentLOP]	Value of -LOP in the most recent action.
[FMP-CurrentMax]	Value of -Max in the most recent action.
[FMP-CurrentRecID]	Value of -RecID in the most recent action.
[FMP-CurrentRecord-Count]	Total number of records in the database.
[FMP-CurrentRecord-Number]	Number of the current record within the currently selected set.
[FMP-Field]	Value of a database field. Parameters: 1 (required): The name of a field in the layout specified in the -Lay variable of the last request. 2 (optional): Encoding— Raw, URL, HTML (default), or Break.

TABLE 11-2. Database Elements

Looping

Retrieving information from a database and inserting it into text or a form is a major part of the work that you do with

FileMaker Pro databases on the Web. But the syntax described so far only allows you to place values from the current record into the HTML file that is being constructed by Web Companion. The Shopping Cart example shown previously is repeated in Figure 11-1.

In many cases, you want to extract values from a number of records and show them in a single window—such as the list of specials from the Shopping Cart example shown in Figure 11-2. In this case, you need the ability to sequentially display the data from each of the records located in a Find action.

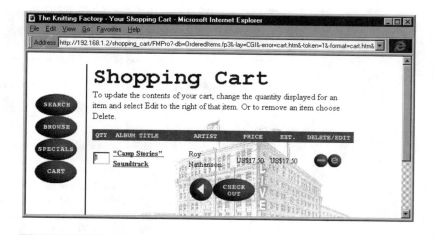

FIGURE 11-1. Shopping Cart: Single-Record Display

FMP-Record

This is such a common situation that CDML provides syntax for dealing with it by providing elements to let you work with the set of records returned by a Find action. The technique is very simple:

1. You create a table that will be used to display the data.

2. You specify one row of the table, indicating which fields from the database will be placed in the table data cells (TD elements). You use the [FMP-Field] elment to do this.

3. You then use the [FMP-Record] element, consisting of the [FMP-Record] starting tag and [/FMP-Record] ending tag, to bracket the table row. When Web Companion encounters the [FMP-Record] element, it will create a row for each record that has been found in the current selection.

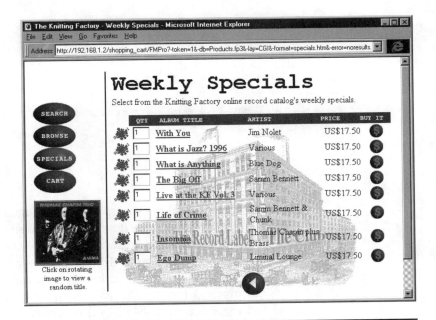

FIGURE 11-2. Weekly Specials in the Shopping Cart

The code that makes this possible is described in detail in "Using Forms," starting on page 289. A relevant section is excerpted here from prodlist.txt. The [FMP-Record] element tags are shown in italics; the [FMP-Field] elements that are used to place data from each record into a table cell are underlined.

```
<P>
<TABLE BORDER=0 CELLSPACING=0 CELLPADDING=2 WIDTH=495>
[FMP-RECORD]
<TR>
    ...quantity and title omitted from the example...

    <TD WIDTH=135>
    <P>
        [FMP-FIELD: Artist]
    </P>
    </TD>

    <TD WIDTH=80>
    <P>
        [FMP-FIELD: Formatted Price]
    </P>
    </TD>

    ...Buy It image omitted from the example...

</TR>
[/FMP-RECORD]
</TABLE>
</P>
```

Unlike traditional programming languages, you do not write loops to iterate through the data (although you use the [FMP-RECORD] element to show the block of code that is repeated for each record). You define a single action that is to be applied to each record and let Web Companion worry about iterations and loops. The values (if any) that you have provided for -Skip and -Max in the action that invokes this format file will be used to limit the data retrieved. (Remember that your format files are always invoked as part of an action.)

Note that it is not necessary to display the data in a table—you could simply display it as rows of text. However, in almost every case, multiple records from a database are presented in a table for ease of reading.

FMP-Portal

In addition to looping through the data retrieved by an action, you can loop through the data defined by a relationship—the data that would be visible in a portal in FileMaker Pro. The syntax is remarkably similar, as this excerpt from the Shopping Cart example (checkout.htm) demonstrates:

```
<TABLE BORDER="0" CELLPADDING="2" CELLSPACING="0"
    WIDTH="445">
[FMP-portal:Ordered Items]

<TR>
    <TD ALIGN=LEFT VALIGN=MIDDLE NOWRAP WIDTH="35">
    <FONT SIZE="-1">   
        [FMP-field:Ordered Items::Quantity]
    </FONT>
    </TD>

    <TD ALIGN=LEFT VALIGN=MIDDLE NOWRAP WIDTH="150">
    <FONT SIZE="-1">
    <B>
        [FMP-field:Ordered Items::Product name]
    </B>
    </FONT>
    </TD>

    <TD ALIGN=LEFT VALIGN=MIDDLE NOWRAP WIDTH="120">
    <FONT SIZE="-1">
        [FMP-field:Ordered Items::Artist]
    </FONT>
    </TD>
```

```
<TD ALIGN=RIGHT VALIGN=MIDDLE NOWRAP WIDTH="70">
<FONT SIZE="-1">
    [FMP-field:Ordered Items::Formatted Price]
</FONT>
</TD>

<TD ALIGN=RIGHT VALIGN=MIDDLE NOWRAP WIDTH="70">
<FONT SIZE="-1">
    [FMP-field:Ordered Items::Formatted Total]
</FONT>
</TD>
</TR>
[/FMP-portal]

<TR>
    <TD ALIGN=RIGHT VALIGN=TOP COLSPAN="4">
    <FONT SIZE="-1">
    <B>Total Cost:</B>
    </FONT>
    </TD>

    <TD ALIGN=RIGHT VALIGN=TOP>
    <FONT SIZE="-1" COLOR="#ff0000">
    <B>
        [FMP-field:Formatted Total]
    </B>
    </FONT>
    </TD>
</TR>
</TABLE>
```

In this case, instead of the [FMP-Record] element, the [FMP-Portal] element is used to loop through the relevant records. (Note that the [FMP-Portal] element requires you to name the relationship involved in the portal. You also need to specify the database from which each of the related fields is drawn. The [FMP-Field] elements are underlined.)

The structure of the code is identical to that shown previously, with each row of the portal being put into its own row of the table. A difference is that an additional row (after the [/FMP-Portal] element) is added to display a total field. You can do this with the [FMP-Record] element, too. (The [FMP-Field] element from this additional row is shown with a double underline.)

FMP-Repeat

The [FMP-Repeat] element lets you do exactly the same thing to a repeating field: the [FMP-Field] element is repeated once for each of the repeating instances of the field, with its data being placed either as text or as a table row.

FMP-LayoutFields

Finally, the [FMP-LayoutFields] element lets you loop through the fields of the current layout (specified in the -Lay variable of the request).

The looping elements are shown in Table 11-3.

Note that [FMP-CurrentFind] and [FMP-CurrentSort] are also looping elements of a kind. They are described in "Tags for Finding and Sorting" on page 261. [FMP-ValueList] is another looping element; it is described in "Lists" on page 263.

CDML	Description
[FMP-Portal] [/FMP-Portal]	Brackets replacement elements (usually [FMP-Field-Name]) to be placed in text or table rows for each portal record. Required parameter: name of the relationship.
[FMP-Record] [/FMP-Record]	Brackets replacement elements (usually [FMP-Field-Name]) to be placed in text or table rows for each record found in the current action (subject to -Skip and -Max variables).
[FMP-Repeating] [/FMP-Repeating]	Brackets replacement elements (usually [FMP-Field-Name]) to be placed in text or table rows for each repeating instance of a variable. [FMP-Repeating] takes a single parameter, which is the name of the repeating field.
[FMP-RepeatingItem]	The value of the field to repeat. Since the field name is provided as a parameter to [FMP-Repeating], [FMP-RepeatingItem] appears in the CDML where [FMP-Field] does for [FMP-Portal] and [FMP-Record].
[FMP-LayoutFields] [/FMP-LayoutFields]	Brackets the [FMP-FieldName] replacement element to be placed in text or table rows for each field in the current layout.
[FMP-FieldName]	The name of a field in the layout. It must appear within an [FMP-LayoutFields] element. The optional encoding parameter can have the value Raw, URL, or HTML (default).

TABLE 11-3. Looping Elements

If Elements

Together with loops and iterators, conditional statements—ifs—are a basic part of programming. CDML provides elements to support the basic conditional paradigm,

```
if (this is true)
    do this
else
    do that
```

The [FMP-If] element has three required parameters:

1. The variable or field being tested

2. The comparison to make

3. The value to compare against

In the example code above, the three test elements would be:

1. "this"

2. "is"

3. "true"

Variables and Fields to Test

You can use environmental and database variables as well as database fields as the basis for your conditional statements. Format files are always invoked in conjunction with a database (that is, they are specified in a request that also contains a -DB variable). Any field in that database's layout (either default or specified with the -Lay variable) can be referenced simply by using its name. Any field in a related database can be referenced by using its qualified name,

```
relateddatabase::fieldname
```

just as you normally do in FileMaker Pro.

Remember that the association between the format file and the database layout occurs when the request is made. You can create a format file that works with a number of different database layouts—provided, for example, that each layout contains a field called "name" and another called "address." Reusing format files with several databases becomes a little trickier when you are using fields from related databases: the field names and the databases in the relationship need to be identical. It is relatively easy to use a single format file for several databases, each of which contains a "name" and "address" field; it becomes a little more complicated—but far from impossible—when you refer to related fields such as "product::itemnumber" and "inventory::itemNumber." You may need to implement such a project in two steps—see "Links" on page 255 for some ideas in this area.

You can also use the environmental and database variables listed in Tables 11-1 and 11-2 as the basis for your comparison. When used in an If element, these variables are referenced directly, not through their CDML element. Thus, the CDML element [FMP-CurrentRecord] is used in a conditional element simply as

```
CurrentRecord
```

Note that this rule applies also to the [FMP-Field] element. To reference a database field within an If element you use the syntax

```
Field: myfieldname
```

(replacing *myfieldname* with whatever your field name is).

The reason for this variation is that the If element—like all CDML elements—is bracketed with [and]. A] at the end of an embedded CDML element would cause errors during processing. This is worth remembering

since the] character in other locations (such as within a string of charac-
ters to use as part of a comparison) can cause problems as well.

Additionally, the Range variable from Table 11-10 can be used, as can the Cookie variable, which is described in Table 11-14.

Finally, there are four additional variables that can be used as the basis for comparisons; they are shown in Table 11-4.

Variable	Description
CanDelete	Password in use allows deletion.
CanEdit	Password in use allows editing.
CanNew	Password in use allows new record creation.
IsSorted	Database is sorted.

TABLE 11-4. Additional Variables for If Elements

Comparisons

Having identified the variable or field to be tested, you next need to specify the comparison. CDML defines the comparison operators shown in Table 11-5.

Not all operators are valid for all types of values. The third column of Table 11-5 lists the types of values to which you can apply each operator.

Operator	Meaning	Comparison Values
.eq.	equals	True, False, numbers, text, dates, times, and Internet addresses. The constant Checked can also be used with .eq. for value list items (see "Lists" on page 263).
.neq.	not equal to	True, False, numbers, text, dates, and times.
.gt.	greater than	Numbers, text, dates, and times.
.gte.	greater than or equal to	Numbers, text, dates, and times.
.lt.	less than	Numbers, text, dates, and times.
.lte.	less than or equal to	Numbers, text, dates, and times.
.cn.	contains	Text.
.ncn.	does not contain	Text.

TABLE 11-5. Operators for [FMP-If]

Testing Values

The right-hand side of the conditional element—the value to test the variable or field against—can be any of the data types listed in the third column of Table 11-5, depending on the type of operator used. In each case, a literal value can be placed in the expression—a number, text string, date, etc. In the cases of numbers and text, you can also place a field name in the right-hand side of the element; the comparison will be performed between the variable or field on the left and the variable or field on the right.

The format of the If element is traditional: the tags involved are shown in Table 11-6. The [FMP-Else] tag is optional. If it is present, it is placed between [FMP-If] and [/FMP-If]. As in the standard if-else-endif construction in many other languages, If statements cannot be nested within one another, nor can they be compound (if this and that and the other thing then…).

However, IP addresses and domain names when used in comparisons with .eq. may be placed in a list, separated by commas; the OR operator is assumed. You can also use * as a wildcard for part of an IP address or a domain name. In these ways, you can test if an address is equal to given strings (or partial strings) as in these two examples:

```
[FMP-If: ClientIP .eq. 192.168.1.*, 10,10,10,10]
    …the user is logged on from either any address
    at 192.168.1.n or at 10.10.10.10…

[FMP-If: ClientAddress .eq.
    *.philmontmill.com, *.philmontmill.*]
```

CDML	Description
[FMP-If] [/FMP-If]	Required tags to bracket the HTML and CDML code to be performed in case of a positive outcome. The [FMP-If] tag has three required parameters: the variable or field for the left side of the comparison, the operator, and the value or field for the right side of the comparison.
[FMP-Else]	If present, the [FMP-Else] tag introduces the HTML and CDML code to be performed in case of a negative outcome. It is optional.

TABLE 11-6. If Elements

File Manipulation with CDML

The linguistic elements shown in Table 11-7 are used to join HTML and CDML files together. The [FMP-Include] element has a single parameter, which is the name of a file to insert within your format file. The contents of the included file are merged with the text in your format file as part of Web Companion's process of creating the dynamic HTML that it returns in response to a request.

The ability to include files within files is very important for two reasons:

1. Commonly used code can be included on many pages. Typically, this consists of a set of logo, address, and navigation elements that are common to all pages on a site (or part of a site). By physically including a single file, you can guarantee that all pages have the same appearance. Furthermore, changes to any of this common information can be made in a single place.

2. HTML and CDML files quickly become very big and very hard to read. It is often particularly hard to decipher the overall structure of a file. Editors that reformat and color syntactic elements help with this, but the biggest help is splitting the files up. In that way, you can have individual files for small parts of pages. This structure is very commonly used in conjunction with the [FMP-If] element.

The FileMaker Pro Web examples use the [FMP-Include] element extensively. The files are particularly easy to read—and to modify for your own purposes. In large part this is due to the use of included files.

The [FMP-Image] element is used to create a URL that points to an image: that URL is used wherever a URL for an image would normally be used—typically in the HREF attribute of an anchor or in an IMG SRC element. The single parameter to the [FMP-Image] element is the name of a container field in the database in use. This enables you to take an image from a record of the database and display it on the page that is being created by Web Companion.

CDML	Description
[FMP-Include]	Include the contents of the file specified by the single required parameter.
[FMP-Image]	Generate an image URL from the image in the container field that is the required parameter. [FMP-Image] is most commonly used in the HREF attribute and IMG SRC element.

TABLE 11-7. File Manipulation Elements

Links

The power of the Web is due in large part to its links. CDML lets you create and modify links that you can use (most often in the HREF attribute of an HTML anchor). The basic element is the [FMP-Link] element, which creates a URL based on the address of the page on which it is placed; that address includes the entire request—including the searchinfo parameters, if present (that is, the parameters that follow the ?).

You use the [FMP-Link] element to create a modified URL that is most often placed in the HREF attribute of an anchor. Thus, the following code creates an anchor with a link to the page on which it is placed:

```
<A HREF="[FMP-Link]">
```

This may seem a rather pointless adventure: clicking on that link will simply reload the current page. What makes this element useful is the ability to omit specific parts of the existing URL and replace them with new ones in the link. In this way, you can change almost all of the existing URL to new values. You simply omit a part of the URL's syntax and then replace it with a new value. Thus,

```
<A HREF="[FMP-Link: r]&-Format=Detail.htm">
```

creates a link to the current request; it omits the existing format file (the meaning of the r parameter) and adds a new format file to the request. Table 11-8 lists the parameters that you use to omit various parts of the URL.

Note that the URL parts need not be replaced. For example, you can simply remove sorting criteria and leave the database unsorted in the newly constructed URL. Note also that you can combine parameters; if you do so, you simply include each additional letter. For example, [FMP-Link]: rm omits the Format and Max sections of the existing URL.

Parameter	Section of URL Request to Omit
a	Action (such as -Find, -View, etc.)
d	Database (-Db)
f	Find
k	Skip (-Skip)
l	Layout (-Lay)
m	Max (-Max)

TABLE 11-8. Link Parameters

Parameter	Section of URL Request to Omit
R	Format file (-Format)
s	Sort
t	Token (-Token)

TABLE 11-8. Link Parameters

The most frequent modification to a request is a repositioning—repeating the request for the next or previous batch of records or for the first or last batch of records. (This is what the Top, Back, Next, and Last buttons in the Instant Web Publishing browser do—see "The Browser Window" on page 109.) Rather than manually modify the URL, you can use several CDML elements that do this positioning for you. [FMP-LinkFirst], [FMP-LinkNext], [FMP-LinkPrevious], and [FMP-LinkLast] create requests that return the same number of records as the current request with the appropriate repositioning.

In this area, another element is frequently used. The [FMP-LinkRecID] element is used to create a URL that points to a specific record. Often used within an [FMP-Record] element, [FMP-LinkRecID] is commonly used to implement a Display Details function. A format file is a required parameter; an optional second parameter is a layout file. (This is because detail displays often use different formats and layout from lists.)

Table 11-9 shows the link elements.

An example of the use of link elements is given in the following code. At $\bar{1}$, you can see the link that is generated to the previous batch of records. $\bar{2}$ is the start of the [FMP-Record] element that will be repeated for all of the records retrieved in the current request. The various statements marked $\bar{3}$ display data from database fields. (Note that these statements

CDML	Description
[FMP-Link]	Creates a URL pointing to the page on which it is placed. Parameters let you modify the new URL; they are listed in Table 11-8.
[FMP-LinkFirst]	Creates a link to the first batch of records using the current request. An ending tag ([/FMP-LinkFirst]) is required. Typically, the content of the element is a phrase such as "First" or "Top"; alternatively—or additionally—a graphic can be used.
[FMP-LinkLast]	Same as above, but applies to last batch of records.
[FMP-LinkNext]	Same as above, but applies to next batch of records.
[FMP-LinkPrevious]	Same as above, but applies to previous batch of records.
[FMP-LinkRecID]	Creates a URL to the current record. Typically used within an [FMP-Record] element. A pathname to a format file is a required first parameter; an optional second parameter is the path to a layout file.

TABLE 11-9. Link Elements

are within an HTML form; the INPUT TYPE element cannot stand on its own. For more details, see "Using Forms" starting on page 289.)

At $\bar{4}$ you can see the use of the [FMP-LinkRecID] element to let users see more details on the current record. Finally, at $\bar{5}$ you see how the [FMP-LinkNext] element is used after the [FMP-Record] element ends to display the next batch of records.

This code is very common. You are probably used to this sort of browsing as you use the Web yourself.

1 `[FMP-LINKPREVIOUS]`
    Click here to see the previous page of records.
`[/FMP-LINKPREVIOUS]`

2 `[FMP-RECORD]`

3 `<P>Date Entered:`
    `<INPUT TYPE=text NAME="Date Entered"`
        `VALUE="[FMP-FIELD:Date Entered]" SIZE=30 entered>`
`</P>`

3 `<P>From:`
    `<INPUT TYPE=text NAME=From VALUE="[FMP-FIELD:From]"`
        `SIZE=45>`
`</P>`

3 `<P>Company:`
    `<INPUT TYPE=text NAME=Company`
        `VALUE="[FMP-FIELD:Company]" SIZE=45>`
`</P>`

3 `<P>Subject:`
    `<INPUT TYPE=text NAME=Subject`
        `VALUE="[FMP-FIELD:Subject]" SIZE=45>`
`</P>`

`<P>Start of Message:`
    `<INPUT TYPE=text NAME=Message`
        `VALUE="[FMP-FIELD:Message]" SIZE=45>`
`</P>`

4 `<P>Want to see`
    `<A HREF="[FMP-linkrecid: layout=Form View,`
        `format=Detail.htm]">`
        `Record Details`
    `</A>?<BR><HR>`
`</P>`

`[/FMP-RECORD]`

5 `<P>[FMP-LINKNEXT]`
    Click here to see the next page of records.
`[/FMP-LINKNEXT]`
`</P>`
`<P>`

Range Elements

Along with the functionality of Next/Previous/Top/Bottom record displays, it is useful to provide additional feedback to users about where they are in a database. An example of a commonly found tip is

```
Displaying records 6-10 of 94 records found.
(5 records displayed).
```

To place such a message in the HTML file generated by Web Companion, you use the elements found in Table 11-10. Their use is demonstrated in the following code (which generates the tip shown previously):

```
Displaying records [FMP-RANGESTART] through
    [FMP-RANGEEND] of [FMP-CURRENTFOUNDCOUNT] records found.

([FMP-RANGESIZE] records displayed).
</P>
```

CDML Tag	Description
[FMP-CurrentFound-Count]	Number of records found in the last request.
[FMP-RangeEnd]	Ending record number of last Find request.
[FMP-RangeSize]	Number of records returned in the last Find request. (-Max).
[FMP-RangeStart]	Starting record number of last Find request.

TABLE 11-10. Range Elements

Tags for Finding and Sorting

Just as it is common to provide information about where in a database the currently displayed data is found (as described in "Range Elements" on page 260), it is common to provide information about the current sort and search criteria used in a database.

If you are using sorts and searches that you have defined, this is very easy. However, if you have allowed the user to generate ad hoc searches and sorts, you do not easily know what the search and sort criteria are.

The [FMP-CurrentFind] and [FMP-CurrentSort] looping elements let Web Companion do this for you. They are looping elements just like those described in "Looping" on page 241. Within the [FMP-CurrentFind] or [FMP-CurrentSort] element, you provide the text and replacement tags for the information that you want the user to see. This may be for informational purposes only, or it may be as a helpful clue when a search has failed—as this slightly abridged excerpt from the Employee Database example shows:

```
There are no employees that match your search.

Modify your search criteria and try again.

<P><TABLE>
   <TR>
      <TD ALIGN=center>
      <P>Search criteria ([FMP-CURRENTLOP]):</P>
      </TD>
   </TR>

   <TR>
      <TD ALIGN=center>
      <P>
         [FMP-CURRENTFIND]
            <B>[FMP-FINDFIELDITEM: HTML]</B>
            [FMP-FINDOPITEM: Long]
```

```
            [FMP-FINDVALUEITEM: HTML]<BR>
        [/FMP-CURRENTFIND]
    </P>
    </TD>
  </TR>
</TABLE>
```

The italicized section shows the use of the [FMP-Current-Find] element. All the find criteria the user has selected will be shown. Each field in each criterion will be in bold (the underlined text); the comparison operator and comparison value will be shown normally.

The additional code in this snippet demonstrates the use of a table with two rows and a single column—one table data cell in each row—to format and align information.

Table 11-11 shows the elements used in reporting information about searches and sorts.

CDML Tag	Description
[FMP-CurrentFind]	The element that encloses text and replacement tags for all criteria within the current find.
[FMP-CurrentSort]	The element that encloses text and replacement tags for all criteria within the current sort.
[FMP-FindFieldItem]	The name of the field used in a single criterion; must be placed within an [FMP-CurrentFind] element. Encoding parameter: Raw, URL, or HTML (default).

TABLE 11-11. CDML Elements for Sorting and Finding

CDML Tag	Description
[FMP-FindOpItem]	The name of the operator used in a single criterion; must be placed within an [FMP-CurrentFind] element. Encoding parameter: Short, Long (default), or Display.
[FMP-FindValueItem]	The value used in a single criterion; must be placed within an [FMP-CurrentFind] element. Encoding parameter: Raw, URL, or HTML (default).
[FMP-SortFieldItem]	The name of the field used in a comparison; must be placed within an [FMP-CurrentSort] element. Encoding parameter: Raw, URL, or HTML (default).
[FMP-SortOrderItem]	The sort order used in a comparison; must be placed within an [FMP-CurrentSort] element. Encoding parameter: Raw, URL, HTML (default), or Display.

TABLE 11-11. CDML Elements for Sorting and Finding (Continued)

Lists

One of the most useful data entry tools of HTML is the ability to create selection lists—prepared lists from which users can select one or more items. When the range of choices is relatively small (less than two dozen, usually), it is much easier to choose from existing items than to enter data manually. This eliminates many mistakes caused by keystroke errors; it also standardizes input (for example, eliminating the possibility of Ukraine and The Ukraine both being entered into a database when one would do).

Selection Lists

The HTML specification allows for the creation of selection lists; their actual visualization is determined by the browser that you use. Typically, a selection list that allows single selections is shown with a pop-up menu, and one that allows multiple selections is shown in a scrolling list; these choices are shown in Figure 11-3. (You can also specify that radio buttons and other formats be used for the selection list.)

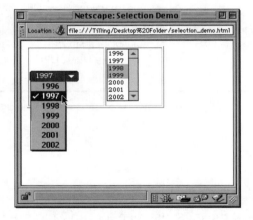

FIGURE 11-3. Single and Multiple Selection Lists in Netscape Communicator

The two selection lists shown in Figure 11-3 are both created with essentially the same HTML:

```
<SELECT NAME=Year MULTIPLE>
          <OPTION>1996
          <OPTION>1997
          <OPTION>1998
          <OPTION>1999
          <OPTION>2000
          <OPTION>2001
          <OPTION>2002
</SELECT>
```

The list at the right—which allows multiple selection—contains the attribute MULTIPLE, which is shown in italics in this code snippet. The list at the left—which does not allow multiple selection—omits the MULTIPLE attribute. Each element of the list is entered as an OPTION element within the SELECT element. (OPTION elements do not require an end tag, </OPTION>, but it can be used to improve readability.)

The selections shown in Figure 11-3 have been made in the browser. However, it is possible to specify that certain elements of the selection list are preselected. To do so, you use the attribute SELECTED in the OPTION element. Thus, to force the browser to open the selection list with the selection shown at the left in Figure 11-3, you would use the code

```
<OPTION SELECTED>1997
```

In the case of the multiple selection list shown at the right, you would use the code

```
<OPTION SELECTED>1998
<OPTION SELECTED>1999
```

Of course, once the browser has displayed the page, the user may modify the selections as needed.

As noted previously ("Value Lists" on page 66), FileMaker Pro implements this sort of functionality as part of its databases: you can specify a value list to be used for a given field. Users can then choose from among the values when entering data. FileMaker Pro value lists can be of two types:

1. They can consist of explicit values.

2. They can consist of values dynamically extracted from a particular field of a database.

Furthermore, in either case you can allow users to modify the value list—or not—as they are entering data. CDML provides functionality to map value lists to HTML selection lists. That syntax is described in this section.

The simplest way to integrate FileMaker Pro's value lists with HTML selection lists is to use the [FMP-Option] element. It allows you to specify a field name (and optionally a value list name); Web Companion then automatically fills in the options of an HTML SELECT, as in the following code snippet from the Employee Database example:

```
<SELECT NAME="Department">
    [FMP-option: Department]
</SELECT>
```

A pop-up menu will be shown; it contains the values from the value list associated with the field Department. If the MULTIPLE attribute had been set in the SELECT element, a scrolling list would be shown instead.

Looping through Items in Value Lists

Sometimes you need to handle each item in a value list individually. That is the case when you want to create a radio button or check box for each one or where you want to indicate the currently checked values. The heart of this syntax for CDML is another repeating element—[FMP-ValueList]. Within the bounds of the [FMP-ValueList], you specify the format of each list item, using the [FMP-ValueListItem] element to identify each one. Web Companion fills in as many items as are present in the value list according to your specifications.

Figure 11-4 shows another page from the Shopping Cart example. At the right, you see a selection list displaying categories of music. This list is created using the [FMP-ValueList] element; it is based on a value list in the database.

The code that implements the list is the simplest type of selection list. It is shown here:

```
<SELECT NAME="Category" MULTIPLE SIZE=9>
        [FMP-valuelist:Category,list=Categories]
        <OPTION>[FMP-valuelistitem]
        [/FMP-valuelist]
</SELECT>
```

FIGURE 11-4. Selection List from Shopping Cart Example

The [FMP-ValueList] tags are italicized; [FMP-ValueList-Item], which is repeated for each item Web Companion finds in the database, is underlined. (The syntax for the list elements is shown in Table 11-12.)

What this means is that the dynamically changing list of categories is maintained in the FileMaker Pro database; as new categories are added—either by users or by the database designer/administrator—the lists in Web pages are dynamically reconfigured. This is an enormous time saver. The power of database-driven Web sites is that the HTML needs to be changed far less frequently than traditional static HTML, even though the underlying data may be changing constantly.

You need not use the [FMP-ValueList] element in a typical HTML selection list. Sometimes you just want to present a list of choices, as shown in Figure 11-5.

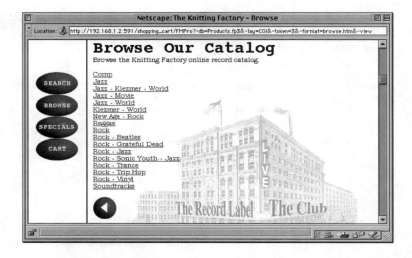

FIGURE 11-5. Choices Not in a Selection List

An extract of the code for this page is shown here:

```
<P>
    <FONT SIZE="+4"><B><TT>
        Browse Our Catalog
    </TT></B></FONT><BR>

    Browse the Knitting Factory online record catalog.
</P>

<P>
    [FMP-VALUELIST: Category, LIST=Categories]
        <A HREF="FMPro?-token=[FMP-currenttoken]&
```

```
           -db=Products.fp3&-lay=CGI&-format=hitlist.htm&
           -error=noresults.htm&-max=10&-sortfield=name&
           -sortorder=descending&
           -category=[FMP-valuelistitem,url]&-find">
      [FMP-VALUELISTITEM: Always, HTML]
   </A><BR>
 [/FMP-VALUELIST]
</P>
```

As in the previous example, the tags comprising the [FMP-ValueList] element are italicized; the [FMP-ValueListItem] element is underlined. They are not placed within a selection list; instead, the value list is used to create a simple list of links to each category that is found. In HTML terms, for each item in the value list, an anchor is created with an HREF attribute pointing to the location of the category. That anchor code is shown in bold in the previous code.

Note two points about the anchor:

1. It includes the [FMP-ValueListItem] element—look for the ending tag (</A>).

2. The [FMP-ValueListItem] element is used twice within the anchor: once as part of the URL that is generated for the HREF attribute and again for its text value that is displayed. URL encoding is used in the first case, since it is part of the HREF attribute (a URL). HTML encoding is used in the second case, since it must be understandable to people.

Looping through FileMaker Pro Value Lists

Finally, you sometimes need to loop through the value lists associated with a database. This lets you implement ad hoc searching procedures for users in which they can choose among value lists such as product names, sizes, and loca-

CDML	Description
[FMP-Option]	This element provides an implicit loop through all items in a FileMaker Pro value list; each is placed in the HTML output from Web Companion. This element should be placed within a standard HTML SELECT element. The first parameter (required) is the name of the field with which the list is associated; the second (optional) is the name of the value list.
[FMP-ValueList]	The loop element in which value list items are repeated. The ending tag ([/FMP-ValueList]) is required. The first parameter is the name of the field name to which the FileMaker Pro value list is attached. (The field name is required so that current values of that field can be properly reflected in the HTML code that is generated.) The optional second parameter is the name of the value list.
[FMP-ValueList-Checked]	Use this element to indicate that the HTML CHECKED attribute should be generated for a value list item that corresponds to the current field value.
[FMP-ValueListItem]	This element provides the value of a value list item; it must be placed within an [FMP-ValueList] element. It has two optional parameters. The first lets you filter out those values not currently selected in this database field. In other words, if the value of the database field is not equal to the current value list item, it is skipped. The two values for this parameter are Checked and Always, indicating whether this filtering should be done. The second parameter lets you specify the encoding for the resulting string. The choices are Raw, URL, and HTML (default).

TABLE 11-12. Value List Elements

tions. You don't have to do any coding whatsoever—you just rely on the value lists that you (or the database designer) have created.

The elements for value list looping are shown in Table 11-13.

CDML	Description
[FMP-ValueName-Item]	This element returns the name of a value list. It is valid only within an [FMP-ValueName] element. Optional encodings are Raw, URL, and HTML (default).
[FMP-ValueNames][/ FMP-ValueNames]	This is the element in which FMP-ValueNameItem is placed. The code within this element is repeated for each value list in the current database.

TABLE 11-13. Value Name Elements

Cookies and Headers

Cookies are one approach to dealing with the statelessness of HTTP and HTML. A cookie is a body of data that is stored on the user's computer by the browser, usually in response to a request from the remote Web server. A cookie can consist of the password that you have entered when browsing a specific site: in that case, the browser can check if the cookie exists and, if it does, use the stored password so that you do not have to reenter it each time you request that password-protected Web page.

Cookie Data

A cookie can contain your preferences with regard to the display of a site—anything from page layout of dynamic pages to color schemes that are under your control. Theoretically, cookies can contain any information at all. The data to be placed in a cookie is downloaded from a Web page and uploaded as a package to that (or another) Web page on demand.

In addition to their encapsulated data, cookies can have the following attributes:

- Each cookie has a name; the name is provided by the Web page and is used in retrieving the cookie at a later time.

- A cookie can have an expiration time on it. Many cookies are stored only while you are browsing a Web page; others are automatically purged when you quit your browser. Still others may last for a day, a month—or even years.

- A cookie can have a domain name associated with it; typically, this is the domain name of the Web server that places the cookie on your disk.

Cookies are implemented by browsers, and their behavior is often subject to user controls. Most browsers allow users to refuse all cookies categorically; other options let you limit cookies based on expiration times and domain names. Thus, what actually happens when a Web page tries to place a cookie is a combination of the Web page author's requests, the user's preferences, and the way in which the browser combines all of them.

Cookies and Security

Such limits are placed on cookies because cookies can represent a serious security problem. When a cookie that contains the password to your bank account is stored on your hard disk, you may welcome the fact that you can check your balance without having to reenter the password each time.

However, anyone else who uses your computer can check your balance just as easily. Of course, you can solve this problem by putting a password on your computer or locking it up. But there are still problems.

A Web page author who knows how a cookie is identified can retrieve a cookie left by another Web page in many cases. Since data inside cookies can be encrypted, this is not always a serious problem, but it is a very real danger in many cases. Most people do not realize that the fact of browsing a Web page can allow a remote Web server to retrieve data from their hard disk. But there are even more problems.

You can store anything in a cookie. You can retrieve data from a FileMaker Pro database and store individual fields into a cookie. As with the password example, this may make life easier for users who have information readily available (through the cookies) that otherwise would have required a data access. But all of the issues involving data security and normalization come into play. What if the data in the database has changed since the cookie was stored? What legal and moral issues exist when data is extracted from a database and disseminated to people who do not even know that they are receiving it? You may have required a password to let people gain access to your site, but once your data has been downloaded via a cookie, anyone with access to your users' computers can see data that you thought was protected.

Cookies are very useful. When their information is purely preferential—page layout, fonts, etc.—it is hard to argue that their existence is a serious threat (although the presence of certain cookies can reveal where you have been pointing your Web browser). When you store information that is otherwise confidential in a cookie, be aware that you may be courting disaster.

CDML Implementation of Cookies

Cookies are part of the HTTP specification—not part of HTML. They are part of the HTTP header information that is sent back and forth between Web servers and clients.[1]

Table 11-14 shows the cookie elements as well as two associated CDML elements.

CDML	Description
[FMP-Cookie]	This element retrieves the cookie with the given name. The parameters used in [FMP-SetCookie] (Expires, Path, and Domain) are managed by the browser before this command can be executed. The encoding parameter can have the values Raw (default) and URL.
[FMP-SetCookie]	This is the element that creates a cookie. Its four parameters are named (e.g., Expires=60) just as the variables in URL requests are (see the previous chapter). The first parameter is whatever you want to name the cookie. The other parameters and their names are Expires, Path, and Domain. The value of the first parameter (cookiename) is any text string of less than 1024 characters; you can use Field:fieldname, where fieldname is a database field name to insert data. Expires is the expiration of the cookie measured in minutes from the present. Path is the URL path to which the cookie applies. Domain is the domain name for the cookie. Other than the cookie name and value, the parameters are optional.

TABLE 11-14. Cookie Elements

---

1. For further information about cookies, see RFC 2109, "HTTP State Management Mechanism."

CDML	Description
[FMP-Header] [/FMP-Header]	This element lets you specify the header that will be emitted by Web Companion. The text you provide completely replaces the default text. If used, it must precede the [FMP-SetCookie] element.
[FMP-ContentMime-Type]	The single required parameter in this element is the MIME type to be placed in the HTTP header that is created by Web Companion. The default—as in most Web pages—is text/html.

TABLE 11-14. Cookie Elements

Summary

CDML lets you create Web pages with all the functionality of FileMaker Pro. You can create it directly or use it implicitly through Home Page. You can also use FileMaker Pro's CDML tool to create snippets of CDML to paste into your own format files. The following chapter discusses that tool.

CDML Tool

12

The Web Tools folder that ships with FileMaker Pro contains the CDML Reference, CDML Tool, and a subfolder of CDML template files. The CDML Reference (a FileMaker Pro database) provides full details on the CDML syntax. CDML Tool is another FileMaker Pro database that interacts with CDML Reference and your own databases to provide you with an easy way of developing format files for Custom Web Publishing.

This chapter provides a guide to CDML Tool.

Note that CDML Tool relies on the presence of CDML Reference in the same folder in which it is located. Because both are FileMaker Pro databases, you may be tempted to explore them to see how they work—that is good. You may also be tempted to "improve" or customize them—that may not be such a good idea.

Using CDML Tool

When you open the CDML Tool database, you see the introductory window shown in Figure 12-1. (Names and version numbers may be different in your version.)

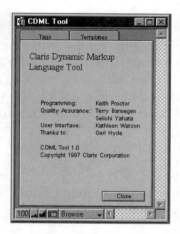

FIGURE 12-1. CDML Tool Introduction

After a few moments, the window's contents change to reflect the FileMaker Pro databases that you have open. Figure 12-2 shows CDML Tool with the Asset Management example that ships with FileMaker Pro.

CDML Tool combines CDML syntax definitions from CDML Reference with the meta-information of a database (field names, layout names, etc.); it merges these into snippets of CDML code that you can paste into your format files.

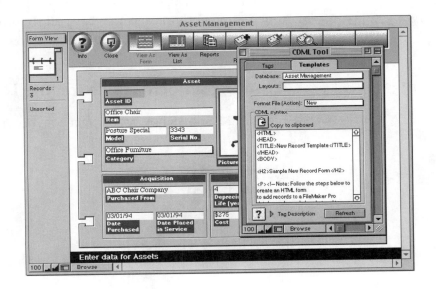

FIGURE 12-2. CDML Tool in Use

The Database pop-up menu at the top of CDML Tool lets you choose from among your open FileMaker Pro databases. You need not have any database open, but if you do, the code snippets that are generated will use the fields and layouts from that database since CDML Tool can read that information from the selected database.

Templates

The right-hand tab at the top of CDML Tool lets you access a number of templates that you can use as starting points for basic format files. These templates come with extensive documentation and notes as to what you should modify.

Creating a Format File for the New Action

Figure 12-3 shows how you select a layout in CDML Tool.

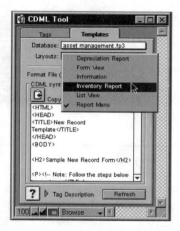

FIGURE 12-3. Selecting a Layout in CDML Tool

Having selected a database and a layout, you select the action for the format file that you want CDML Tool to create. This is shown in Figure 12-4.

CDML Tool will merge the appropriate template with the database and layout producing code that is shown in the window at the center of CDML Tool. You can use the mouse and menu commands or the Copy to Clipboard button to copy that HTML code and paste it into your HTML editor.

FIGURE 12-4. Selecting an Action for a Format File in CDML Tool

The Resulting Format File

The code is heavily annotated, as the following example shows. It is the code that is generated from the steps shown here—the Inventory Report layout of the Asset Management database used to create a New action format file. Note the underlined lines, which show the automatic incorporation of information from the layout and database.

```
<HTML>
<HEAD>
<TITLE>New Record Template</TITLE>
</HEAD>
<BODY>

<H2>Sample New Record Form</H2>
```

<P><!-- Note: Follow the steps below to create an HTML form
to add records to a FileMaker Pro database. An angle bracket
and two hyphens indicate comments; comments are not displayed by the Web browser.-->

<P><!-- STEP 1. SPECIFY THE FORM ACTION
The form action is already set to "FMPro." When submitting
this form, the Web server is notified to pass this format
file to FileMaker Pro 4.0 for processing.-->
<P><FORM ACTION="FMPro" METHOD="post">

<P><!-- STEP 2. SPECIFY THE DATABASE
If you've chosen a database in the CDML Tool, the database
name should already be specified within the Database CDML
tag. If the database name has not been specified or is
incorrect, delete the database name specified in the Value
section of the CDML database tag below and type a new database name within the quotation marks.-->
<P><INPUT TYPE="hidden" NAME="-DB"
    VALUE="<u>Asset Management</u>">

<P><!-- STEP 3. SPECIFY THE LAYOUT
If you've chosen a database and layout in the CDML Tool, the
layout name should already be specified within the Layout
CDML tag. If the layout name has not been specified or is
incorrect, delete the layout name specified in the Value
section of the CDML Layout tag below and type the appropriate layout name within the quotation marks.-->
<P><INPUT TYPE="hidden" NAME="-LAY"
    VALUE="<u>Inventory Report</u>">

<P><!-- STEP 4. SPECIFY THE FILENAME FOR RESPONSE FILE
Update the path specified in the value section of the CDML
Format tag below, which indicates the location of the next
format file that is displayed after the Web user submits
this form. In the example below, the "newreply.htm" format
file will be displayed next.-->
<P><INPUT TYPE="hidden" NAME="-FORMAT"
    VALUE="path-to-file/newreply.htm">

```
<P><!-- STEP 5. ADD TEXT FIELDS
In the CDML Tool, first choose a method to add fields in the
Category pop-up menu. Next, choose the HTML tag to display
the data (text field, radio button, etc.). Select the field
name, then drag the CDML syntax below this comment. The HTML
tag that creates a blank text field is: <INPUT TYPE="text"
NAME="Field Name1" VALUE="" SIZE=25> -->

<P><!-- STEP 6. SPECIFY THE BUTTON ACTION
The Submit button adds a record to the FileMaker Pro data-
base. To customize the button text, delete the button text
specified in the Value section of the -New CDML tag below
and type the replacement text within the quotation marks.-->
<P><INPUT TYPE="submit" NAME="-NEW" VALUE="New Record">
<P><INPUT TYPE="reset" VALUE="Clear Form">

<P><!-- STEP 7. SAVE FILE
Save this file to a project folder within the Web folder in
the FileMaker Pro 4.0 folder.-->

</FORM>
</BODY>
</HTML>
```

Tags

The other tab at the top of CDML Tool lets you generate specific CDML tags, either as syntax examples (if no database is open) or as ready-to-use code that you can paste into format files. (Note the italicized section in the generated code shown in the previous section: it indicates where such tags are to be inserted.)

You choose the category of tag that you want to create by using the Category pop-up menu which is shown in Figure 12-5.

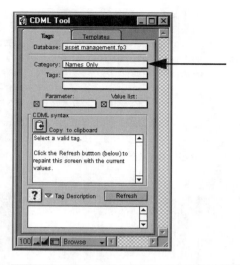

FIGURE 12-5. Category Pop-up Menu in CDML Tool

Once you have chosen a category, the CDML tags in that category are listed in the Tags pop-up menu, as shown in Figure 12-6. You choose the type of tag in which you are interested and then select the specific field from your database in the Fields pop-up menu, as shown in Figure 12-7.

The menu may be blank—as it is in that figure. If it is, just click the Refresh button, which is highlighted in Figure 12-7. CDML Tool will reload the fields from your database, producing the full pop-up menu shown in Figure 12-8. Select the field in which you are interested, and the CDML code will be generated in the window in the center of CDML Tool—as shown in Figure 12-9.

The steps will become a simple pattern:

1. Select the database.

2. Click the Tags tab if it is not already clicked.

3. Select the category of tag.

4. Select the individual tag.

5. If necessary, click the Refresh button.

6. Select the field.

7. Copy the code from CDML Tool to your CDML format file. (If you are using Home Page, make certain that you are in Edit HTML Source mode in order to be able to paste the code in.)

FIGURE 12-6. Contents of Tags Pop-up Menu in CDML Tool

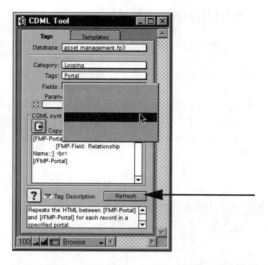

FIGURE 12-7. CDML Tool Needing Refreshing

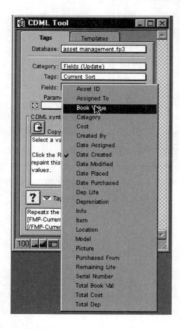

FIGURE 12-8. Fields for Tags in CDML Tool

FIGURE 12-9. Generated Code for Individual Tag in CDML Tool

Summary

If you are experienced with databases and have little experience with Web page authoring, CDML Tool can be an excellent way of negotiating the sometimes arcane syntax of HTML and CDML without having to really think about it very much. And even if you have years of experience with HTML, CDML Tool can keep you from forgetting the loose ends that can trip you up.

Using Forms

The World Wide Web was conceived initially as a way of navigating through information from sites all over the world. It quickly became clear that in addition to being used as a delivery vehicle for information, it could also be used as a simple and easy collection vehicle for data. The FORM element was devised to make data entry easy.

Like the Web, databases can be used both for storage and retrieval as well as for data entry and updating. As you have seen, FileMaker Pro has a number of built-in data validation routines that can be used to help ensure the quality of data. The HTML FORM element mixes well with FileMaker Pro. This chapter shows you how to do it.

Forms versus Tables

Both forms and tables are used to structure information. Typically, you use HTML tables to display data that is retrieved, whereas you use HTML forms to collect data that is being entered. In addition, you can use tables to organize information—whether retrieved or entered—on a single Web page.

A Table Example

For example, Figure 13-1 shows an HTML table that is used to display records retrieved from a FileMaker Pro database.

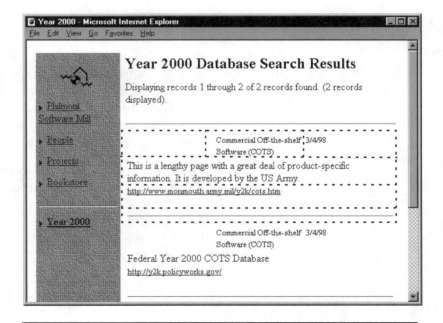

FIGURE 13-1. Table Used to Display FileMaker Pro Data

The table that is shown here is more complex than some of those shown previously in which a single FileMaker Pro record was displayed in a single row with one column for each field. The dotted lines that have been superimposed on the screenshot in Figure 13-1 show that for each FileMaker Pro record, there are four rows of three cells each.

- The first row contains three cells, each of which contains one field's data. The first two cells are filled only if their contents are not blank. This provides a very slight performance improvement: less HTML code is generated by Web Companion when the fields are blank and that means less code to transmit and less code for the user's browser to process. However, the mechanism for excluding data can be used in other circumstances and for other purposes.

- The second row contains a single field's data that spans the three cells.

- The third row contains another field's data that once again spans the three cells. It is an anchor containing a link—an HTML HREF attribute.

- The fourth row contains a carriage return (<BR>) and a horizontal rule (<HR>) spanning the three cells.

HTML for the Table Example

For review, the code is provided here. Note the [FMP-Record] and [/FMP-Record] tags, which delimit a single File-Maker Pro data record. Everything within them is repeated for each record; thus, each retrieved record will generate four table rows.

```
<P>
<TABLE BORDER=0 WIDTH="100%">
[FMP-RECORD]
    <!--first row-->
    <TR>
        <TD VALIGN=top WIDTH="31%">
            <P>[FMP-IF: Product .neq. ]
                <FONT SIZE="-1">[FMP-FIELD: Product]</FONT>
                [/FMP-IF]
            </P>
        </TD>

        <TD VALIGN=top WIDTH="31%">
            <P>[FMP-IF: Subject .neq. ]
                <FONT SIZE="-1">[FMP-FIELD: Subject]</FONT>
                [/FMP-IF]
            </P>
        </TD>

        <TD VALIGN=top WIDTH="31%">
            <P>
                <FONT SIZE="-1">[FMP-FIELD: Date Entered]
                    </FONT>
            </P>
        </TD>
    </TR>

    <!--second row-->
    <TR>
        <TD COLSPAN=3 WIDTH="93%">
            <P>[FMP-FIELD: Message, Break]</P>
        </TD>
    </TR>
    <!--third row-->
    <TR>
        <TD COLSPAN=3 WIDTH="93%">
            <P>[FMP-IF: Reference .neq. ]
                <P>
                    <A HREF="[FMP-FIELD: Reference]">
                    <FONT SIZE="-1">[FMP-FIELD: Reference]
                    </FONT></A>
                </P>
            <P>[/FMP-IF]</P>
        </TD>
```

```
    </TR>

    <!--fourth row-->
    <TR>
        <TD COLSPAN=3 WIDTH="93%">
            <P><BR><HR></P>
        </TD>
    </TR>

[/FMP-RECORD]
</TABLE>
</P>
```

As you can see, a table can be used as a very complex way of displaying formatted data from a database; it need not be evident that it is a table (for example, the table cells in Figure 13-1 have no borders that identify them as being table data cells).

A Form Example

Forms, on the other hand, are usually used for data entry. Figures 13-2 and 13-3 show a data entry form used to enter data to the same database shown in Figure 13-1.

By contrast with the table, the form shows a single record at a time. Furthermore, while the table suppresses field and record boundaries, the data entry fields in the form are clearly outlined. (This is an option in both designs, but typically forms explicitly show the fields and tables often do not.)

Even more important, the form is designed for user interaction: note the New Record and Clear Form buttons at the bottom of Figure 13-3.

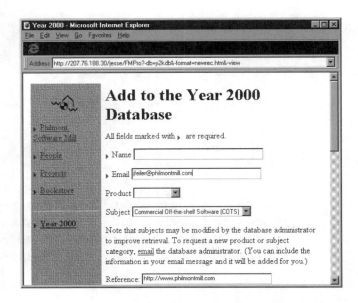

FIGURE 13-2. Form for Data Entry (1)

You can combine tables and forms. In addition to being used to display data with the [FMP-Record] element, tables can also be used to position objects on a page. (The data entry screens shown in Figure 13-2 and 13-3 actually show a table—the left-hand navigational panel is a single data cell of the table and the right-hand cell contains the data entry form.)

FIGURE 13-3. Form for Data Entry (2)

Example Code for a Form within a Table

You have seen the mingling of tables and forms previously—for example, in "Weekly Specials in the Shopping Cart" on page 243. Here is the section of code that was referred to there. (You may wish to refer back to the figure on that page to remind yourself of what this will look like.)

The italicized table data cell contains a form (the syntax of which will be described in "What Is a Form?" on page 298). The boldfaced line of code later in this code snippet submits the form. The point of this example is that you can combine the physical structuring of tables with the functionality of forms for data entry.

```
<P>
<!--Begin Include: prodlist.txt-->

<TABLE BORDER=0 CELLSPACING=0 CELLPADDING=2 WIDTH=495>
[FMP-RECORD]
<TR>
    <TD WIDTH=35>
    <P>
        [FMP-IF: Special.eq.Yes]
            <IMG SRC="images/special1.gif" ALT="Special!"
                WIDTH=29 HEIGHT=24 BORDER=0 ALIGN=top>
        [/FMP-IF]
    </P>
    </TD>

    <TD WIDTH=40>
    <P>
        <FORM METHOD="POST" ACTION="FMPro"
            NAME="prodform[FMP-field:ID]">
        <INPUT TYPE="hidden" NAME="-token"
            VALUE="[FMP-currenttoken]">
        <INPUT TYPE="hidden" NAME="-db"
            VALUE="OrderedItems.fp3">
        <INPUT TYPE="hidden" NAME="-format"
            VALUE="cartok.htm">
        <INPUT TYPE="hidden" NAME="-lay"
            VALUE="CGI">
        <INPUT TYPE=hidden NAME="Product ID"
            VALUE="[FMP-field:ID]">
        <INPUT TYPE=hidden NAME="Order ID"
            VALUE="[FMP-currenttoken]">
        <INPUT TYPE=hidden NAME="-new" VALUE="">
        <INPUT TYPE=text NAME=Quantity VALUE="1"
            SIZE=2> </FORM>
    </P>
    </TD>
    <TD WIDTH=165>
    <P>
        <A HREF="[FMP-linkrecid:layout=CGI,
            format=detail.htm]"
            onmouseover="self.status='View Detail.';
            return true">

            <B>
```

```
                    [FMP-FIELD: name]
                </B>
            </A>
        </P>
        </TD>

        <TD WIDTH=135>
        <P>
            [FMP-FIELD: Artist]
        </P>
        </TD>

        <TD WIDTH=80>
        <P>
            [FMP-FIELD: Formatted Price]
        </P>
        </TD>

        <TD WIDTH=40>
        <P>
            <A HREF="javascript:document.prodform[FMP-field:ID].
                submit()"
                onMouseOver="return setimg
                    ('buy.[FMP-field:ID]',true)"
                onMouseOut="return setimg
                    ('buy.[FMP-field:ID]',false)">
            <IMG SRC="images/buy1.gif"
                NAME="buy.[FMP-field:ID]" ALT="Buy"
                WIDTH="24" HEIGHT="24" BORDER="0">
        </P>
        </TD>
    </TR>[/FMP-RECORD]
</TABLE>
</P>


<CENTER>
    <A HREF="javascript:history.go(-1)"
        onmouseover="return setimg('back',true)"
        onmouseout="return setimg('back',false)">
    <IMG SRC="images/back1.gif" ALT="Go Back"
        WIDTH=41 HEIGHT=41 BORDER=0 ALIGN=bottom
        name=back>
    </A>
```

```
    <BR>
    <BR>

    <A HREF="http://www.claris.com/filemakerpro/">
    <IMG SRC="../images/powered_by_fmp.gif"
        ALT="Powered by FileMaker Pro" WIDTH=114 HEIGHT=43
            BORDER=0 ALIGN=bottom>
    </A>
</CENTER>

<P>
    <!--End Include: prodlist.txt-->
</P>
```

What Is a Form?

A form is a container for controls. **Controls** are normally those data entry elements with which users interact. In addition to being a container for controls, forms have attributes that enable them to interact with programs on a remote computer:

- Forms have a **method**. The method instructs the browser how to transmit the data from the form to the action program. The most commonly used methods are GET and POST, which were discussed in "Controlling Your Database with HTML" starting on page 207.

- Forms have an **action** associated with them. The action is the name of a program (and the path to get to it); the program is executed when the user submits the form. (See "Actions" on page 221.)

Other characteristics of a form are usually less important to you. They include the following:

- Forms may be named.

- A form's character encoding determines what characters it will accept and how they will be transmitted.

- The content type of a form specifies how data submitted with the POST method is transmitted. (If you are transmitting graphics and other nontextual material, you must use the content type attribute.)

Form Tags

The starting tag for a FORM element must contain the form's method and action. Here is a typical starting tag:

```
<FORM METHOD="POST" ACTION="FMPro">
```

The action for all FileMaker Pro forms that will be sent to Web Companion is always FMPro. If you are sending a form from a Web page on a different computer than the one running Web Companion, you must include the address, such as

```
ACTION="http://192.168.1.1/FMPro"
```

Everything that appears after the starting tag until the ending tag (</FORM>) is part of the form. Like most HTML elements, forms may also be named. Naming your forms makes the code more readable and can allow you to manipulate them using controls located outside the form on the same Web page (see "Controlling Forms and URL Requests with Scripts" on page 326).

Controls

Controls are the elements of a form with which a user interacts. Most of them are coded in HTML using the INPUT element. The types of controls and their attributes are described in this section.

Types of Controls

Controls are familiar to users of any graphical interface.

- Buttons may be either general or the Submit and Reset buttons which have special meanings within a form. Other buttons may be used to launch scripts.

- Check boxes allow yes/no choices.

- Radio buttons can be grouped (by giving several of them the same name). Only one of a group of radio buttons can be on at one time.

- Menus provide single and multiple selections from a designated list of options.

- Text controls (such as the Name field in Figure 13-2) allow entry onto a single line.

- Text areas (such as the Message field in Figure 13-3) allow entry into a larger multiline area.

- Special text fields for passwords are defined; typing in them does not display the characters that you type.

- Image controls display an image.

- Hidden controls have no visible representation, but they can contain data that is submitted with the form.

The code snippet shown in the previous section uses a number of hidden controls. (They will be explained in "Hidden Controls" on page 302.)

- Object and file select controls are also part of the HTML specification. Consult an HTML reference for more details about them.

Attributes of Controls

Control attributes let you manipulate your form's controls. The attributes that matter most to you are these:

- TYPE. You must specify a type (such as radio, text, hidden) for the control so that the user's browser knows how to display it.

- NAME. Each control has a name. It is used to identify the control within the form and the control's data within the message that is transmitted to the action program. When you are collecting data within a form that will be sent to a CDML action, the control names are normally the names either of database fields or of requests (such as -db or -lay). (An enhancement to HTML lets you associate an ID attribute with a control and add a LABEL element that places a label on that ID.)

- VALUE. Each control has a value. You specify an initial value (often blank, as in VALUE=""), but normally users can enter new values. (Buttons, which cause actions, have no data values in this sense; the value of a button is the text that is displayed on it.) The data transmission when the user submits the form includes pairs of NAME=VALUE. Thus, your form may combine control names and values to transmit data, such as the following:

```
firstname=John
-db=students.fp3
```

Other attributes let you specify such characteristics as the size (width) of the control, the maximum number of characters for a text or password control, and whether or not a radio button or check box is checked.

Note that controls flow down the page just like all other data elements do. To position them from side to side or in more complex manners, place them within a table. Note also that controls can be commingled with other HTML elements within a form—as the instructions in Figures 13-2 and 13-3 are.

This basic code snippet—

```
<INPUT TYPE=x NAME=y VALUE=z>
```

—will work its way into your fingers very quickly.

Hidden Controls

Hidden controls are used frequently in forms that update databases. A hidden control has the same three attributes that all other controls do—its type ("hidden"), a name, and a value. Just like other controls, a hidden control is transmitted as part of the data when a form is submitted. Its transmission is exactly the same as that of other controls:

```
controlname=controlvalue
```

This is the way in which data can be transmitted to the database without having been entered by the user. You can create hidden fields and set their values to the values of fields in the current or other databases (using the [FMP-Field] element); you can also set the values of hidden fields to dates, times, or other items that you construct or calculate when the Web page is displayed.

Hidden controls are a specified type of control: you cannot hide radio buttons, text fields, or menus. A hidden control has no visual representation, and so only its name and value matter. There is a distinction between a hidden control and a control of another type that is placed so that it is not visible.

Submitting a Form

A user can do any of three things with a form:

1. It can be submitted—the contents of its controls are sent to the action program using the specified method.

2. It can be reset—all entered values are replaced with the values specified in the VALUE= attribute of each control.

3. It can be ignored—the user can move on to another page or another activity.

The SUBMIT input type (<INPUT TYPE=SUBMIT>) is used for a button that submits the form. The value of this control is used as the name for the button.

Likewise, a RESET input type is used for the button that will reset the form's values. Its value is used for the button name.

In the example given previously in this chapter ("Example Code for a Form within a Table" on page 295) you will notice that no SUBMIT or RESET input types are present. This will be explained in the following chapter ("Controlling Forms and URL Requests with Scripts" on page 326).

What Happens When a Form Is Submitted

Forms that go to FileMaker Pro's Web Companion normally contain an action. In the example given previously, the underlined line of code specifies that a new record is to be added to the database:

```
<INPUT TYPE=hidden NAME="-new" VALUE="">
```

The actions discussed on page 221 are all valid for form submission. Although this chapter emphasizes the use of forms to collect data for entry to a database, you can use a form to collect the values that will be used to search a database using one of the -find actions.

Form Design Issues

As soon as a form gets larger than a few fields, design issues come into play. There are many references available concerning the design of graphical user interfaces. Perhaps the most important point to note is that there is no substitute for usability testing: not everyone follows directions, and not everyone behaves the way you do. Furthermore, telephone calls interrupt people while they are working, cats stretch out on computer keyboards, and a host of other events happen that may interfere with filling in your form.

Size of Forms

In general, forms should be as small as possible. The complexity of a large form is daunting, whether it be on the computer or on paper.

Scrolling and Screen Size

When possible, a form should be able to be seen with as little scrolling as possible. Although this is hard to do when you are designing forms for devices ranging from desktop computers to palm-size products, try to keep as much information visible as possible. Often, you can do this by using a table within your form so that the various data entry fields are arrayed across the page as well as down.

Logical Size

Try to keep your form to the smallest part of your Web page. In general, a form that consists of an entire Web page is too big. Forms can contain text, graphics, and other HTML elements, but if they are not to be submitted as data, it is best to keep them out of the form. Lay out your page—with its graphics, links, etc.—and place the form within a small section of it. The examples that ship with FileMaker Pro and Home Page adhere to this practice. It makes the code easy to maintain and read.

One trick to accomplishing this design is to create the page without the form. Lay everything out and precede it with something like "here is a form" instead of the actual form. When you are happy with its layout, replace "here is a form" with the <FORM> element.

Managing Large Forms

Sometimes, you simply do need to have a lot of data on a form. One way to do this is to split the form into several separate screens. On the first screen, place the first batch of data fields. Using the GET method, send those fields and their data to the next screen. Place them in hidden fields on that screen, and let users enter the visible fields.

In this way, you can have a reasonable number of entry fields on each screen (perhaps 10), and accumulate the entries from prior screens into hidden fields on each current screen. The final submission will send all data from both hidden and visible fields for processing.

Help and Assistance

Do not forget the need for help and assistance with the forms that you create. You can integrate instructions (both graphical and textual) with the form elements, but this can take up valuable space. One way of solving the problem is to place links on the names of the various fields, linking to definitions of the fields.

Place the links on the field names, not on the fields themselves.

Automating Forms

You can automate many aspects of forms—from computing values for fields to performing edit checks and submitting forms without a Submit button. These are covered in the next chapter, "Using Scripts," starting on page 311.

An E-mail Example

You often want to generate e-mail automatically in conjunction with a form submission. The Shopping Cart example demonstrates how to do this. When the user checks out, it is by submitting a form that displays the order. As part of that form, hidden fields are transmitted that generate e-mail.

Here is the code that does that:

```
<INPUT TYPE="hidden" NAME="-mailhost"
    VALUE="smtp.yourhost.com">
<INPUT TYPE="hidden" NAME="-mailfrom"
    VALUE="yourname@yourhost.com">
<INPUT TYPE="hidden" NAME="-mailto"
    VALUE="[FMP-field:Customers::Email]">
<INPUT TYPE="hidden" NAME="-mailsub"
    VALUE="Knitting Factory Online Order">
<INPUT TYPE="hidden" NAME="-mailformat"
    VALUE="emailorder.txt">
```

Note that these fields are transmitted with the POST method to the FMPro action program. Other fields in the same form's transmission specify the database and the action to take. The e-mail message is not a separate action.

The -mailhost variable needs to be replaced with the name of your e-mail host—the e-mail address from which you send all outgoing mail. (You may also have a POP address—the e-mail address to which all incoming mail is sent.) If you are unclear what this should be, ask your network administrator or Internet service provider.

If you are running your FileMaker Pro databases on a computer other than the computer on which your primary Internet site is located, be careful to check that you are using the appropriate SMTP mail host. In order to cut down on spam, some ISPs do not allow access to their mail host from any program running on another computer. If this is the case, you may need to use the SMTP mail host on your FileMaker Pro database's computer. If you explain the situation to a technical representative of your ISP(s), you should be able to get a simple answer. It doesn't really matter what SMTP host you use—your return address is specified in the -mailfrom variable.

You also need to replace the -mailfrom variable with your return address.

Note that the recipient's address (italicized) is specified by a value from the database.

The boldfaced type specifies a format file which is normally separate from the form and its data. The format file is a regular CDML file containing text and replacement elements.

When it comes time to send an e-mail message, the data is filled in just as it would be for a Web page.

Here is the format file referenced by the code in this example:

```
<P>Thank you for your order. Your order is number
[FMP-FIELD: Order ID] placed on [FMP-FIELD: Order Date].

Here are the items you selected:
Quantity | Product Name | Price | Extended Price
------------------------------------------------
[FMP-PORTAL: Ordered Items]
    [FMP-FIELD: Ordered Items::Quantity] |
    [FMP-FIELD: Ordered Items::Product Name] |
    [FMP-FIELD: Ordered Items::Formatted Price] |
    [FMP-FIELD: Ordered Items::Formatted Total]
[/FMP-PORTAL]
The total for your order: [FMP-FIELD: Formatted Total]

Here is the contact information we have for you:
------------------------------------------------
Customer ID:
[FMP-FIELD: Customers::Customer ID] Name:
[FMP-FIELD: Customers::FirstName]
[FMP-FIELD: Customers::LastName]
    [FMP-IF: Customers::Organization.neq.]
        Organization: [FMP-FIELD: Customers::Organization]
    [/FMP-IF]
Address:[FMP-FIELD: Customers::Address]
    [FMP-FIELD: Customers::City],
    [FMP-FIELD: Customers::StateProvince]
    [FMP-FIELD: Customers::PostalCode] Email:
    [FMP-FIELD: Customers::Email]

If there is a problem, please call us.
Thank you.</P>
```

A full description of the CDML used for generating mail is found at "Mail Requests" on page 228. Generating e-mail is really this simple: you add the five hidden fields to the form (-mailhost, -mailto, -mailfrom, -mailsub, -mailformat) and construct a CDML format file.

E-mail is generated in conjunction with another database action—normally viewing, adding, or editing a record. It can serve as a confirmation (as in the Shopping Cart example) or as a transaction log of database accesses. There is no separate mail action. This doesn't prevent you from viewing a database record with a format file that displays no fields (thereby showing nothing to the user and appearing to do nothing). But you must use the correct database in order to properly fill in an e-mail format file. In other words, if your e-mail format file will need a name and address, you need to generate mail from an action involving a database that contains (or is related to) those fields.

Summary

Forms are the easiest way to collect data to be sent to File-Maker Pro Web Companion. They can combine user-entered data with hidden fields that you generate in any of a number of ways, sending everything to be processed when it is complete.

You can further extend the power of forms by providing scripts that perform error checking, validation, and automatic submission. The next chapter deals with some of those issues.

Using Scripts

Scripts extend HTML, allowing Web pages to do more than just sit there in a browser where they are statically displayed. There is a scripting interface to HTML, which is language independent; you can use the standard HTML scripting syntax to integrate scripts written in JavaScript, Visual Basic, Tcl, or other scripting languages (including those that you create).

This chapter provides an overview of HTML scripting in general as well as a guide to some specific uses of JavaScript with FileMaker Pro databases. (JavaScript is used in the Web examples that ship with FileMaker Pro; you can use your favorite scripting language if you want—such languages are remarkably similar, although their proponents would have apoplexy if you said this out loud.)

You can use scripts for many purposes. The three most basic ones for which scripts are used in conjunction with File-Maker Pro Web sites are as follows:

1. Scripts can be used to manipulate data that users enter into forms; it can be edited, copied to hidden fields, and so forth.

2. Scripts can be used to control the submission of forms and to generate complex URL requests.

3. Scripts can be used to enhance the interface, for example, highlighting objects as the mouse moves over them or changing colors of buttons.

Examples of each of these three types of scripts are given later in this chapter.

This is not a complete guide to HTML scripting or to JavaScript. It is designed to give you a feel for some of the things that you can do with scripts as well as to give you an overview of the logic behind scripts. As with so much of HTML, a lot of your work will consist of modifying existing code written by other people to do what you need it to do. Such work is much easier than starting with an empty piece of paper (or computer screen) and writing a script from scratch.

Scripts and HTML

Scripts are downloaded with Web pages—just as text or graphics are. They are written in a scripting language of your choice and are designed to be executed by a browser, which reads the script and carries out its actions as needed.

Scripts provide a way to significantly enhance the user experience of Web pages; much of the development work that is going on today is devoted to these kinds of enhancements. Specifications (usually in the form of draft specifications) are proliferating; if you are planning on working on the cutting edge of this technology, make certain that you have the latest information. However, the techniques that are described in this chapter are among the most basic; you can use them without looking over your shoulder to see if the specifications have changed since yesterday.

Scripts differ from applets (such as those written in Java) in that applets are not interpreted by the browser; their code is read and interpreted (compiled) before they are attached to Web pages. What is downloaded to the browser are the instructions (byte-code) to be executed by a "virtual machine"—an imaginary standard computer that is implemented on each actual computer.

The process of changing a human-readable scripting or programming language into computer code is thereby done once, rather than each time the page is displayed. This means that applets can run faster (there is less work for the browser to do); it also means that they are somewhat more complex than scripts.

(Java actually uses an intermediate route: the preliminary compilation produces something called byte code which is interpreted by a Java Virtual Machine that your browser contacts as needed.)

This section describes the basic object model that underlies HTML scripting as well as the syntax for the HTML SCRIPT element.

The Object Model

Scripts designed to work with HTML are much less complex than programming languages, which usually are designed to work in many different environments with many types of data. Thus, HTML scripts need not start at a primitive level of defining variables for you to use (those pesky things that are often called i or x or temp); instead, they start at the more sophisticated level of HTML objects. They recognize concepts such as documents, windows, forms and HTML controls. Scripting languages do let you create variables like i or x or temp, but you use them in addition to the more sophisticated constructs.

Furthermore, they come complete with simple mechanisms for asking a question of a user ("Are you sure you want to continue?") as well as of posing alerts or warnings ("Beware—this action may cause serious problems"). They also often incorporate fairly sophisticated tools for manipulating the user's browser environment.

Using HTML Objects

Modern scripting languages build on the concepts of object-oriented design. In this type of structure, the data and procedures or functions of old-fashioned languages are linked to objects that are recognizable—documents, windows, forms, buttons, and so on.

Scripting languages usually let you refer to HTML objects by using their HTML NAME attribute. (If an ID attribute has also been provided, you can use it, but the NAME attribute takes precedence over the ID when both exist.) This, then, is the reason why it was suggested in the previous chapter that you name forms—by naming a form, a script can then refer to it. (See "What Is a Form?" on page 298.)

Objects at Rest

Each object that you deal with has a number of attributes; you can think of attributes as adjectives that refer to nouns— the objects. Attributes are sometimes called fields or properties. Not surprisingly, the attributes of a named HTML object (such as a form, a button, or an input control) can be accessed by scripting languages. In addition, other attributes may be defined by the scripting language—or by you—and you can access these as well.

One of the most frequently accessed attributes is the VALUE attribute of input controls. As noted in the previous chapter, you frequently write HTML code like this to create an input control and to set its initial value:

```
<INPUT TYPE=TEXT NAME=City VALUE="">
```

Once the user has entered a value into the City text field, it is automatically submitted as part of the form that it is on. However, before submitting the data, you can use a scripting language to manipulate the entered data in some way. For example, you can test to see that it is not blank, that it contains at least a certain number of characters (useful for checking passwords), that it differs from or matches some other field's value, or any of a host of other operations.

Some attributes and properties can be read and changed; others can only be read.

Objects in Action

In addition to their attributes and properties (the adjectives of objects) objects can participate in actions (verbs). Just as in life (and language), they can act and be acted upon.

FUNCTIONS AND METHODS Scripting languages let you define functions (sometimes called procedures or subroutines) that can be executed in different cases. (These are the actions that objects perform.) For example, any of the data manipulation functions described previously could be written as a function. The advantage of doing so is that the function—such as determining that a field is not blank—can then be used for many different fields.

Sometimes you create such functions, procedures, or subroutines and place them in the HEAD element of an HTML page: any script on that page can then use those functions. In other cases, you may want to tie a function closely to an object; in those cases, you can create a function that is a **method** of an object such as an input control or form—it is callable only by that particular object.

Do not worry too much about how to create functions, procedures, subroutines, or methods. In most cases, you take an example of the scripting language that you are working with and modify existing code. Knowing the broadest outlines of the architecture is sufficient to let you cut out the one line of code that obviously counts the number of characters in a field and replace it with another line of code that checks that no blanks appear in the field.

EVENT HANDLERS In addition to performing actions themselves, objects can be acted upon—that is, events can occur to them. Events are defined in HTML for many types of actions that can occur to an HTML element. Note that these definitions are not specific to individual scripting languages; these are part of the HTML standard and should be supported regardless of the scripting language that you use.

Since they are general, the basic events defined in HTML 4.0 are provided in Table 14-1. They are the glue that cause scripts to be executed (although scripts can be executed in other circumstances, this is the most common case). Often, they are user events—mouse clicks, for example. For events that apply to only certain HTML elements, those elements are listed in the third column; a blank means that the event applies to most HTML elements.

Event Name	When the Event Occurs	Elements to which It Applies
onload	On completion of loading a page or all frames in a frameset.	BODY FRAMESET
onunload	On unloading a page or all frames of a frameset.	BODY FRAMESET
onclick	When the mouse is clicked over the element.	
ondblclick	Same, but for a double click.	
onmousedown	The first half of a mouse click event.	
onmouseup	The reverse of onmousedown.	
onmouseover	As the mouse moves over an element, if no clicking occurs.	
onmouseout	When the mouse moves out of the bounds of an element.	
onmousemove	When the mouse is moved while over an object (not necessarily entering or leaving the object).	
onfocus	When the element is focused—for text, that means available for data entry (the cursor is blinking).	LABEL INPUT SELECT TEXTAREA BUTTON

TABLE 14-1. HTML Events Designed for the Scripting Interface

Event Name	When the Event Occurs	Elements to which It Applies
onblur	When focus is lost to another element (as when tabbing to another field).	LABEL INPUT SELECT TEXTAREA BUTTON
onkeypress	When a key is pressed and released over an element that has focus.	
onkeydown	When the key is depressed (and held) over an element.	
onkeyup	When the key is released over an element.	
onsubmit	When a form is submitted.	FORM
onreset	When a form is reset.	FORM
onselect	When any text is selected (using the mouse or the Select All menu item within a field).	INPUT TEXTAREA
onchange	When focus is lost and data has been entered or changed in the control. (The onkey… events can track data changes before data entry is complete and focus is lost.)	INPUT SELECT TEXTAREA

TABLE 14-1. HTML Events Designed for the Scripting Interface (Continued)

SCRIPT Elements

You can type script commands into your HTML file in many places. The most convenient way to use scripts is to place them within a SCRIPT element.

The HTML SCRIPT element is composed of a starting tag, content (the script), and an ending tag. The starting tag (<SCRIPT>) can take several attributes:

- As with other elements (such as IMG), you can specify the SRC attribute as the location of the script's content. In such a case, the ending script tag (</SCRIPT>) immediately follows the starting script tag.

- The TYPE attribute specifies the content type of the script as a MIME type such as text/javascript, text/tcl, or text/vbscript. This is a new feature of HTML; it supplants the LANGUAGE attribute (which is used in the examples that ship with FileMaker Pro 4.0). Either attribute may be used, but TYPE is preferred.

- The DEFER attribute can be set to true or false, indicating whether or not this script will modify the document. If it will modify the document as it executes, the browser must stop its imaging in order to execute the script and incorporate its content into the page. If DEFER is true, the browser has an indication that no content will be modified or generated and imaging of the page can therefore continue, leaving the execution of the script until after it is complete. This attribute is provided for optimization purposes, and you need not worry about it.

The content of the script is placed between the starting and ending tags (or is incorporated from the location specified by the SRC attribute. This script must adhere to the standards of whatever language is specified in the TYPE or LANGUAGE attribute. A script can contain a single line of code or a number of functions.

One of the useful features of JavaScript is demonstrated in the examples that ship with FileMaker Pro. Comments within JavaScript are limited to a single line that starts with //. The entire script can be placed within an HTML comment (starting with <!-- and ending with -->). This hides it from browsers that might be tempted to display the script on the page that they are imaging (a common problem with older browsers or those that do not recognize the scripting language that you use).

Manipulating Data with Scripts

There are many reasons to manipulate data with scripts, but most of them fall into these two categories:

1. You can automatically copy data from one field into another as it is entered.

2. You can analyze data as it is entered, possibly modifying it as a result of your analysis.

Copying Data

There are many cases where you want to copy data automatically. One of the most frequent involves a page like that shown in Figure 14-1.

This figure shows a page with three forms. The first, at the top, contains fields for first and last names. The second lets you enter billing information and subscribe to a periodical. The third lets you simply browse one issue for free. Both the subscribe and browse forms need the name information; rather than repeat those fields several times on the page, the common information can be placed at the top and automatically filled in as needed.

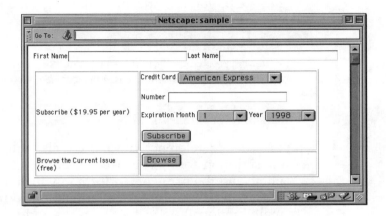

FIGURE 14-1. Subscription Form

How to Do It with Script Commands

You can copy data with script commands by creating hidden fields within the subscribe and browse forms and filling them with scripts from the fields at the top of the page. You already have seen how to do this. For each field, you need to specify its type, a name, and an initial value. The code for the First Name field is this:

```
First Name <INPUT TYPE=text NAME=firstnm VALUE="" SIZE=30 >
```

The code for the hidden first name field in the subscribe form is

```
<FORM ACTION="FMPro" METHOD=POST>
<INPUT TYPE=HIDDEN NAME=firstnmsubscribe VALUE="" SIZE=30>
```

After data entry, the value of the firstnm field will be whatever the user has typed in. You can access the VALUE attribute from a script. Armed with the full name of the hidden field, you can add the following code to those two lines (additions are shown in boldfaced type):

```
First Name
<INPUT TYPE=text NAME=firstnm VALUE="" SIZE=30
    onchange="subfrm.firstnmsubscribe.value=this.value">

<<FORM name = "subfrm" ACTION="FMPro" METHOD=POST>
<INPUT TYPE=HIDDEN NAME=firstnmsubscribe VALUE="" SIZE=30>
```

In order to reference the INPUT element that is inside the subscription form, you need to be able to identify it by its name and the name of the form in which it is located. This is why you have to get used to naming forms (which is normally optional). In using this recipe, add the boldfaced lines of code and modify the underlined words to reflect the names you give your forms and input fields.

You do not have to name the input field from which data will be taken; the event handler can simply refer to it as "this," as in the code here.

How to Do It with a SCRIPT Element

The onchange event handler can easily be added to the input field as shown in the previous section. However, when you have a longer script, it is easier to use the SCRIPT element.

Here is the same code implemented as a SCRIPT element with a function:

```
<SCRIPT NAME=changer TYPE=text/javascript>
    function changer (theField1, thefield2)
```

```
    {
        thefield2.value=theField1.value
    }
</SCRIPT>
```

It is invoked by the onchange event handler just as before; this time, though, the function is called to do the work. This can make the code more readable, and it also means that you can use and reuse the function with many fields, calling changer(name2,name1), changer (firstname, hiddenfirst-name), etc., as you see fit.

Here is the changed event handler code:

```
<INPUT TYPE=text NAME=name1 VALUE="" SIZE=30
    onchange=changer(name2,name1)>
<INPUT TYPE=text NAME=name2 VALUE="" SIZE=30>
```

To make the script itself into a comment so that it is not inadvertently displayed by browsers that do not support Java-Script, you can bracket it with comments as shown here:

```
<SCRIPT NAME=changer TYPE=text/javascript>
    <!--
    function changer (theField, thefield2)
    {
        thefield2.value=theField.value
    }
    //-->
</SCRIPT>
```

This is unnecessary if you are certain that people will not be using old browsers; however, adding those two lines is not a problem for most people and it can forestall problems.

Analyzing and Editing Data

FileMaker Pro has excellent data validation routines, but it is much more efficient to use a script for validation if you can.

In practice, this means relying on FileMaker Pro for edits that require database accesses, but relying on scripts for such things as determining that a field on a form is not blank—which requires no database access.

*You can make a distinction between **validity edits** (those which can be done based simply on the characteristics of the data that is entered—such as a minimum number of characters) and **quality edits** (those which involve comparison with data in the database). Note that validity edits may involve data comparisons—they just don't involve comparisons with data in the database. Checking to make certain that the Total field on a form is actually the sum of its elements is a validity edit. Checking to see that the total amount purchased by the customer is within a specified credit limit is a quality edit and requires a database access. A further distinction is that validity edits normally cannot be overridden, whereas quality edits are the sorts of edits that can be overridden by a manager or supervisor.*

You may need to build on the example given previously if you need to compare the contents of a field with the contents of another field. As long as the fields are named (and their forms are named if they are not in the same form), you can use the VALUE attribute to test them. JavaScript provides a number of operators and functions that let you compare values.

How to Do It

Here is a simple example of a JavaScript edit. A text input field (field1) is compared with another field (called field2). If the value of field2 is greater than the value of field1, field1's value is changed to the value of field2. (In other words, field1 will wind up with the larger number.)

Here is the code. It is implemented as an onchange event handler:

```
<INPUT TYPE=text VALUE="" SIZE=30
    onchange="if (field2.value > this.value)
        this.value=theform.field2.value">
```

Just as in the previous example, you use the name of the other field and the word *this* for the field from which you are working (the field to which the event handler is attached).

You can go very far with this line of code. You can even do some edits that you might normally think required database accesses. For example, you might download a limit for purchase amounts and store it in a hidden field; you can then let someone know that a proposed purchase is over the limit without making that limit obvious. (Hidden fields can be seen by sophisticated users, so you should not consider this to be a secure solution.)

Of course, if you are going to reject data or change it in any way, it is appropriate to let the user know. You can enhance the previous code by adding an alert:

```
<INPUT TYPE=text NAME=name1 VALUE="" SIZE=30
    onchange="if (field2.value > this.value)
        {
        alert ('The value is automatically being changed');
        this.value=nafield2me2.value
        }">
```

The alert function is built into JavaScript; it poses an alert dialog that the user must dismiss by clicking an OK button. The text that you enter is displayed in that dialog. Note that when an If statement contains multiple statements (in this case the alert and setting of this.value) they must be bracketed as shown here with { and } and separated by a semicolon between them (only between—it is not required after the final statement).

Controlling Forms and URL Requests with Scripts

In the last chapter, you saw an example of a form that was submitted with a script. (The code is given in "Example Code for a Form within a Table" on page 295; the screenshot is repeated here for convenience as Figure 14-2.)

FIGURE 14-2. Weekly Specials

The reason for submitting a form from a button outside the form is that a table is created in which each row corresponds to a database record. A form is created dynamically for each record's data. If you want to buy the item described in that record, you click on the image to the right of that row. The Web page designer has no idea how many records will be retrieved. For this to work, the Buy button must be able to submit the form that it is next to.

How to Do It

The code in question is repeated here (the full code is found in "Example Code for a Form within a Table" on page 295).

Here is the beginning of the form for each record:

```
<FORM METHOD="POST" ACTION="FMPro"
    NAME="prodform[FMP-field:ID]">
```

The form is named, and that name is constructed from "prodform" as well as a field from the FileMaker Pro database for that record. Thus, each form on the page has a unique name that is generated automatically.

Later—beyond the bounds of the dynamically created form—you can submit that form. Here is that code:

```
<A HREF=
    "javascript:document.prodform[FMP-field:ID].submit()"
    onMouseOver="return setimg('buy.[FMP-field:ID]',true)"
    onMouseOut="return setimg('buy.[FMP-field:ID]',false)">
<IMG SRC="images/buy1.gif"
    NAME="buy.[FMP-field:ID]" ALT="Buy"
    WIDTH="24" HEIGHT="24" BORDER="0">
```

What happens here is that an anchor is created; clicking on it submits the form that is identified by this name. You as the Web page designer do not know what the form's name will be: all you have to do is make certain that the naming of the form and the naming in the submit statement match.

You can use this code safely without knowing any more than this. Insert the boldfaced lines of code and make certain that the underlined words match in the form name and in the submit statement.

Enhancing the Interface with Scripts

Perhaps the most common use of scripts is to enhance the interface. As you move the mouse over a button, you can change its image or display a paragraph that describes what the button does. Or both.

As you look at various Web pages, you can see what techniques are most useful and attractive to you. Get in the habit of critiquing the pages you view. And watch out for overuse of these techniques. For example, it is all well and good to display information only when the mouse is moved over an area of the page, but can you be certain that the user will move the mouse over that area?

Decide What to Do

This section uses the Shopping Cart default.htm page as an example. It is shown for reference in Figure 14-3. There are two sections of the page that are hot, that is, that cause visible changes when the mouse is moved over them. They are outlined with dotted lines in Figure 14-3.

The visible change is the Enter button—it changes from green to red when the mouse is moved either over it or over the Knitting Factory graphic outlined above it. When the mouse is moved out of either outlined area, the Enter button reverts to green. This is an interesting example of the use of interface-enhancing scripts, since actions in two separate areas of the page have the same effect on one object (the Enter button).

(This page was discussed previously in "The HTML Source Code" starting on page 195.)

FIGURE 14-3. Shopping Cart Default Page

How to Do It

Once you have decided what you want to do, you need to plan how to implement it. Most interface enhancement scripts start from the onmouseover and onmouseout events—the first is triggered when you move the mouse into a control's area, and the second is triggered when the mouse leaves. Remember, there is no guarantee that a user will move the mouse over the area in question; there is also no guarantee that onmouseout will be triggered (the user can go to another page without moving the mouse from the area).

Onfocus and onblur are another pair of events that are prime candidates for interface-enhancing scripts. You can also use a single event as a trigger for your script, modifying the page when the user moves the mouse over an area and leaving that modification in place. (This can make for an interesting game that will make those idle Web-browsing hours pass quickly.)

Here are the steps to take:

1. Locate the object that will be hot.

2. Identify the object that will be changed.

3. Write the script(s) that will be triggered.

4. Associate the script(s) with the hot object.

Locate the Object That Causes Script Activity

In this case, there are two objects that need to cause script activities. The first one is the Enter button itself. Here is an excerpt of the code from this page:

```
<A HREF="FMPro?-db=Orders.fp3&-format=search.htm&-new">
<IMG SRC="images/enter1.gif" ALT="Enter"
    WIDTH=75 HEIGHT=41 BORDER=0 ALIGN=bottom name=enter>
</A>
```

This is the code that creates the anchor for the Enter button. Inside the anchor element the HREF attribute is set to a URL request that asks FileMaker Web Companion to use the Orders.fp3 database for the -new action (with results shown in the search.htm format file). If you click on the Enter button (the anchor), this link will be requested. The content of the anchor is an image, whose source is images/enter1.gif.

So the first step is done—the object that will be hot is this anchor. (If you look at the code in "The HTML Source Code" starting on page 195, you should be able to identify the anchor for the Knitting Factory graphic—it starts at $\overline{11}$.)

The object that will start the script executing must be an HTML object such as an anchor. If you want an area of the page to be hot that is not an object, you will need to create an object (perhaps one with no content) so that you can make it hot. This situation rarely occurs, however, because it is generally poor interface design to surprise the user—which is what making an invisible object hot does.

Identify the Object That Will Be Changed

The script will need to change the image of the Enter button from a green button to a red one. The only way that a script can do such a thing is for the object that will be changed to be identifiable. Note in the code shown previously that the NAME attribute has been supplied for the IMG element; images are not normally named, but there is no harm in doing so and it will be necessary to have a name (or ID) in order to carry out the script.

In the code shown previously, the object that will be changed (the image) is named "enter" by the line that is underlined.

Write the Script(s) That Will Be Triggered

For this step, you need to know something about the scripting language you are using. For many people, it is quite sufficient to have a few simple recipes on hand to do what you need to do. Here is the recipe for changing an image. It is one of the most frequently used pieces of JavaScript.

```
active_button=new Image;
active_button.src = 'images/enter2.gif';
document['enter'].src = 'active_button.src';
```

You can use it without understanding how it works. All you need to do is to customize two sections:

1. The underlined text should be the location of the image to which you want to change the object. It can be a complete URL (however, since retrieving images from other sites tends to degrade performance, it usually will be a relative URL to an image on the same site). In this case, it is a file called enter2.gif which is located in the images folder on the site (a common location).

2. The italicized word should be changed to whatever the name of the object to be changed is. That is, it should be the name that you have set in the previous step.

You can use this code snippet over and over. All that you need to do is to attach it to a specific event on the object that will start the process, as detailed in the next step.

If you are curious, the code works in this way. First, a new image object is created; it is placed in a variable location called "active_button" (it could be called anything). In the second line, the SRC attribute of that object is set to the file name. In the third line, the object named "enter" on the current document has its SRC attribute set to the evaluated value of "active_button.src."

Associate the Script(s) with the Hot Object

This is the final step in the process. The code shown previously is enhanced by adding an onmouseover event handler to the anchor. The added code is italicized in the following snippet:

```
<A HREF="FMPro?-db=Orders.fp3&-format=search.htm&-new"
    onmouseover="
        active_button=new Image;
        active_button.src = 'images/enter2.gif';
        document['enter'].src = eval('active_button.src');"
>
<IMG SRC="images/enter1.gif" ALT="Enter"
    WIDTH=75 HEIGHT=41 BORDER=0 ALIGN=bottom name=enter>
</A>
```

To change the image back, you can add an onmouseout handler. The code is identical, but you need to use a different image (the green Enter button in the Shopping Cart example is images/enter1.gif, in case you want to use it).

Example: Animating a Button

You can repeat the steps shown here whenever you want to change an image. In the Shopping Cart example, the scripts are more sophisticated. Rather than repeat the code each time, several functions are created that make it even easier to manage this sort of interface change.

This is actually the most complex example in this chapter. If it frightens you, feel free to stick with the recipe shown previously. You may type more lines of code, and you may increase the time it takes to test and trouble-shoot your pages, but it may be worth it if this section scares you.

As you can imagine, things can get complicated fairly quickly when you are dealing with multiple images for interface elements. To make it simpler, the Shopping Cart example creates a few rules:

- Each image has two versions—the highlighted (or active) one and the normal one. They are in files with identical names except for the digit 1 or 2 at the end. Thus, the green (unactivated) Enter button is in the file enter1.gif, and the red (activated) Enter button is in the file enter2.gif. There are two Browse buttons—browse1.gif (unactivated) and browse2.gif (activated). This makes keeping track of files easier.

- Rather than repeat the lines of code shown previously, a function is created that does the generic work. It is called "setimg", and it takes two arguments—the basic name of the image and true/false, indicating whether or not the active version is required. If you call setimg with the parameters enter and true, it will look for a file called enter2.gif; if you call it with the parameters browse and false, it will look for a file called browse1.gif. This enables you to write the event handlers as follows:

```
onmouseover="setimg('enter',true)"
onmouseout="setimg('enter',false)"
```

- The script is placed in the HEAD element of the page. Its functions execute only when called; however, it has some statements that execute automatically when the page is loaded. They are italicized in the code that follows. They check to see that an appropriate version of the browser is running (one that can interpret the JavaScript). After that, in the italicized lines, new images are created and their SRC attributes are set to the appropriate URLs; they are ready for use whenever one of the script's functions is called. This is the final rule that is established: within the script, the image containing the appropriate image for each button is identified with the _active suffix for the active version.

- A text string is associated with each object (in either the active or inactive form). In the code shown later in this section, it is identified as a localization section—that is because you can often change the language of a script (for example, from French to German) by changing only these lines of text.

Combining these rules, you get the names shown in Table 14-2 for the Browse button animation described here.

Names of Files	images/browse1.gif (inactive)
	images/browse2.gif (active)
Names of Variables That Reference Those Files	browse (inactive)
	browse_active (active)
Name of Variable with Descriptive Text	browse_txt

TABLE 14-2. Browse Button Naming Conventions

In the Shopping Cart example, this principle is used in the nav.js that is included in most of the Web pages for that example. It is also used in the default.htm page, whose code is shown here (the rest of it was shown in "The HTML Source Code" on page 195). There is more to the code than has been described—it generates text for each version of the button, and it allows for extension and expansion into more complex situations. Nevertheless, you should be able to use it as a prototype of a fairly complex script.

All that you need to do is to set up your files with the naming convention of ...1.gif and ...2.gif and to add code as necessary to associate those file names with variables of the form

… and …_active (in the two lines of code that are both italicized and underlined). Then, to use the script, replace the boldfaced code to associate the setimg function with the appropriate event handler and to name the object whose image is to be changed.

You also need to add a variable like enter_txt in the style …_txt; it should be set to the text that you want associated with the object—"Enter the Knitting Factory" in this example.

```
<HTML>
<!--This file created 2/16/1998 12:37 PM by Home Page ver-
sion 3.0-->

<HEAD>
    <TITLE>Welcome to the Knitting Factory</TITLE>
    <META NAME=GENERATOR CONTENT="Home Page 3.0">
    <X-CLARIS-WINDOW TOP=42 BOTTOM=613 LEFT=4 RIGHT=534>
    <X-CLARIS-TAGVIEW MODE=minimal>

  <!--This is the main entry point for the Knitting
      Factory shopping cart solution.  This page simply
      contains 4 images. When two of the images are
      clicked, they'll create a new record and take you
      to the search page.

      The JavaScript™ below is used to animate the entry
      button.  This script is very similar to the nav.js
      script in the includes folder.  Since this page is
      returned directly to the client and not processed
      (STATIC), it was necessary to place it here.  In the
      remainder of the solution, the FMP-include tag is
      used to automatically insert the script.-->

    <SCRIPT LANGUAGE="JavaScript">
    <!--Hide from older browsers
        var app;
        ((navigator.appName == "Netscape") &&
            (parseInt(navigator.appVersion) >= 3)) ?
            versionOK=true : versionOK=false;
```

```
    // Localize here...
    enter_txt = "Enter the Knitting Factory.";
    // ...end localize

    if (versionOK)
    {
        enter = new Image();
        enter_active = new Image();

        enter.src = "images/enter1.gif";
        enter_active.src = "images/enter2.gif";
    }

    function helptxt ( name )
    {
        self.status = eval(name + "_txt");
        return true;
    }

    function setimg ( name, activate )
    {
        if (versionOK)
        {
        if (activate)
                document[name].src =
                    eval(name + "_active" + ".src");
            else
                document[name].src = eval(name + ".src");
        }
        return helptxt ( name );
    }
//End hiding-->
</SCRIPT>
</HEAD>
```

```
<BODY BGCOLOR="#6666CC" BACKGROUND="images/headerbg.gif">
<CENTER>
<TABLE BORDER=0 CELLSPACING=0 CELLPADDING=10 WIDTH="100%">
    <TR>
        ... comment removed ≥
        <TD ALIGN=center VALIGN=top BGCOLOR="#FFFFFF">
        <P>
            <A HREF="FMPro?-db=Orders.fp3&
                -format=search.htm&
                -new"
                onmouseover="return setimg('enter',true)"
                onmouseout="return setimg('enter',false)">
            <IMG SRC="images/kf.gif"
                ALT="The Knitting Factory"
                WIDTH=341 HEIGHT=250 BORDER=0
                ALIGN=bottom>
            </A>
            <BR>

            <A HREF="FMPro?-db=Orders.fp3&
                -format=search.htm&
                -new"
                onmouseover="return setimg('enter',true)"
                onmouseout="return setimg('enter',false)">
            <IMG SRC="images/enter1.gif"
                ALT="Enter"
                WIDTH=75 HEIGHT=41 BORDER=0
                ALIGN=bottom name=enter>
            </A>
        </P>
        </TD>
    </TR>
    <TR>
        <TD ALIGN=center VALIGN=top>
        <P>
            <NOBR>
            <IMG SRC="images/BannerAnim.gif"
                ALT="Powered by FileMaker Pro"
                WIDTH=230 HEIGHT=90 BORDER=0 ALIGN=top>
            <IMG SRC="images/header.gif" ALT="4.0"
                WIDTH=99 HEIGHT=67 BORDER=0 ALIGN=top>
            </NOBR>
        </P>
        </TD>
```

```
        </TR>
    </TABLE>
    </CENTER>
    </BODY>
    </HTML>
```

Summary

Scripting is built into current versions of HTML. It relies on an object model that lets you access HTML elements and their attributes. Scripting languages like JavaScript implement functionality that may be specific to individual browsers.

This chapter has provided an overview of the sorts of things that you are likely to do with scripts and FileMaker Pro databases. It is only a start, but the examples shown here can be used as templates for a great deal of productive work.

Testing and Troubleshooting Custom Web Publishing

All of the issues that apply to Instant Web Publishing apply to testing and troubleshooting Custom Web Publishing (see Chapter 7 starting on page 155 for more details). But Custom Web Publishing comes with a host of other issues you need to consider. Those issues are centered on these areas:

- Custom Web Publishing relies on dynamic HTML: the pages that are displayed are created on demand.

- Instant Web Publishing pretty much takes care of errors and exceptions for you. With Custom Web Publishing, you need to develop (and test!) error and exception handling code.

Dynamic Web Pages

Traditional Web pages are very easy to test: you display them on monitors of various sizes using the current and immediately prior versions of several browsers. You can usually look at a static Web page and see if there are problems—if not, you can just check off that particular test.

Dynamic Web pages pose a much trickier problem since they are assembled from a multitude of sources on demand. And that demand is not under your control in most cases: users can use your Web site in many ways that you may not have thought of.

Keeping Track of All the Pieces

The place to start is to keep track of all of the items that a single Web request may need. For each Web page that you create (free-standing Web pages as well as format files), you need to identify everything that is needed. Those items normally are as follows:

- Format files (including error files) that may be included in URL requests and in form submissions.

- Files that you include with the [FMP-Include] element.

- Scripts that are located either in the format or included files.

- Forms that are located either in the format or included files.

- Images, scripts, and objects that are included using the SRC= attribute.

- The database (if any) that is accessed before the CDML is executed—in other words, the database for which this page is a format or error file. Note that not every file has a database, and that you can use a single page with several databases (if field names are consistent).

For each of these items, you should have the following information:

- The name

- The purpose of the object

- The type of object (HTML page, format file, script, form, mail format file, etc.)

- The language in which it is written (HTML, JavaScript, CDML, etc.)

- The language version in which it is written

- Where the object is located (filename, for example)

- Restrictions (copyrighted material is used, confidential information is present, etc.)

- The date it was created

- The person who created it

- The date it was last modified

- The person who last modified it

- The date it was verified or tested on its own

- The person who did the verification or testing

- Comments, notes, bug reports, etc.

The reason for keeping track of this information is so that you can quickly locate work that has already been done when you are testing—or when you need to create a new page. Fortunately, you have an excellent tool for keeping track of these objects: this is what FileMaker Pro does best. You can create a simple database using the fields identified in this section.

Armed with this database, you can quickly locate everything that uses HTML 4.0 or all forms that are used for accounting purposes (provided the purpose field is filled in appropriately). If you create a more sophisticated database in which you can keep track of which objects refer to other objects, you can quickly produce a list of things to test when a given form, script, or page changes.

You will soon see that this database runs into trouble when objects are not named. As noted previously, you do not have to name objects such as forms, but doing so makes life easier.

Prepare a Test Plan

In addition to your database of objects, you should prepare a test plan for your Web site. This is a set of steps that you execute in sequence each time the site is changed. It should be your final step before uploading files to your server—and your first step after you have done so (to make certain that the upload was successful). Remember that—even on an intranet—you are not alone and it is far better to catch errors yourself than to hear about them from others.

Part of your test plan should involve testing the complete site in a test environment as well as on your final Web site. You may have to work with your ISP or network administrator to temporarily create a separate test environment, but it will be worth it.

What Does It Look Like Today?

Finally, Custom Web Publishing often entails creating requests and names of objects (like forms) on the fly from database fields. (You might create a form called "buyboots" from the string "buy" and the contents of a database field called "product.") In your test plan, document every case in which this is done, and make certain that you review the database periodically to make certain that these generated names are legitimate. "Buyboots" may work as the name of an object, but if you create a form called "buy gloves (pair)" you may find that the parentheses cause problems down the line—particularly if you have not specified URL encoding when you are creating a URL.

If you allow online updates to your database, you need to come up with a quick browsing routine that lets you be reasonably assured that your database has not been corrupted by bad data. Some people think it is a joke to enter spurious data (even obscene or offensive) into a public database. If it is your database and it is on your site, you should act quickly to remove the data that should not be there.

As part of your database monitoring, keep track of the number of records in the database. A database that grows by 30 records on an average day should not grow by 2000 records overnight without a good explanation.

Error Handling

Your Web site should be able to handle every possible error. Protect your database by placing validation edits on every field with the FileMaker Pro options. You may well go beyond that and place further validations on fields that are entered via the Web (using scripts, in most cases). It does not matter that the FileMaker Pro validation edits will never fail (since errors will be caught by the scripts). Leave them in place as a second line of defense.

Test Error Handlers

Then comes the fun part: test the error handlers. Try using your Web site without following the instructions; in fact, try using it by deliberately disobeying the instructions. Enter your address in the name field; enter an invalid telephone number. See how many errors are caught—but look carefully for those errors that get through and subsequently cause serious problems.

Manage Disconnects

If you are developing an application like the Shopping Cart example, you need to consider what happens when people stop in the middle of a transaction. You cannot assume that you will have completed orders in all cases. What happens to the orphaned records? Does someone who logs in with the same user name suddenly get a half-filled shopping cart?

Download Databases

Finally, if you are allowing updates to your databases, periodically download them and reupload them. Check them for consistency and browse through them to see what you have. Look carefully at bad records—incomplete parts of relationships, for example. Try to figure out how they may have materialized.

Complexity

Projects that use Custom Web Publishing tend to be larger and more complex than those that use Instant Web Publishing. You should watch out for some of the problems that occur with increased complexity.

Monitoring Performance

Monitor the database's performance continually. Publishing information on the Web (or an intranet) is useless if response time is too slow. Have a feedback form on your Web site and encourage users to give you the information that you can use to help you improve the site.

This is a very good exercise if you want to develop a form. Make certain that you automatically capture the date and time of the feedback: that may help you to determine when you have performance problems. (See "Environmental Elements" on page 236 for CDML elements that display the date and time; you can use them in generating an e-mail message.) As a rule, you get more negative feedback than positive feedback, and there is nothing like poor response time to generate negative feedback.

Modify Your Database for Performance

If you need to improve performance, you can modify your database in some cases. The simplest modification to make is to move relationships that are not used. (Often a relationship is used to assist in data entry and is not needed during information retrieval.) This can be very dangerous unless you have seriously planned your environment so that you can be certain that the relationship is restored when databases are used for updating on a local computer.

You can also consider permanent database modifications that denormalize your database to reduce disk accesses. Remember that in general each access of a database record requires access to disk—and that can be a bottleneck on some servers.

In any performance modifications, however, be careful that what you do actually does improve performance and that it does not corrupt the database. Often people speculate about what is causing performance problems, and they solve the problems about which they have speculated: not those that exist.

Summary

With a dynamic Web site, your work does not end when the Web pages are uploaded. You need to continually monitor the site to see how it is assembling itself in response to user queries and to database updates.

Custom Web Publishing with Home Page

16

Working with Home Page

This part of the book focuses on Home Page—the tool that is most intimately related to FileMaker Pro. Home Page has an assistant that will build a Web site for you based on the database that you select (Chapter 17 deals with that process). It also has enhancements to its graphical user interface that allow you to modify CDML elements as well as standard HTML (Chapter 18 covers those issues).

This chapter provides a quick reference to the features of Home Page. It is not a step-by-step tutorial: a lot of examples, tutorials, and online help screens ship with the product. Rather, this is a walk through some of the features that you may find most useful.

Sites and Pages

As discussed in "Home Page Overview" on page 81, Home Page lets you edit individual Web pages as well as entire sites. Home Page can keep track of your upload location and can automatically upload changed files (or an entire site).

Home Page also handles included files that you use with the CDML [FMP-Include] element. In addition to the FileMaker Pro Connection assistant, Home Page has two libraries of CDML elements that you can easily insert into your documents. They are accessible from the File menu, as shown in Figure 16-1.

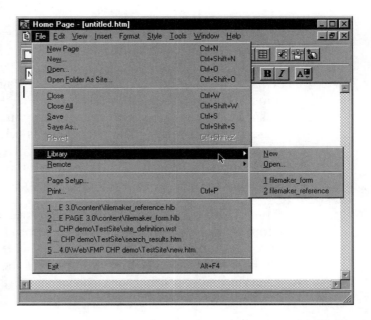

FIGURE 16-1. Home Page File Menu

The FMP Form Library and FMP Reference are discussed later in this chapter (for more details see "Using the FMP Reference Library" on page 360 and "Using the FMP Form Library" on page 361).

Viewing and Editing Pages

The core of Home Page is accessible from the View menu on Windows, as shown in Figure 16-2, and from the Window menu on Mac OS, as shown in Figure 16-3.

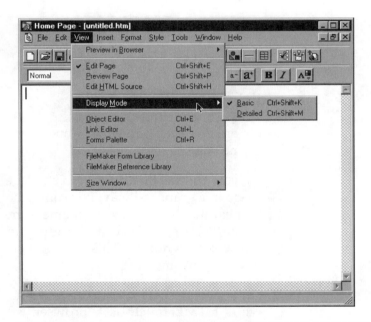

FIGURE 16-2. View Menu

There are two sets of commands that you constantly use: the three commands in the second section of the menus shown in

Figures 16-2 and 16-3 let you edit pages; the three commands in the fourth section of the menu let you edit objects within those pages.

FIGURE 16-3. Mac OS Window Menu

Editing Pages

There are three ways in which you can view your Web pages in Home Page:

1. If you choose Edit Page, Home Page displays your page in a graphical way; it is somewhat like what will appear in a browser, but editable elements (forms, for example) are outlined and highlighted in ways that browsers do not do. This enables you to select them, move them, and edit them.

2. If you choose Preview Page, Home Page displays your HTML much as a browser would. Note that Home Page is not a browser and does not contain all the functionality of a browser. This is an approximation of what the page might look like. For a truer version, the Preview in Browser command lets you

launch any (or all) of several browsers that you have installed and defined for Home Page. The page you are working on will automatically be opened.

3. Finally, the Edit HTML Source command lets you view the source code behind your page. Home Page highlights syntactic elements so that you can easily follow the code.

Most people switch back and forth between the Edit Page and the Edit HTML Source modes.

Editing Objects

Three palettes are available that let you inspect and manipulate objects with which you are working:

1. The Object Editor provides information about whatever object is selected. It lets you add extra HTML to each object through its palette. Some people prefer never to use the Edit HTML Source mode and only to work with the Object Editor. You can find examples of the use of the Object Editor in Chapter 18, "Editing CDML Pages with Home Page," starting on page 393.

2. The Link Editor lets you create and edit links. You can browse files to locate a link, and the correct path will be automatically created. It also provides a handy reference for the formats of different types of links. There is more information in Chapter 18 in the section on "Managing Links" on page 400.

3. The Forms Palette lets you easily insert form elements into your page from a floating palette.

Working with Forms

As you can see from Figure 16-4, the Insert menu lets you insert a variety of objects into your page. Perhaps the most frequently inserted objects are those related to forms.

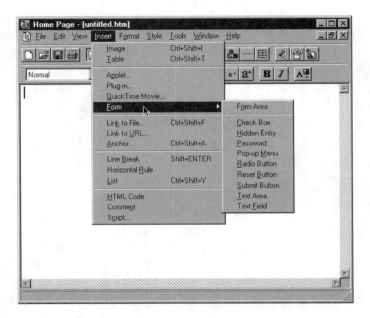

FIGURE 16-4. Insert Menu

Forms are an essential way of collecting information that will be sent when the form's Submit button is clicked. Remember that tables are used for physically organizing information on a page, whereas forms are used for logically organizing the information for an HTTP request that is submitted by the form's Submit button. You can have several forms on a single page.

Using the Tools Menu

The Tools menu has a number of important commands—not the least of which is the Spelling command. Remember that the Web is public (even intranets are public in their own way). Typographical errors and spelling mistakes are not a good idea in public media.

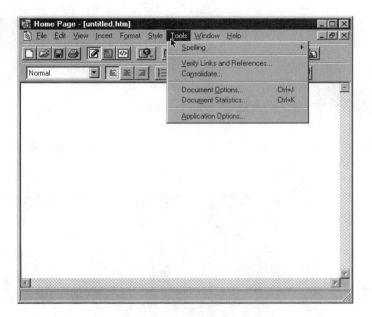

FIGURE 16-5. Tools Menu

Even more essential are the Verify Links and References command and the Consolidate command. Each can be used on an individual page, and both should be used for your entire site before you upload it. These tools prevent dead links and errors of that sort. It quickly becomes impractical to manually check all of the links on even a small Web site: use these tools to present a polished and professional appearance to the world.

The Document Statistics command is another helpful tool that can make your site more appealing. It estimates the download time for individual pages or a site. Unless you are certain that your site will only be viewed by people with high-speed connections, it is essential to make certain that your content does not overwhelm the available bandwidth (that is, that it doesn't take forever to download a cute graphic that really isn't so cute after it's been downloading for four minutes).

Using the FMP Reference Library

The FMP Reference Library is shown in Figure 16-6.

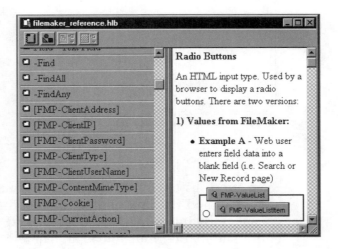

FIGURE 16-6. FMP Reference Library

It is an alphabetical listing of all the CDML elements. You can highlight the elements at the right (for example, you could highlight the [FMP-ValueList] element at the lower right of Figure 16-6), copy them, and then paste them or drag them into your pages. You then double-click the CDML elements and customize them with your database, layout, field names, etc. (This is discussed further in Chapter 18.)

Using the FMP Form Library

Although the alphabetical listing of the CDML tags in the FMP Reference Library may be just what you are looking for, the FMP Form Library may serve you just as well if not better. The same information is presented in the FMP Form Library but it is organized by logical operation, as shown in Figure 16-7.

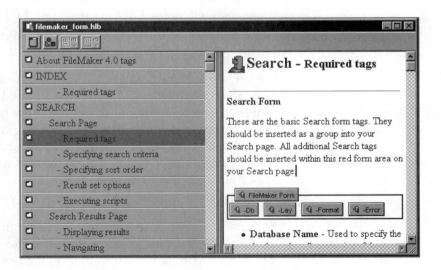

FIGURE 16-7. FileMaker Pro Form Library

As with the FMP Reference, you can copy the elements into your files.

Compare the FMP Library and FMP Reference with the CDML Tool in FileMaker Pro: since it is part of FileMaker Pro and since it examines your open databases, the CDML elements that you copy from it contain the appropriate field names from your database. You can also compare all three of these tools to the FileMaker Pro Connection assistant discussed in the next chapter: it integrates a specific database with the appropriate CDML and actually generates a Web site for you.

Summary

If you are familiar with Web page authoring, Home Page should be a convenient tool to work with—for standard pages as well as for FileMaker Pro and CDML. If you do not like the graphical user interface, you can always stick to the HTML editing window.

If you are not familiar with Web page authoring, take an hour to explore Home Page. Use a tutorial or one of the templates to create a Web site. Do not start by creating the site that you are planning. Start by creating a site that you will throw out. Explore the different styles and experiment with different graphics. See what the difference between a text area and a text field is (text areas are multi-line with scroll bars, text fields are short). Then start on your project.

For many people the FileMaker Pro Connection assistant—described in the next chapter—is the easiest way to develop a site, which you can always customize later. As many authors know, anything that you can do to avoid facing a blank page moves you well on the road to getting the work done.

Using the FileMaker Connection Assistant

The FileMaker Connection assistant in Home Page creates a Web site for you based on an existing database and the answers that you give to its questions. This chapter walks you through the FileMaker Connection assistant process, showing you how your choices are visualized in the resulting Web pages.

The process is in four steps:

1. **Getting started.** You choose the FileMaker Pro database with which you want to work.

2. **Setting up the CDML files and fields.** You select the layouts and fields that you will use for searching, data entry, and display.

3. **Choosing the Web site style.** You use (and modify) Home Page settings to customize the look of your site.

4. **Finishing the site.** You review the pages that have been created, modify the CDML and HTML code if necessary, and upload them to your Web server. Once the Web pages have been created, you can modify them further with your own customizations. Alternatively, you can take these pages—or portions of the HTML and CDML—and simply paste them into you own Web pages.

Using the FileMaker Connection assistant is often the easiest way to see how to write certain types of code. You can create a Web site that you will throw away and examine how the assistant has implemented searching, editing, and other functions.

Getting Started with the FileMaker Connection Assistant

To get started, you select a FileMaker Pro database and open it so that Home Page can examine its fields and layouts. In this chapter, the databases in the Integrated Solution example are used for demonstrations.

Figure 17-1 shows the main menu of the Integrated Solution. Many FileMaker Pro databases have such a menu; when you convert the database to a Web-based system, this menu screen can be totally replaced by standard HTML code.

FIGURE 17-1. Integrated Solution Main Menu

Your first step in building a Web-based solution is to open one of the databases that contain data for the Integrated Solution. Figure 17-2 shows the Products database.

The vendor information (in the lower right of Figure 17-2) is from a related database. The database that you want to use for your Web site must be open to use the FileMaker Connection assistant. It should be accessible from the computer on which you are running Home Page. That means that you must know the IP address of the computer on which FileMaker Pro is running; if it is running on your own computer, you can click the This Computer button to have the FileMaker Connection assistant automatically connect to your own IP address.

(For a review of this process, see "Using FileMaker Pro Web Companion" on page 141.)

FIGURE 17-2. Products Database

Start by choosing New... from the file menu. Click the Use Assistant radio button at the top of the screen and choose FileMaker Connection Assistant as shown in Figure 17-3.

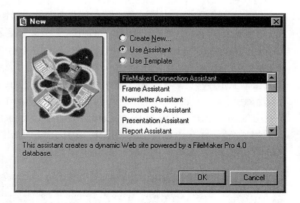

FIGURE 17-3. FileMaker Connection Assistant

When you click OK, you will see the overview screen shown in Figure 17-4.

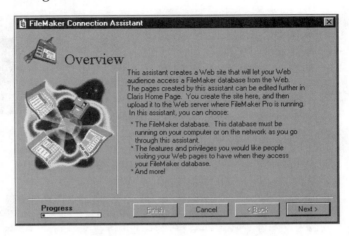

FIGURE 17-4. Overview

The overview continues with the Before You Begin screen shown in Figure 17-5.

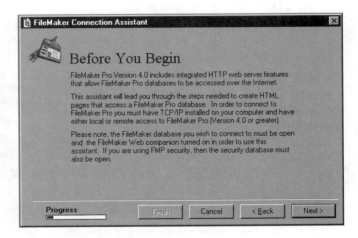

FIGURE 17-5. Before You Begin

When you click Next, the screen shown in Figure 17-6 prompts you to select the database you want to use.

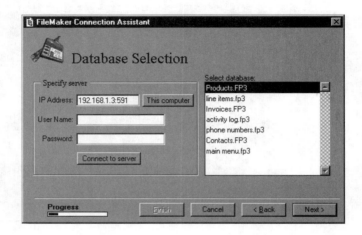

FIGURE 17-6. Selecting a Database

If you click the This computer button, the assistant will fill in the IP address of the computer on which you are running. If FileMaker Pro is configured to use a port other than 80, you will need to add that port number to the IP address that is shown. (For more information, see "Setting Up FileMaker Pro Web Companion" on page 143.)

When you click the Connect to Server button, you will see a list of all open FileMaker Pro databases that are enabled for sharing or for Web publication. If the database you are interested in is not in the list, check that it is configured properly for Web access (i.e., that it is marked for sharing if on the same computer or for publication using the Web Companion).

If you have problems, open one of the Web examples (Shopping Cart, Employee Database, or Guest Book). Then, click Connect to Server. If you do not see that database, your copy of FileMaker Pro has not been configured properly—see Application Preferences. If you see the Web example, FileMaker Pro is properly configured, but your own database has not been—see "Using FileMaker Pro Web Companion" on page 141.

Setting Up the CDML Files and Fields

You start the process by selecting a layout to use. The assistant shows you the layouts available in your database as well as the fields that are included in each one, as shown in Figure 17-7.

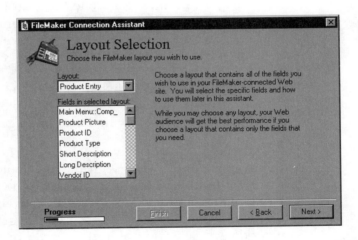

FIGURE 17-7. Selecting a Layout

You should choose the layout that contains all of the fields that you want to use but no others, even if that means creating such a layout specially for your Web site. The layout is used to select the fields that will be used and the formatting of those fields that will be used; the other aspects of the layout—its graphics, for example—are not used in Web publishing.

The FileMaker Connection assistant lets you select only one layout for your Web site, even though a separate layout can be used for each request (remember that Instant Web Publishing asks you to select a layout for each of its actions—see "Layouts for the Web" on page 132—and that Custom Web Publishing with CDML allows you to specify a layout with the -lay variable in each request—see "FileMaker Pro Web Companion Requests" on page 218). There are several ways to use multiple layouts with the FileMaker Connection assistant:

- You can run the assistant several times, each time selecting a different layout and creating different sorts of pages (a search page one time, an entry page the next, etc.). You can then combine them into one site (see "Consolidating Files from Several Sites" on page 387).

- You can manually adjust the layout in the CDML that has been generated by the FileMaker Connection assistant (see "Modifying Files" on page 388).

At this point, however, you select the one layout that you will use as you proceed with the assistant. When you click the Next button, you see the screen shown in Figure 17-6, which you use to select the features that you want included on your Web site. You can let users search your database, enter data, delete and duplicate records, or edit existing data.

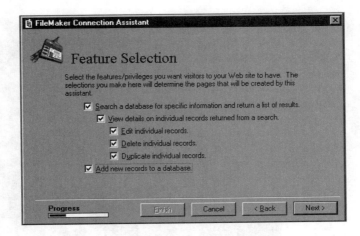

FIGURE 17-8. Selecting Features for Your Web Site

The features that you select will be reflected in the site that is created. Figure 17-9 shows the home page for a site in which the search and add features are both enabled (as is the case for the site created from the options shown in Figure 17-8).

The style of the pages is generated according to the options that you choose later in the assistant's sequence (see "Choosing the Web Site Style" on page 382). Notice that the name of the database (Products.FP3, in this case) is automatically inserted at the top of the page. Note also that in addition to the formatting, there is ample descriptive text for the user that explains what these options are all about.

You can modify this page later using the graphical user interface of Home Page or the HTML that has been generated. Both techniques are discussed with regard to this particular page in "Modifying Files" on page 388.

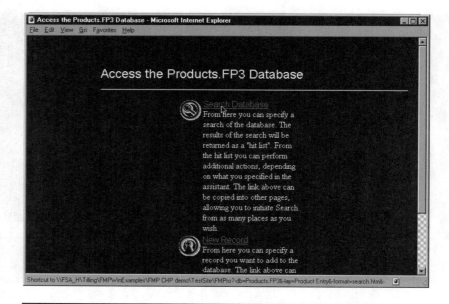

FIGURE 17-9. Home Page for the Web Site

Search Pages

If you requested the search feature as an option in Figure 17-8, the assistant will create the pages necessary to search your databases, starting with the page shown in Figures 17-10 and 17-11. The physical layout of the page varies depending on the style that you will choose later on; the fields that can be used to search are determined by you in the next FileMaker Connection assistant screen, which is shown in Figure 17-12.

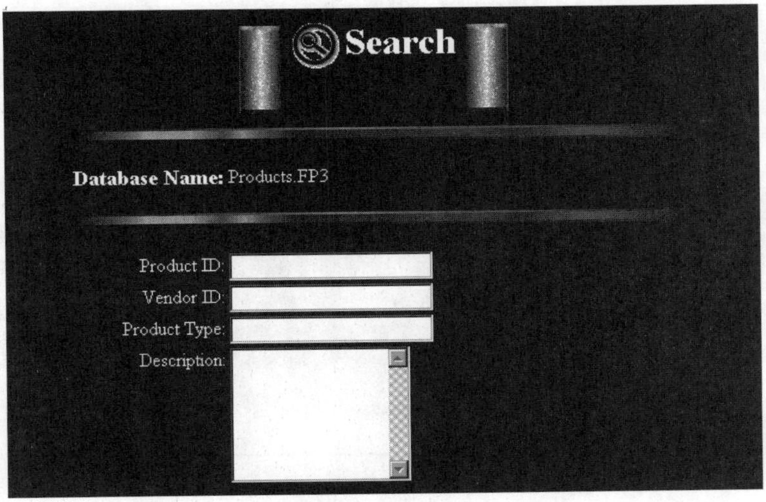

FIGURE 17-10. Search Page (top half)

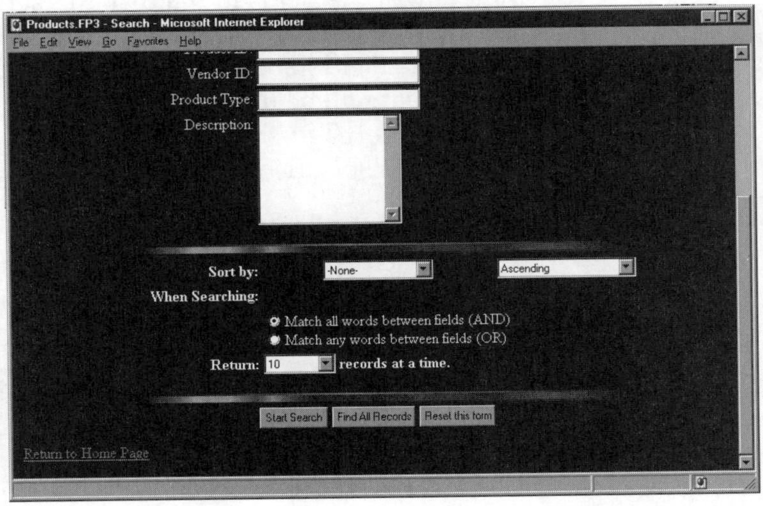

FIGURE 17-11. Search Page (bottom half)

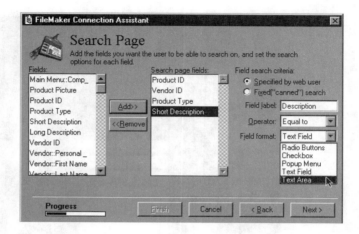

FIGURE 17-12. Selecting Search Fields

You select each field that you want to be used in a search from the list in the first column and then click the Add button to place it in the Search Page Fields list at the center. Highlight any of the fields in that list and set the search criteria at the right. Note that you can retitle a field on the search page (using the Field Label entry), and you can specify the type of format that will be used for that field on the page that is generated. (The page shown in Figures 17-10 and 17-11 is the page that is specified in Figure 17-12.)

Depending on the options that you have selected, there may be other screens on which you specify the fixed ("canned") searches that users can execute.

Once you have specified how searches can be constructed, you specify how the results are to be shown: you do this using the next screen, which is shown in Figure 17-13.

This screen lets you select the fields that are shown (again, based on the fields in the layout that you have selected). These fields will be shown in a table format on the HTML page that is generated.

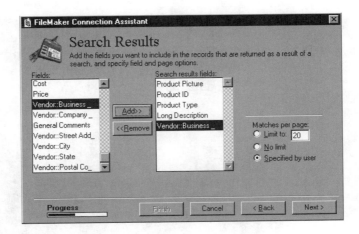

FIGURE 17-13. Specifying Search Results

The page built from the parameters in Figure 17-13 is shown in Figure 17-14.

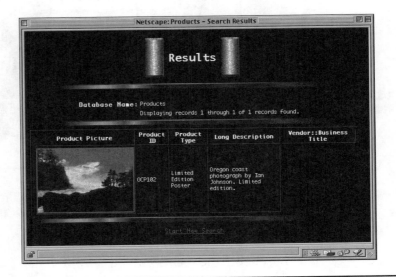

FIGURE 17-14. Search Results Page

This is the FileMaker Connection assistant's version of Instant Web Publishing's Table view (see "Table View" on page 110). Each database record is shown in one row of the table; at the left is a link you can click on to see a detailed display of the data, as shown in Figure 17-15.

FIGURE 17-15. Detailed Record Display

Notice that this display can quickly become very wide—even with only a few fields shown. For that reason, consider limiting the display of data in this page to information that identifies the record. Users can scan the information quickly (without scrolling from left to right on each line) and can click on the record that they want displayed in full.

You specify the contents of the details page in the screen shown in Figure 17-16.

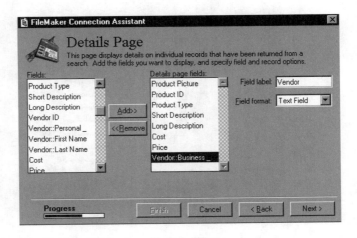

FIGURE 17-16. Specifying the Details Page

Adding Records

If you specified that users can add records to the database, the FileMaker Connection assistant will create a page like that shown in Figure 17-17 for you.

This page is generated based on the same sort of information that you supply for searching. The screen on which you enter it is shown in Figure 17-18. As before, you select the fields from the list at the left, using the Add (and Remove) button to place them in the list at the center. You can retitle the field labels at the right, and you can specify the type of field to be used on the page.

FIGURE 17-17. Adding a Record

One of the most useful features of the FileMaker Connection assistant is its ability to incorporate your database's value lists into its data entry pages. Using a value list helps to keep your database clean, since you know that the entries made will not have typographical errors (they may be wrong, but they will be from the known collection of values in the value list). The page shown in Figure 17-17 allows people to type anything that they want into the Product Type field at the top of the form.

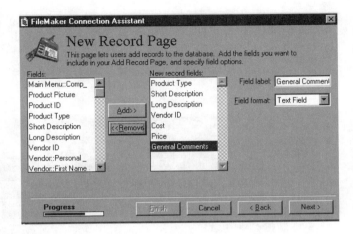

FIGURE 17-18. Specifying a Page for Data Entry

The database has a value list that is set up with known values for product types; Figure 17-19 shows the value lists in the Product database that is used in the examples in this chapter as they are shown in FileMaker Pro.

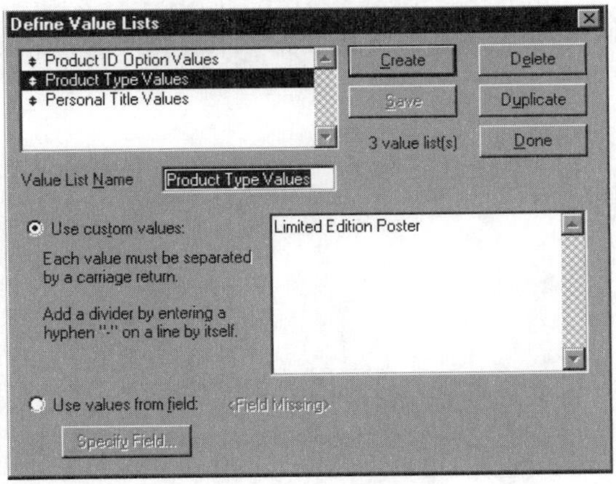

FIGURE 17-19. Value Lists in the Database

You can specify a value list by selecting the Popup Menu field format as shown in Figure 17-20. If you select Popup Menu, you will be presented with fields that let you enter the name and behavior of the value list to use.

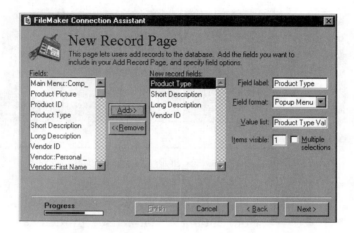

FIGURE 17-20. Using a Value List on the Web Page

Given the information shown in the previous figures, the data entry page that is generated is shown in Figure 17-21.

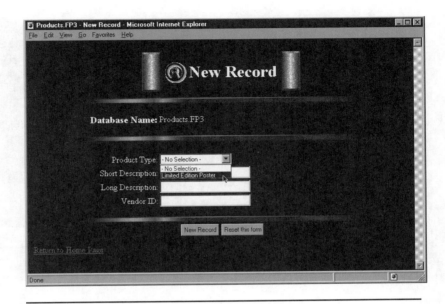

FIGURE 17-21. New Record Page with Value List

Creating Other Pages with the FileMaker Connection Assistant

Depending on the choices that you have made along the way, the FileMaker Connection assistant may generate other pages for you and may need further input. The next screen (shown in Figure 17-22) alerts you to this fact and introduces the screens that may appear next.

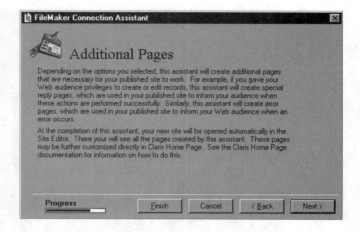

FIGURE 17-22. Additional Pages

Choosing the Web Site Style

Home Page comes with a number of built-in styles for Web sites, as shown in Figure 17-23. If you choose to customize the style, you can change the following items:

- The colors of links (active, visited, and normal)

- The color of text

- The color for the background of pages

- An image to be used for the background of the pages

Do not fret over these settings at this point: you can easily change them in Home Page once the assistant has completed its work.

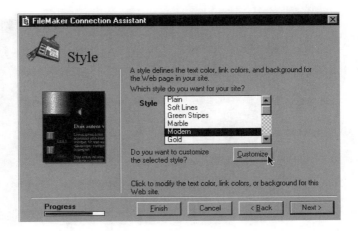

FIGURE 17-23. Selecting a Web Site Style

Finishing the Web Site

The last steps in finishing your Web site start with automatic prompting from the FileMaker Connection assistant. Figure 17-24 shows the screen with final information on it that you see at the end of the process. When you click the Next button, the screen in Figure 17-25 appears, letting you choose a location for your Web site.

The first time you create a site with FileMaker Connection assistant, you should choose to create a new folder. Thereafter, you may update an existing folder. You would update an existing folder if you decide to use the FileMaker Connection assistant a second time to create new pages. You might plan to use it twice—once to create search pages using one layout and a second time with a different layout to create pages to add records.

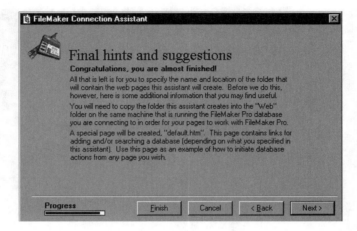

FIGURE 17-24. Final Hints and Suggestions

When you click the Create button on the screen shown in Figure 17-25, you may wait quite some time as Home Page creates all of the pages for your site. Do not worry as time passes: all will be well.

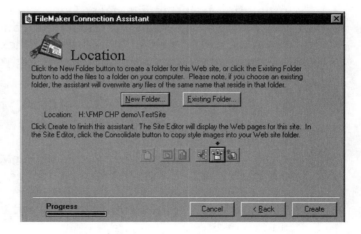

FIGURE 17-25. Setting the Location

What You Will Have

Eventually, you will see the window shown in Figure 17-26—it is your new site definition.

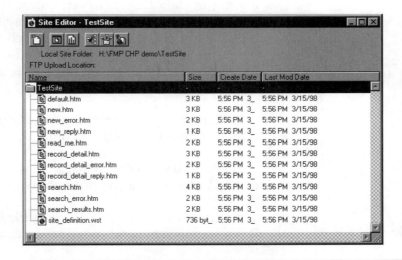

FIGURE 17-26. Site Definition Window

The files that the assistant creates are as follows:

- default.htm is the introductory screen shown in Figure 17-9.

- search.htm is the CDML format file shown in Figure 17-10.

- search_error.htm is the CDML error file for searching. It is a standard file and contains no customization.

- search_results is the CDML file to display search results (shown in Figure 17-14).

- record_detail.htm displays an individual data record. It is the format file used when you click any of the links in the search_results.htm file (Figure 17-15).

- record_detail_reply.htm is generated if you allow editing of data that has been entered. The previous file, record_ detail.htm is used to display the data to be edited and therefore is customized for each database; this is the CDML format file used to display a satisfactory completion message. It is a standard file and contains no customization.

- record_detail_error.htm is the CDML format file used if there is an error on editing data.

- new.htm is the data entry page shown in Figure 17-17 or 17-21 (depending on your options).

- new_error.htm is the CDML error file for data entry. It is a standard file and contains no customization.

- new_reply.htm is the CDML file that is displayed after successful data entry. It contains a link to the current record so that users can check the data that they have entered. The [FMP-CurrentRecord] element is used, so there is no customization of this page (i.e., it displays whatever the current record is).

- site_definition.wst is the file that contains this information.

Various other read_me and informational files may be generated. Note also that the choice of .htm or .html as a file suffix is a Home Page option; you should set it before you use the FileMaker Connection assistant.

Consolidating Files from Several Sites

As prompted in the screen shown in Figure 17-25, you should Consolidate your site as soon as it has been created. When you choose Consolidate from the menu or by clicking the button at the top of the screen shown in Figure 17-26, you open a dialog that is shown in Figure 17-27.

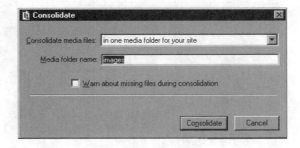

FIGURE 17-27. Consolidate Dialog

The purpose of consolidation is to eliminate references to images and files that are located on your computer; the files themselves are copied into a single location within your Web site—usually a folder called Images (although you can change its name). You can create a consolidation folder for subfolders within your Web site. Before you construct a complicated structure of folders and subfolders, start by creating a simple Web site with a single Images folder. Once you are certain that things work properly, you can then experiment with more sophisticated file structures.

Figure 17-28 shows a typical Web page that is previewed in a browser before consolidation. The images are all missing. Be aware that Home Page itself may display the page correctly, but a browser will often have these problems. Just to make your life more complicated, it is not unknown for a browser looking at the files on your computer (not on a Web server) to correctly be able to locate missing images. Test by using a browser on a computer different from the one on which you prepared the page.

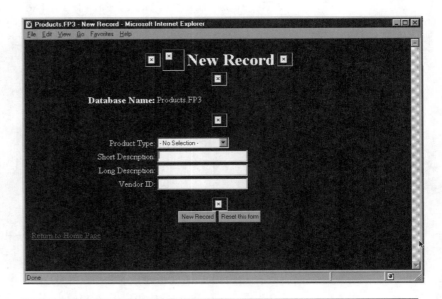

FIGURE 17-28. An Unconsolidated Page

Modifying Files

You can modify the pages created by Home Page by using its normal editing tools. The default.htm page is shown in Figure 17-29 in Home Page; it is similar to the version shown in the browser in Figure 17-9, but the text is editable.

The next chapter examines the process of editing CDML files with Home Page.

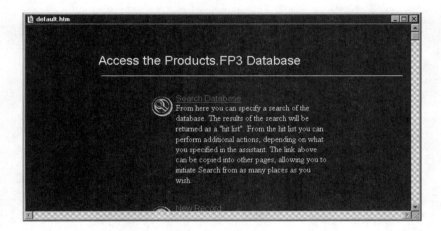

FIGURE 17-29. default.html in Home Page

You can switch to HTML display in Home Page. The same page shown in Figure 17-29 is shown again in Figure 17-30 as HTML. You can modify the HTML as you see fit.

A common modification occurs when you use the assistant multiple times to create a site that accesses multiple databases. The first time, you would create the files listed previously. You might rename them with names such as employee_record_detail.htm (instead of record_detail.htm), employee_new.htm (instead of new.htm), etc. The next time you run the assistant, it will create a new set of these files—which you in turn might rename position_new.htm, position_record_detail.htm, etc. Use the Home Page multiple file search and replace dialog to change the names. Note that the files that are not customized (such as the error and reply files) need not be duplicated or renamed.

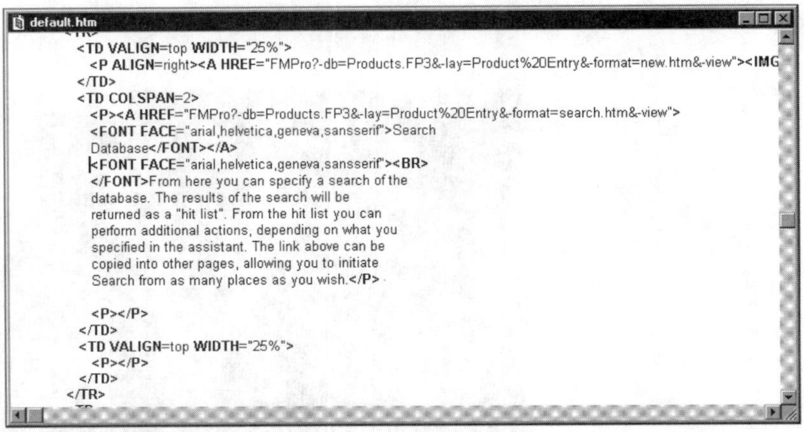

FIGURE 17-30. default.htm in HTML

Home Page highlights HTML syntax for you. Use that highlighting as a tool to debug your pages. It is not an accident if a tag like </TD> is not highlighted as you would expect it to be: a quote may be missing, as may a < or >. The HTML highlighting should be correct before you proceed. If it is not, the page has errors in it.

Summary

This chapter has walked you through the process of creating a Web site with the Home Page FileMaker Connection assistant. Whether you use it to create a Web site, as a customized tutorial to see how you can create CDML code for your own database, or for some combination of these functions, it can be an invaluable tool in quickly creating more sophisticated Web sites than can be obtained with Instant Web Publishing.

The next chapter walks you through the process of editing CDML with Home Page—whether you have written it from scratch, created it with the FileMaker Connection assistant, or used the FMP Library to create the code.

Editing CDML Pages with Home Page

Whether you have created CDML files with the FileMaker Connection assistant or by writing them from scratch, you can use Home Page to edit them. Its graphical user interface has been extended to make the CDML elements easy to see and modify.

You will see how to locate and edit the CDML elements on a page using the graphical interface as well as how to modify the underlying CDML and HTML code. This chapter also provides a look at some of the Home Page features and commands, although it is not designed as a complete guide to that product.

Where Does CDML Come From?

You may be starting from a blank page or from a FileMaker Connection assistant page. Remember that the FileMaker Pro Library (see "Using the FMP Form Library" on page 361) contains templates of code that you can copy and paste into your pages. That is one likely source for the basic form element with blank database, layout, format, and error elements.

Another source is CDML Tool which can provide templates that are filled in with the fields for the database on which you are working. (For more information, see "CDML Tool" on page 277.)

Remember that CDML Tool is part of FileMaker Pro and is located in its Web Tools folder; the FMP Library is part of Home Page and is available from the Library submenu in the File menu.

Starting to Edit the Page

This chapter uses the New Record page created by the FileMaker Connection assistant. It was discussed in the previous chapter and is shown here in Figure 18-1 in a browser.

If you open this page in Home Page, you can choose to edit it using the Edit Page command. The same page shown in Figure 18-1 is shown again in Figure 18-2 in the Home Page editor.

FIGURE 18-1. New Record Page

The first thing to notice in Figure 18-2 is that the elements of the page are made visible. There is a form element that is outlined on the page; at the upper left is an identifier that you can click on to select the entire form.

Modifying CDML Parameters

The CDML on this page—as on most pages—falls into three categories:

1. Hidden CDML elements are used to specify the database, format file, etc.

2. CDML elements that are associated with form fields for data entry.

3. CDML elements that are associated with buttons (particularly the Submit button for the form).

CDML for Hidden Fields

Within the confines of the form are four CDML elements that specify the database (-Db), the layout (-Lay), the format file (-Format) and the error file (-Error).

FIGURE 18-2. New Record in Home Page Editor

If you click the -Db element, you open the dialog shown in Figure 18-3. You can type in a new database name for the -Db element. You use the same technique to modify the layout, format, and error elements.

There are several cases to consider when you want to modify these elements:

- If you are changing the names of the files that are generated by the assistant (into employee_new.htm, for example), you may need to change format or error file names. In the case of the new record page that is automatically generated, both the format (successful reply) and error files are generic and do not need to be renamed.

- If you want to use a different layout than the one you specified in the assistant, you can change it here.

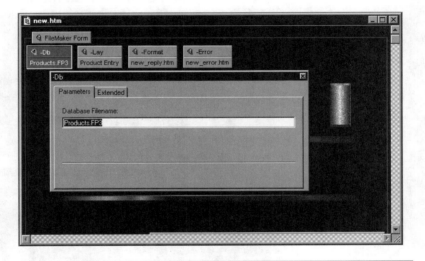

FIGURE 18-3. Database Dialog

If you switch to HTML display, you will see what this interface generates. In the case shown here, this is the corresponding code:

```
<INPUT TYPE="hidden" NAME="-DB" VALUE="Products.FP3">
```

The Extended tab lets you enter anything that you want. Whatever text you type in the Extended parameters field will appear at the end of the INPUT element, as in the following code:

```
<INPUT TYPE="hidden" NAME="-DB" VALUE="Products.FP3"
    additional text of any kind>
```

CDML for Fields

Each data entry field has its own CDML element. In Figure 18-4, you see the CDML element for the Product Type value list. It was generated by the assistant based on the value list that you specified for that field.

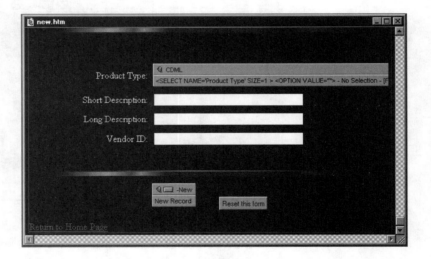

FIGURE 18-4. CDML for a Field

If you double-click the CDML element, you see the dialog shown in Figure 18-5, which contains all of the CDML code that was generated for the value list.

If you want to change the code in any way, this is a simple way to do it. Alternatively, you can switch to the HTML view and look at the code there. That may be easier since the HTML view includes highlighting of syntax elements and better spacing than the dialog.

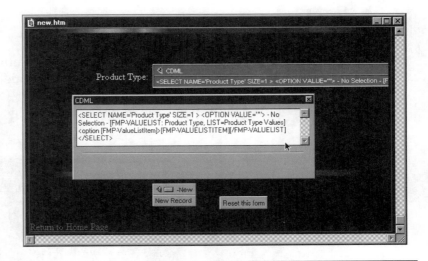

FIGURE 18-5. Code for CDML Value List Element

CDML for a Submit Button

Notice that the button at the bottom of the form (New Record, at the bottom of Figure 18-5) is also a CDML element. If you look at the code that has been generated, you will see why:

```
<INPUT TYPE="submit" NAME="-New" VALUE="New Record">
```

This is standard HTML code, but the Name="-New" section is needed to generate the appropriate part of the request with the -New CDML action. The Reset button that is next to it is not a CDML element since it has standard HTML code with no special features for CDML (it just resets the form as any HTML Reset button would).

Managing Links

At the lower left of this page is a link—Return to Home Page. If you highlight it in Home Page Edit mode, you can open the Link Editor dialog shown in Figure 18-6. (You use the Show Link Editor menu command to do this).

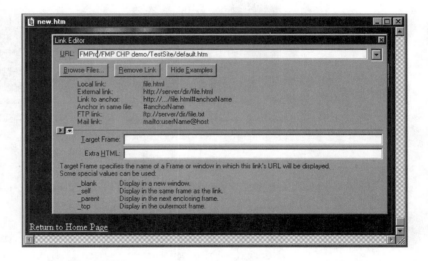

FIGURE 18-6. Link Editor

The Link Editor shows you the link that you have associated with this text. You can change it either by typing in a new link or by using the Browse Files… button to locate the appropriate link. The window also provides you with hints as to the proper syntax for links.

As always, you can switch easily to the HTML code to check exactly what has been generated, as shown in Figure 18-7.

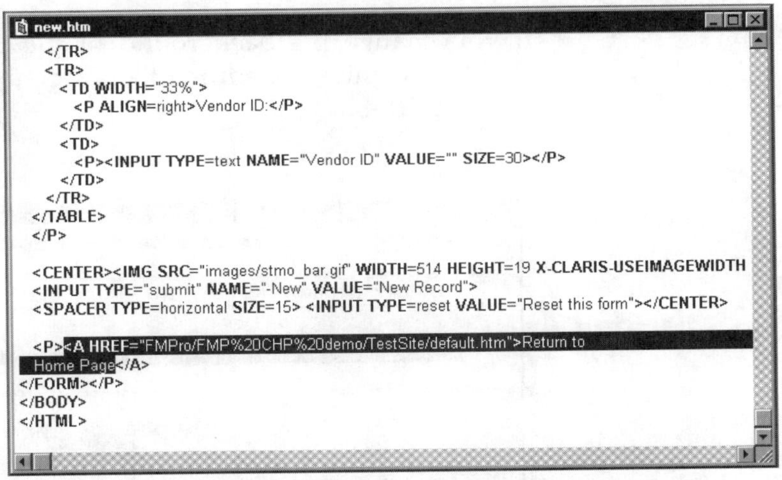

```
new.htm
    </TR>
    <TR>
      <TD WIDTH="33%">
        <P ALIGN=right>Vendor ID:</P>
      </TD>
      <TD>
        <P><INPUT TYPE=text NAME="Vendor ID" VALUE="" SIZE=30></P>
      </TD>
    </TR>
  </TABLE>
  </P>

  <CENTER><IMG SRC="images/stmo_bar.gif" WIDTH=514 HEIGHT=19 X-CLARIS-USEIMAGEWIDTH
  <INPUT TYPE="submit" NAME="-New" VALUE="New Record">
  <SPACER TYPE=horizontal SIZE=15> <INPUT TYPE=reset VALUE="Reset this form"></CENTER>

  <P><A HREF="FMPro/FMP%20CHP%20demo/TestSite/default.htm">Return to
Home Page</A>
</FORM></P>
</BODY>
</HTML>
```

FIGURE 18-7. Link in HTML

If the link that you are using is to a file that is not in the same directory as this page, it is essential that you consolidate files and check references (from the Site Definition window) before you upload your files. This is the area in which you can create something that works on your computer but that fails on another one—or on the Web.

Using Tables with CDML

You can open the Document Options dialog using the Document Options command in the Edit menu or with the button at the top of the page editing window or at the top of the site definition window.

If you change the background of the page shown in this chapter to white, the editing tools are more visible, as shown in Figure 18-8.

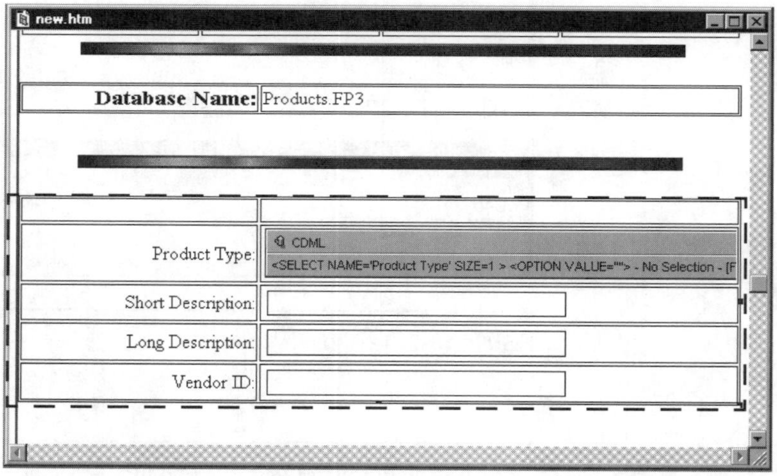

FIGURE 18-8. Page with White Background

The dotted line outlines a table of five rows and two columns. You can use the Object Editor (View Object Editor command) to inspect and modify the parameters for this table, as shown in Figure 18-9.

As discussed previously, HTML tables involve a number of elements, such as <TR> and </TR> tags to specify rows, and <TD> and </TD> tags for each table data cell. This graphical interface to table parameters saves a lot of HTML coding and generates code that is correct.

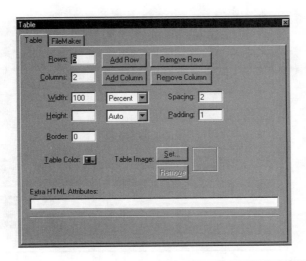

FIGURE 18-9. Object Editor (Table)

If you are using a table as a formatting tool (as is the case here), you can create tables and table cells that align fields and labels in ways that are very difficult to do with nontable formats.

The Object Editor can be used to inspect individual cells in the table. In Figure 18-10, you can see that the upper left cell of the table is selected; when it is, the Object Editor includes a Cell tab, which is shown in the figure.

You can set background colors for cells and rows in the Cell tab of the Object Editor; the Table tab lets you set background colors for the table itself. You can also set spacing and alignment for the rows and cells, as shown in Figure 18-10. (Note that the ability to have a cell span several columns is very useful in laying out pages while maintaining an organized look.)

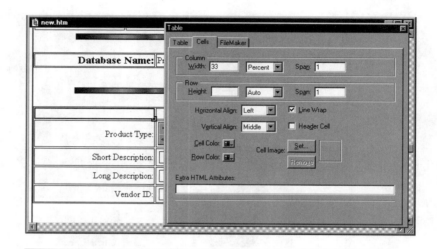

FIGURE 18-10. Object Editor (Cell)

The final tab in the Object Editor is shown in Figure 18-11. This allows you to specify that a table is used for FileMaker Pro results. In practice, setting a table as a results table causes Home Page to insert the [FMP-Record] element around the appropriate row(s).

If you create a table that will be used for results, you must manually insert the fields into the appropriate data cells—either with the FMP Library (Home Page), CDML Tool (FileMaker Pro), or raw CDML code that you type in. However, your work will be confined to filling in the table cells that you need: the overhead and structure will be taken care of for you.

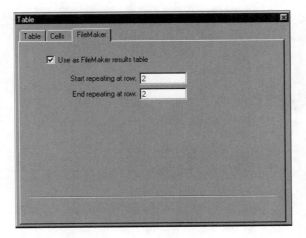

FIGURE 18-11. Object Editor (FileMaker Results Table)

Summary

This chapter has provided an overview of the types of editing of CDML that you can do with Home Page. The CDML tags are shown in Edit mode and can be edited via the graphical user interface; in addition, the raw HTML and CDML code is easily modified when you switch to HTML Source view. In practice, most people switch back and forth between the two views, checking that everything looks right. The next step, as always, is to preview the page in a browser—and then it is time to check the page from other machines, across a network, and on a Web site.

The next part of the book discusses the issues involved in setting up and maintaining your Web site.

Setting Up and Maintaining Your Databases on the Web

Security

Security on a nonnetworked desktop computer is easy to implement: you lock the door to the room where the computer is. In a public and shared environment, however, security quickly becomes a serious issue. You need to address the following issues:

- The security of the data you publish

- The quality of the data that is entered by others through your online system

- The use of your data and databases

- The integrity of your system, including the disk files and security apparatus that you use to manage the database.

This chapter deals with these issues. It starts with an overview of security concerns in general and continues with a summary of FileMaker Pro security features and how to use them. It concludes with a discussion of some of the issues and trade-offs you need to address.

Security in General

The biggest mistake people make with security is ignoring it, thinking that they can add it on at the end of a project. The three aspects of software and databases that cannot be retrofitted are security; version control (discussed in "Version Control" on page 444); and all aspects of networking, file-sharing, and multiuser operations. If you are going to use any security whatsoever at any time in the future, you need to plan for it at the beginning. This does not necessarily mean that you implement all your security at the beginning of your project, but it does mean that you should know what you will need to do later—and what will need to be in place to achieve your security goals.

The second biggest mistake people make with security is thinking that they can "turn it on." Security is not a switch; it is a complex combination of physical and logical attributes implemented in your databases, on your Web server, in FileMaker Pro Web Companion, and in FileMaker Pro itself.

Evaluating Your Security Needs

You start by evaluating your security needs in terms of the four areas previously mentioned. Each area addressed has its own concerns.

Security of the Data That You Publish

In this area you need to consider who has access to the data, what they use it for, and how you control it. Security in this sense is a very broad term: if you are implementing a shopping cart application, the prices that you publish need to be secure in the sense that someone accessing the site tomorrow needs to be able to find a logical reason for a change in price (perhaps a notice at the bottom of each page that "prices are subject to change without notice").

In terms of access, you need to consider who is allowed (or is not allowed) to access your customer database—which may contain credit card numbers. Controlling what information people can access and who can access it also means controlling what information people cannot access and who cannot access it.

It is tempting to divide all data into public and private data, but that distinction is at most only half of the puzzle: you must consider the data to which you and your colleagues need access (for maintenance purposes) as well as the semipublic data to which only certain people have access (an individual user's credit card information, for example). In the case of data needed for maintenance purposes, a set of people have a higher level of security that enables them to manipulate data that is off limits to the general public. In the case of credit card information, it may be only the owner of the data who can access it—even you may not be able to see someone's credit card or password information.

Think about these issues with regard to your data: do not worry yet about FileMaker Pro.

Quality of the Data That Is Entered by Others

If you allow online updates to your database, you need to find a way to maintain the quality of the data in your database—particularly if those updates are immediately accessible to others. Even if the data is not available to others, you need to implement security procedures to prevent someone from using your shopping cart application to order 15 gross of an item and sending them to someone who refuses delivery.

In the case of data that will be available to others, your procedures reflect the nature of the data. You may want to use the built-in mailing actions in CDML to mail a copy of database updates to yourself or someone else. Those e-mail messages may contain all of the data or just a notice that an update has occurred. Alternatively, you can use the Web Companion log feature to keep track of what has happened. In the first case, you (or your delegate) are notified automatically of updates; in the second case, you (or your delegate) must decide to check the log for updates. (See "Mail Requests" on page 228 and "Logs" on page 427 for more information.)

The only thing worse than discovering that hackers have filled your online database with gibberish or pornography is to be given this information in public. Even if you rely on logs and/or e-mail, establish a regular routine for checking your published database to look for trouble.

Use of Your Data and Databases

This is an area that takes on increasing importance in the world of the Internet, where many people have access to your data (unless you protect it). The publication of the addresses and telephone numbers of individuals without their permission can cause problems; even the publication of e-mail addresses on Web pages can open those accounts to unwanted e-mail.

When considering what sort of security to implement, take a moment and think of the worst use that could be made of your data by the worst possible person.

Relying on the supposition that no one would care enough about your data to hack it is always a poor choice!

Integrity of the System

Finally, you need to consider the integrity of the entire system. Many a security scheme has been put in place only for the owners to discover that they are locked out. As you construct a security structure, you need to simultaneously look for holes that can be exploited by people who want to get around your security as well as look for ways for you to carry out your legitimate database housekeeping chores.

If you are dealing with data of significant intrinsic value (as is true in the financial services industry), you may already be constrained by rules and procedures. All of these are thwarted, however, if your database backups are stored on an open shelf in a neat row of correctly labeled backup tapes.

Part of the need for building security into your work from the beginning is that if you do find yourself in a situation where someone may be jeopardizing your data, the mere suggestion of the implementation of security may be enough to cause serious problems. People who deal with human resources issues will tell you that the time to set out a policy on drug use in the workplace is when you have hired someone who appears to be a saint—not when you have hired someone about whom you have suspicions.

Cheer Up

In many ways, security runs against the tide you are riding with on the Web and with FileMaker Pro: most of your work is aimed at addressing access, making things easy, and providing as much as possible to the people who visit your database and your Web site. In this sense, security is a negative issue.

Nevertheless, it is essential. You must understand the issues and implement security in the most effective way possible—and the way that least intrudes on what you are trying to accomplish. Fortunately, FileMaker Pro provides you with a multitude of options.

FileMaker Pro Security Features

The FileMaker Pro security tools fall into four groups:

1. FileMaker Pro supports passwords and access control; this is unchanged in FileMaker Pro 4.0 and unchanged in Web Companion. It is the heart of the security system (but by default it may be off, and it may never come into play on your databases).

2. Web Security databases are designed for use by Web Companion in publishing your databases. Web Security databases work to a limited degree with Instant Web Publishing (names, passwords, and user permissions, but not for script permissions or field restric-

tions) as well as to their fullest extent with Custom Web Publishing. They do not affect people who access your databases directly with FileMaker Pro.

3. Remote administration lets you control access to Web Security databases and the format files contained inside your Web folder.

4. Logs permit you to monitor what happens with your database.

All of these tools are controlled from the Web Companion Configuration screen, shown in Figure 19-1.

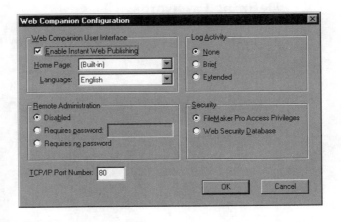

FIGURE 19-1. Web Companion Configuration

FileMaker Pro Access and Passwords

The basic FileMaker Pro access control uses passwords and groups to specify levels of access. You manage FileMaker Pro access from the Access Privileges submenu in the File menu. The choices you will find there are

- Define Groups

- Define Passwords

- Overview

(These commands are discussed in the sequence in which most people use them rather than in the order in which they appear in the menu.)

Defining Passwords

You start by defining one or more passwords on the screen shown in Figure 19-2.

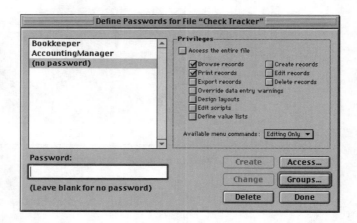

FIGURE 19-2. Define Passwords

In the example shown here, someone with no password can open the database, but only to view the data. The password AccountingManager provides full access to the file, and the

Bookkeeper password allows access to all features except the abilities to override entry warnings, design layouts, and edit scripts.

To create a new password, type it in the box at the bottom left. When you click the Create button, it will appear in the list at the left. You can then highlight it (or any other password in the list) and choose the access privileges for that password.

In addition to a variety of general access privileges, you will also be able to choose the type of menus to be shown when FileMaker Pro opens the database with that password. You can select no menus, editing only, or the normal menu structure. Within the menus you have chosen, some commands may be disabled due to the access choices that you have made.

When you make changes, remember to click the Change button: changes are not automatically saved when you click the Done button, and you are not warned about unsaved changes. If your access changes do not "take," redo them and make a special effort to click the Change button.

If you create passwords for a database, FileMaker Pro will force you to create at least one password (the master password) that has full access to the file. If you have created any passwords that have less than full privileges, you will see the warning shown in Figure 19-3 when you try to close the Define Passwords dialog.

FIGURE 19-3. Password Confirmation for Full Access

Access Overview

The passwords that you create for FileMaker Pro databases facilitate record-level activities (such as creating, editing, and deleting records) as well as some global privileges (such as menus). You cannot use passwords to control the access to individual fields within a database.

However, with Web Security databases you can implement both record-level access and field-level access (see "Web Security Databases" on page 422); you can also implement field-level security with groups and the Access Privileges dialog shown in Figure 19-4.

The next section discusses the creation of groups. For now, all you need to know is that a group is a collection of passwords.

You can select a group and then assign passwords to it, define access for layouts, and define access for fields. The symbol to the left of each item in the Access Privileges window toggles among the three choices shown at the bottom of the window—accessible, not accessible, and read only.

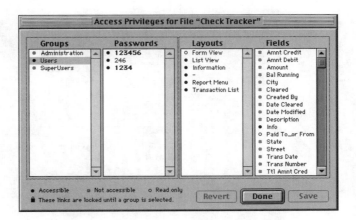

FIGURE 19-4. Access Privileges Overview

Figure 19-5 shows how field-level security can appear to a user. A number of fields on the layout are grayed out such as the Date field, the City, and the Payee Address. Another field—Paid To or From—has been marked as read only. Its data ("cat") is visible, but if the user tries to change it, the dialog shown in the figure is displayed.

Note that this is implemented based solely on the Access Privileges specified for the database. You do not have to modify the database or its layouts to get this functionality, nor do you have to write any scripts or If statements in them to check if someone has access.

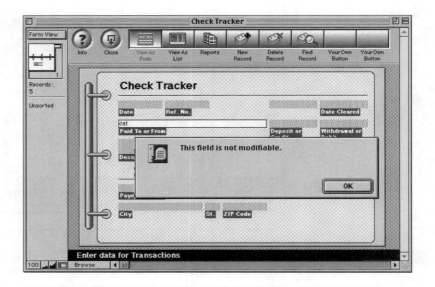

FIGURE 19-5. Field-Level Security in Action

Defining Groups

The groups that are used in the Access Privileges window are defined in the Define Groups window shown in Figure 19-6. You define the groups here and then assign passwords and access privileges to them in the Access Privileges window.

This may be a slightly different structure than those you are used to: passwords do not belong to specific groups in the way in which users may belong to groups on a network. Each password has access privileges set for it with regard to each group, and passwords can wind up in multiple groups. Experiment with the Access Privileges window to see how this works. Note also that one level of security that you may be used to—user names—does not exist in this structure; it does exist in the Web Security database structure discussed in the following section.

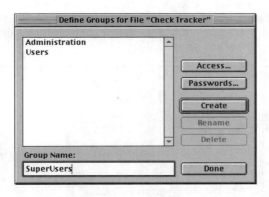

FIGURE 19-6. Define Groups

Default Passwords

You can create a default password for a database; you use the Document Preferences window shown in Figure 19-7 to do so. Note that one of your preferences is a default password to be used when opening the database. If you have set this preference, that password will always be used unless you hold down the option key while you are opening the database (in which case you will be asked to supply a password—which can be different from the default password).

If you are having security difficulties—particularly those in which you seem to have set access correctly but the database appears to have a mind of its own—check the default password on the database. From a user's point of view, it is impossible to tell the difference between opening a database with no password and no security and opening a database with a default password and some security.

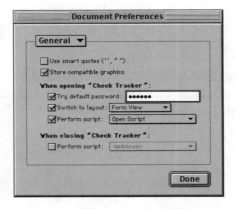

FIGURE 19-7. Setting a Default Password

Web Security Databases

You can use Web Security databases to implement security for the databases you publish on the Web. These can be used instead of traditional FileMaker Pro access or in addition to it. The chief difference between the traditional FileMaker Pro access mechanism and the Web Security databases is that the traditional access mechanisms include not just database security (at both the field and record level) but also control of FileMaker Pro functionality (the types of menus that are used, whether a user can create layouts, etc.). Web Security databases address only the database security issues.

There are three databases, located in the Web Security folder of the FileMaker Pro folder, that implement this functionality:

- Web Security

- Web Fields

- Web Users

These databases implement security for all of the FileMaker Pro databases that are published by FileMaker Web Companion on that computer.

The Web Security database is shown in Figure 19-8.

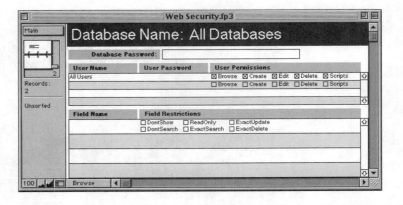

FIGURE 19-8. Web Security Database

This is the default record in the database that controls access to all databases for all users; it ships with FileMaker Pro. You can then add records for individual users and individual databases that narrow this access.

In a production environment, you might want to modify this record to provide limited access to all users and all databases. In that case, the records that you add for individual users and individual databases would broaden the default (limited) access.

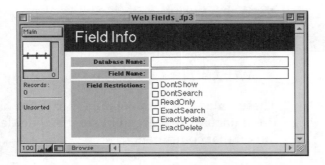

FIGURE 19-9. Web Fields Database

There are two portals that allow you to browse and enter data into the related files: Web Fields and Web Users. You need not access those files except through this database, but in case you are interested, they are shown in Figures 19-9 and 19-10.

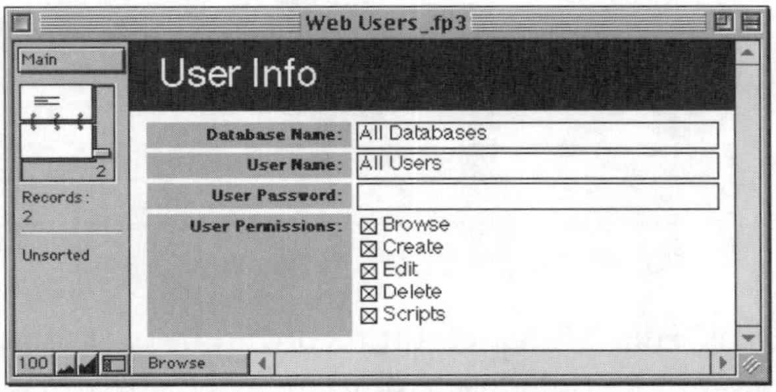

FIGURE 19-10. Web Users Database

You start as shown in Figure 19-8, with a user name called All Users. By default, that user has no password and has all access privileges. Typically, you start by redefining All Users to remove most if not all of the access. You then create additional users (such as Accounting Manager and Bookkeeper in the example earlier in this chapter). Each of those users has permissions beyond the wholesale browsing that you assign to all users. In this case, Accounting Manager would have all of the permissions that were assigned to All Users in Figure 19-8; Bookkeeper would have permissions to browse, create, edit, and delete records (but not for scripts); and All Users would have access only to Browse records.

The field permissions shown in Figures 19-8 and 19-9 let you restrict access in fairly standard ways—allowing or disallowing display, the use of the field in searching, and modification. The three final privileges (Exact Search, Exact Update, and Exact Delete) implement privileges for the record based on a field's value. If one of these privileges is set, the operation (searching, updating, or deleting) can only be performed if the value of the field exactly matches the value in the database. This enables you to implement a form of record locking based on field values—such as passwords known only to the person who enters the record being required before the record can be deleted.

The Web Security database is used only by Web Companion: if you open a database directly with FileMaker Pro, only the FileMaker Pro access security is used. Because of this combination of security systems, you need to decide what security is implemented where. This can be a significant issue for databases that are accessed directly, over an intranet or local area network and over the Internet. (See "Security Issues for Intranets and Other Networks" on page 454 for a more detailed discussion of the issue.)

Remote Administration

Since the Web Security database is itself nothing but a File-Maker Pro database, it can be subject to the same security controls that you can apply to any other database. On the Web Companion configuration screen (Figure 19-1), you have the ability to allow remote administration of the Web Security access: your choices are to disable it, to enable it with a password (that you supply), or to enable it with no password.

All that remote administration does in the configuration screen is to apply the same kind of security to the Web Security database that you apply to your own databases: specifically, whether a password should be required for access to the database. This password is used in combination with the user name Admin for access to the Web Security database.

If you have turned on remote administration, you first move the Security folder containing the format files for the Web Security database to the Web folder so that you can access it across the Internet. Then, you connect to the Web Security database as you would to any FileMaker Pro database on that computer: with a URL that includes that computer's IP address. If you are using an IP address like 192.168.1.2, the address of the page that accesses that database is

`http://192.168.1.2/Security/default.htm`

(As always, if Web Companion has been configured to use a port other than 80, you must add that to the IP address.)

If you have specified a password, log in as Admin with the password that you created.

Logs

The final option that Web Companion provides for you with regard to security is its logging feature. Some people would argue whether this is more of a debugging tool or a security tool, but the point is that it allows you to keep track of what FileMaker Web Companion is doing.

If you turn logging on, you can choose either brief or extended entries. All entries are written to a file called Web.log, which is kept in the folder with FileMaker Pro. Web Companion continually adds log data to the end of this file: if you choose to keep it around forever, sooner or later your hard disk will be full. Purging the file (in practical terms copying it elsewhere) is your responsibility. You can simply move (or remove) the file: if it is not there when Web Companion needs it, it will create it.

Here is what a typical log looks like:

```
3/26/1998 3:52:42 PM 192.168.1.2 /FMRes/FMPro
3/26/1998 3:52:42 PM Got search argument.
3/26/1998 3:52:42 PM -db=bid%20comparison&-max=1&token=25&-
    format=FormVw.htm&-findall
3/26/1998 3:52:42 PM Sending reply.      Elapsed time: 59
    millisec.
3/26/1998 3:52:44 PM 192.168.1.2 /FMRes/FMPro
3/26/1998 3:52:44 PM Got search argument.
3/26/1998 3:52:44 PM -db=bid%20comparison&-max=1&-
    token=25&-format=New.htm&-find
3/26/1998 3:52:45 PM Sending reply.      Elapsed time: 70
    millisec.
3/26/1998 3:52:46 PM 192.168.1.2 /FMRes/NwRcdHdr.gif
3/26/1998 3:52:46 PM /FMRes/NwRcdHdr.gif
3/26/1998 3:52:46 PM Sending reply.      Elapsed time: 5
    millisec.
```

The sections in bold indicate a request to use the Bid Comparison database with the -findall action. This is followed by a reply along with the amount of time it took to create the reply. Later on you can see an access to NewRecHdr.gif—the image for the New Record button in Instant Web Publishing. You can follow the sequence of user actions and Web Companion responses.

There are several points to note in looking at log entries:

- They are listed in the sequence in which Web Companion has processed them. Each entry is stamped with the date and time, but there is no guarantee that these will be in chronological order (for example, the computer's clock may have been reset).

- The entries reflect what Web Companion is doing. The example given here was for a single user accessing a database with Instant Web Publishing. If several people are accessing several databases at the same time, their entries will be intermingled.

- Finally, remember that the log imparts information about your database and security. *The log should perhaps be considered the most secure FileMaker Pro document on your computer.* Although it may be tedious, someone up to no good can learn a great deal about your database configuration by reading the log.

The log feature can be very useful when you are analyzing problems—be they performance, errors, or security difficulties. In order to be of the greatest use, though, turn on the log briefly when there are no problems so that you get a sense for what it should look like. That way, when you look at a log that is reporting aberrant behavior, you have a chance of recognizing it.

Security Issues in FileMaker Pro

For some people, security is like a wonderful strategic game of chess; for others, it is a big nuisance. Your job is to find the balance that is appropriate to your project and your data. Here are some further security issues you may want to think about.

Using Address Information for Security

The CDML elements discussed in "Environmental Elements" on page 236 can be helpful in your security considerations. You can use specific IP addresses together with [FMP-If] elements to limit access to various sites. You can test for addresses and partial addresses, as in these code snippets, which are discussed further in "Testing Values" on page 252:

```
[FMP-If: ClientIP .eq. 192.168.1.*, 10,10,10,10]
    …the user is logged on from either any address
    at 192.168.1.n or at 10.10.10.10…
```

and

```
[FMP-If: ClientAddress .eq.

        *.philmontmill.com, *.philmont.*]
```

Related Files and Their Visibility

Related files and their fields are controlled by the FileMaker Pro access of the master (primary) file rather than by their own access controls. If a database is used in a relationship, the database that is relating to it is responsible for security. In this one case, the access controls that you specify can appear to be side-stepped by FileMaker Pro itself.

Be aware of this, and in the case of secure data, consider other means to limit access. Typically this involves removing the relationship and denormalizing the data structures in one way or another. (This is discussed further in "Databases Can Be Normalized" on page 22.)

Exporting Records

The Export Records privilege that you can set in the Define Passwords window (see Figure 19-2) also controls Web publishing. If you can export records from a database, you can publish that database with Web Companion. Thus, anyone to whom you grant the Export Records access privilege has automatically been granted the ability to publish the entire database on the Web.

In the past, exporting records meant nothing more than sending a database's data to a flat file with standard delimiters (such as tabs, commas, quotes). In the world of Web publishing, exporting records means much more than that. If you have existing databases with access controls, you may need to revisit this option in light of these changes. Furthermore, you may need to implement access control where you never did before: publishing a database on the Web is a far cry from copying it into a spreadsheet.

What about Hackers?

A discussion of computer hackers is far beyond the scope of this book; however, it is a subject that you should think about. If you are going to publish information on the Web, presumably that information has some value—or else why would you publish it? (The only exception is a classroom exercise.) If it is valuable to you, to whom else would it be valuable? Beyond the question of who else would like to see it, who else would find it amusing or profitable to change your data?

Approach the hacker issue by first examining your data and its value—to anyone. Next deal with the specifics.

The simplest assumption to make is that no computer and no data is invulnerable if the computer is connected to a network. Your job is to make the hacker's job difficult and/or unpalatable. Many hackers—like burglars—will look for egregious breaches of security. For a hacker to spend a great deal of time trying to get into a well-protected site, there must be some attraction to the site. Having determined how valuable your data is, now sit down and turn the question around—is it really of any interest to anyone else? Most data is valuable to its owner and of no interest to anyone else. (Want to see some baby pictures?)

The fact that a determined hacker can get past any security mechanism should not prevent you from creating the simplest and most powerful security system you can design and afford. Then rely on it.

Don't Lock Yourself Out!

It is very easy to construct a security scheme that prevents you from accessing your database. While FileMaker Pro is careful to ensure that there is always a password that lets you access the entire database, you can easily construct a mechanism that prevents you from doing your work. For example, a common procedure is to divide access and passwords among several people. Thus, one person might have the key to the room in which your Web server is kept, another might have the password to access the computer, and a third might have access to the database.

This simple structure (which is used in many high-security areas) can break down very easily. An office-wide outbreak of the flu can destroy it. In an emergency (flu and hard disk crash), one person will need access to all three security levels. A very large number of security breaches occur in such cases. Before you know it, the password to each computer and database is posted in a secure location (taped to the under-side of the middle desk drawer of the desk on which the computer is located).

If your security scheme is too complex, you will be locked out—or at the first sign of problems it will be thrown out the window.

User Names and Passwords in FileMaker Pro

As noted previously, FileMaker Pro uses passwords but not user names. If you open a database over the Web that requires a password, Web Companion will use your browser's standard name and password dialog to ask for the password. It will ignore the name that is entered.

Summary

Security is something that you should think about from the beginning of your projects. You may not implement it at the start, but it is maddeningly difficult to retrofit security.

FileMaker Pro provides security via its standard password access mechanisms as well as with the Web Security database that Web Companion uses. Both provide security that can be tailored down to the field level.

File Structures for Your Web Site

Managing a Web site quickly becomes a difficult task as files are modified, added, and removed. Managing a Web site that also involves databases is even more complex. This chapter addresses some of the issues that you will encounter and presents a way of organizing and managing your site that will make your life easier.

In this chapter, "folder" and "directory" are used interchangeably. In general, "directory" is the name that is used in character-based environments, and "folder" is the name that is used in graphical user interfaces.

File Structures for Easy Maintenance

On your desktop, you can pretty much put files anywhere you want and call them anything you want. To a large extent that is true on the Web, but in practical terms you will find substantial limits on the freedom you may be used to.

Naming conventions and filing strategies differ from computer to computer—as they do from person to person and from organization to organization. Using a very standard structure will often make it easier for other people to access your files (either for maintenance or with Internet browsers).

Do Not Rename Files

The cardinal rule is never to rename a file. Once you have given it a name, that is its name forever and ever. Adhering to this rule will prevent the broken links that are generated when you rename a file and leave HTML pages pointing to the old name.

Renaming a file includes moving it to a new folder or directory: that changes its name for some purposes. Thus, this rule means that you must put the file wherever it is going to be with the name it is going to carry—forever.

FileMaker Web Companion needs to be able to locate your CDML format files in order to create the HTML that combines the CDML and your database data. If the HTML files are in the same folder as your CDML format files, there will be no problem.

Eight Dot Three

The most restrictive naming convention is that used in DOS (and later in the first versions of Windows)—an eight-character filename followed by a three-character suffix that identifies the file. Examples are schedule.doc, program.exe, and autoexec.bat.

Some operating systems (Mac OS, for instance) incorporate the information from the suffix in the file itself; thus, the filename is not used to identify the kind of file it is. Other operating systems (Windows 95, for instance) use the suffix to help identify the file type and determine the kind of icon to represent it with, but they normally do not display the suffix. Other operating systems (Unix, for example) allow multiple suffixes that can be interpreted in various ways.

Of all of these, the eight-dot-three convention is the most restrictive and therefore will work on most platforms. While you only need a naming convention that will work on your Web server, adhering to this convention will ultimately make it easier to support your files.

The only exception to this is Web servers—often those running Unix—that allow four-character suffixes and which require .html rather than .htm as the suffix for HTML files.

Capitalization

Some systems (like Unix) distinguish between upper and lowercase characters: the file schedule.doc is not the same as Schedule.doc. Others (like Windows and Mac OS) do not make this distinction. For this reason, it is best not to rely on capitalization to distinguish between files.

It is appropriate to use capitalization for your own purposes. One convention that some people use is to name primary databases with capital letters—as in Functs.fp3. Secondary databases (such as related databases) are given names that start with lowercase letters—as in categories.fp3. Anyone who is familiar with this convention can then easily see which databases are designed to be opened directly by users and which are designed to be opened implicitly through the use of relations.

Another such convention is used to identify HTML files and distinguish them from CDML format files and included files. Here, the HTML files—which are designed to be opened directly by users in their browsers—are also capitalized, as in Welcome.html. Included and format files begin with lowercase letters. Note that this convention is not as easy to maintain as the previous one: some Web servers use index.html, home.html, or default.html as special filenames. In the case of a server that recognizes the distinction between upper and lowercase characters, this would require that you reverse the convention—or not use it.

Whatever conventions you use, remember that capitalization should be used only to provide extra information to people and not as a distinguishing characteristic of files.

Keep Track of Files and Folders

Since you are not going to be moving or renaming folders, it makes sense to keep track of what you have. Files and folders have been known to disappear from Web servers: you need to be able to restore what should be there.

The easiest way to keep track of your Web site is to keep an updated list of each file, together with its contents, its update date, and the folder in which it belongs. You can create a small FileMaker Pro database with this information and publish it on your Web site. If you make it accessible with Instant Web Publishing (which should not take much time), you will always be able to keep track of your site.

Note the distinction between a database listing the files that you think should be on your Web site and the directory listing of your Web site, which provides a listing of what actually is there. If you have a housekeeping accident and accidentally delete files or move them to the wrong directory, the database will help you reconstruct what should be where.

Establishing Directories

The principle of not renaming files extends to directories. As a consequence, it will not do to name a directory ClientTst and another one ClientPrd (for test and production environments). Create your directories at a higher level—such as Test and Production—and then place all of the files and folders for your Web site in each folder. That way, nothing will ever have to be renamed. Within the Test, Production, and other folders, you may have duplicate files and duplicated directory structures, but since they are in separate environments, nothing should be confused.

Web servers and FileMaker Web Companion are very good at accessing other files within the same directory as the file that they are currently processing. Most people get into trouble when they try to mix files from other directories.

If you think of each site and area of your site as its own site and place it within its own directory, all will be well. Within each directory, place a default file—called default.htm, index.html, or home.htm according to your Web server's standards.

There are several environments that you can create to make the development and support of your Web site easier.

Production/Server

Ultimately, your files must be placed on a Web server where people can access them. You typically do not have control over the directory in which these files are placed, but you do have control over the subdirectories.

These files are the ones that people access. No files other than your finished files should be in this directory. You may think that a file called private.htm will be invisible to everyone if you do not have a link to it, but it is very easy to list the files in a directory on a Web server.

All of these files should be backed up as part of the Web server's routine maintenance. Unless you are the administrator, you should not be responsible for backing up the files that you have placed on the server.

Production/Mirror

If it is at all possible, you should have a complete copy of the files and folders on your Web site on a single computer that is not the Web server. This is your production/mirror site—the site that you can use for final testing.

This site is on your computer and is under your control. You should be responsible for backing it up whenever changes are made; you should also be responsible for moving files from it to the Web server.

Do not allow your production/mirror site to differ from the production/server site. Sometimes a few files accumulate on one site or another that are not duplicated on the other one. Deal with these either by deleting them or by duplicating them to the site from which they are missing. Keep these two sites identical.

When a file needs to be modified or added to your site, you move that file into the production/mirror environment. You should run through your test procedures there; when you are satisfied, move the file onto your Web server.

Note that you move files into your production/mirror environment: you do not create them or make changes to them there.

Test Environment

A test environment lets you experiment with Web pages and your databases. It differs from the production/mirror environment in that it may not have your entire site on it but only the files on which you are working.

Depending on your security needs and the nature of your site, you may or may not allow modifications to files directly in the test environment. You certainly should never allow such modifications directly in either the production/mirror or production/server environment, and you always allow that behavior in your development environments.

Development Environments

A development environment is just that—an area where you and your colleagues can work on databases and Web pages. All bets are off in these environments: you can rename files, you can move them, and you can change the structure of the site as your ideas evolve. This is the only way to be productive in developing a Web site.

Since you need this kind of freedom, you will need to establish a development environment where this can happen: you cannot do these things in the production or test environments. If you make exceptions (even for yourself), before you know it you will have different file structures in each environment and you will not know what files belong where.

Why It Matters

If you have not worked in a controlled environment before, this may seem like a lot of overhead to you. In fact, it is the standard way of controlling large systems involving multiple files. Before long it will become second nature to you.

If you cut corners, you will soon find yourself with incompatible versions of files all over the place; even worse, you will not know what is the correct combination of files to make your Web site function. Unfortunately, as with disk backups, it usually takes an accident to convince people of the need for such preventive actions. Remember that your Web site—even if on an intranet—is a very public area. Do you really want your boss to ask you why the site is all messed up?

Archives

Another common environment that you may have consists of archives. You should have regular backups of all of the files on your computer, but you may want to make special backups (perhaps on removable media) of your production/mirror environment every time you change it.

Special-Purpose Folders

Within your Web site, you can have any number of subfolders. As noted previously, you can use such subfolders (or subdirectories) for self-contained portions of your site—subsites, in fact. In addition, there often are special folders within each site (or subsite).

IMAGES This folder typically contains all of the graphics used in your site. (Home Page has a Consolidate command that will copy all the needed files to such a folder.) If you use other types of files such as sound files, or video, you may place them in the Images folder or in separate folders named Sound and Video. Try to avoid having a folder with one file in it. If you have one video clip and 14 images, stick the video clip in the Images folder even though technically it is not an image.

DATABASES You may also create a Databases folder. If your Web site uses a FileMaker Pro database that has no related files, there is no need for such a folder. However, if you have related files—or will have them in the future—placing all FileMaker Pro databases in a Databases folder will make your site easier to maintain. Keep everything else—HTML, CDML, images, etc.—out of the Databases folder.

INCLUDE FILES The [FMP-Include] element lets you construct CDML format files from several individual files. It is helpful to place all of these files in a single folder. That way, if you use an included file in several files, you can locate it easily. The Shopping Cart example uses an Include Files folder to share the common JavaScript routines that animate buttons.

Version Control

Even if you properly maintain separate environments for production, test, and development, you still need to provide some kind of version control so that you know which pages and databases work together. A common case involves the addition of a new field to a database: the database must change, and at the same time the CDML format files that display the data and that provide forms for data entry and modification must be changed.

The easiest way to provide version control is to explicitly provde a version for every item on your Web site—HTML files, CDML format files, databases, etc. (If you are using a database to keep track of them, this makes your life even easier.)

Do not try to provide a unified version scheme across all files: making certain that database version 1.4 matches HTML version 1.4 will soon drive you over the brink. You can provide a general version system in which version 1.x is the same for all files and version 2.x is the same for all files, but leave incremental revision numbers to fluctuate separately for each file.

Versioning Your Web Site

If you are using Home Page, use the Document Options from the Site menu to set a version for the entire site. You can place it as part of the text to be placed in the HEAD element.

Versioning the Web Pages

It is normally a good idea to place a version number at the bottom of each Web page. You may also place a date there, but for infrequently updated pages that may suggest that the site is getting a bit old to be relied on (even though with dynamic HTML that displays data from a database the content of the page may be much more recent than the format).

You may want to consider placing the modification date of each Web page as a hidden field that you can view but which is not shown to users.

Versioning the Databases

The safest way to control database versions is to create a global field (one value for all records in the database) that contains the version number. This way, you can retrieve the contents of that field just like any other data field and display it on pages that display database data. This can come in handy in tracking down problems.

Note that a database version typically applies to the database format—its fields and layouts. The database timestamp (which you can create as a separate field) shows the date and time of last update.

Why Not Just Use Dates?

Your database, HTML, and CDML format files may be on different computers—they certainly will be as you move them from the production/mirror site to the production site on the server. Each machine will have its own date and time.

The use of an explicit version identifier provides you with a tool that is independent of each machine's clock.

Summary

This chapter has covered some of the work necessary to construct a Web site that works and that can be maintained and modified as needed. There are other ways of structuring sites, and you should use whatever works for you. The critical issue, though, is creating a site whose maintenance is not a burden to you and on which the distinction between production files—those that you have approved for placement on the Web site—and test and development files is maintained.

Special Issues for Intranets

You can share FileMaker Pro databases on the Web using Web Companion as well as over your own network using the standard file sharing features that have been part of File-Maker Pro for some time. There is a distinction between the Web-based sharing of Web Companion and the network-based sharing of the traditional method.

Furthermore, intranets—which use Internet technology—combine some of the features of both. Extranets also enter into the picture, providing yet another complication.

This chapter provides a look at the differences—in FileMaker Pro terms—between sharing using FileMaker Pro alone and sharing using FileMaker Web Companion. It continues with discussions of the security and scalability of your database projects.

Networks, File Sharing, and File Servers

Networking is used to refer to the communication between and among computers. They may be on a local area network, on the Internet, or on some other medium: networking simply relates to the ability of computers to communicate with one another.

File sharing and file servers concern the ability of computers to share their files over a network—to use files on another computer as if they were on your own computer. (**File sharing** is normally regarded as the process of sharing files that reside on one or more file servers.) A file sharing environment may have a dedicated computer on which all files reside or it may consist of a number of computers, each of which can share its own files with others.

File sharing requires communication among the computers: a network is a prerequisite for file sharing. Networks, however, do not require file sharing. Many simple networks allow just the basic level of communication between computers and printers.

If you have file sharing in your environment, you can use an application program on your computer to open a file on another computer or a file server. For example, you can launch a word processing program on your computer and open a document on another computer to make edits in it. Normally, someone at another computer cannot open the document at that time. When you have closed it, someone at another computer can run their own word processing application and open the same document that you were editing. They can then continue and enhance the work that you were doing. (They may also take out all of your best ideas and leave the document worse than it ever was before: the issues involved in that case are beyond the scope of this book.)

What is important to remember about file sharing are these points:

• Each computer runs its own copy of the application.

• The application opens the document on the file server or remote computer just as if it were on its own computer. This is the essence of file sharing: the ability to use documents on another computer as if they were on your own computer.

• File sharing is implemented at the operating system level. The application program (FileMaker Pro, for example), really has little if any awareness of the fact that the file it is opening is not located on a disk that is physically connected directly to (or inside of) the computer on which it is running.

In addition to this basic way of sharing files, FileMaker Pro supports two sharing mechanisms. They differ from the file sharing described in this section in that FileMaker Pro is actively involved in the sharing—it is not just a function of the operating system that is making a remote disk appear locally to FileMaker Pro.

The two FileMaker Pro sharing mechanisms are direct sharing and FileMaker Pro Web Companion. They are described in the following sections.

This is a slight oversimplification and there are some exceptions, but you do not need to worry about them now. In addition, remember that all of these manipulations of files are subject to the security and access privileges that you have set for the files and the network.

Sharing Databases with FileMaker Pro

FileMaker Pro lets you share databases over a network; this does not rely on the file sharing described in the previous section. Rather, it relies on the basic networking that lets two computers (or a computer and printer) communicate with one another.

Opening

If you open the database using FileMaker Pro's standard Open dialog (as shown in Figure 21-1), you cannot open it with another application—or with another copy of FileMaker Pro. It is not shareable in the file sharing sense.

FIGURE 21-1. FileMaker Pro's Open Dialog

However, you can click the Hosts button at the lower right of Figure 21-1, and FileMaker Pro on your computer will communicate over the network with other copies of FileMaker Pro. You will see the dialog shown in Figure 21-2; it shows computers on your local area network that are running File-Maker Pro; for each one, it lists any databases that have been opened on that computer on for which the multiuser sharing option has been set. You open such a database by clicking the Open button in the lower right of the Hosts dialog.

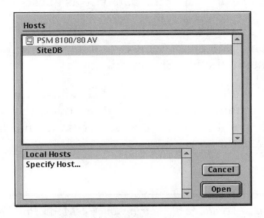

FIGURE 21-2. FileMaker Pro Hosts Dialog Box

This is not file sharing—this is networking: the computer on which you are running FileMaker Pro is sending messages to another computer (the host). Among those messages may be a request to the host to open a FileMaker Pro database file for you as a guest. Although this may appear to be sharing, it is not: only one copy of FileMaker Pro opens the database (with the Open dialog); other copies of FileMaker Pro communicate with that copy of FileMaker Pro (via the Hosts command) and ask it to open a link to the database.

Thus, the host version of FileMaker Pro—which is the only one that has directly opened the database file—can keep track of every guest user of the database, since all of them are communicating with the host version of FileMaker Pro via network messages.

What You Need to Do

In order to share a database that you open with FileMaker Pro, you need to have Export Records set for the password you use to access the database. (Export Records need not be set—and probably should not be set—for the passwords that will be accessing the database as guests.)

You need to have selected a network protocol in the Application Preferences window, and you also need to click Multi-User in the File Sharing dialog.

As the host of the opened database, this copy of FileMaker Pro handles communication over the network with the guests; it also handles all access to the database that it has opened.

You can combine file sharing and FileMaker Pro sharing by opening a FileMaker Pro database over a file sharing connection; if the database is on another computer—and if you are the first FileMaker Pro user to access it—your copy of FileMaker Pro becomes the host for that database. If you then let others share that database, they will implicitly connect to the computer on which the database is located, but the connection will actually be via your computer and its copy of FileMaker Pro. You also will have constructed a very inefficient environment, and performance—particularly for guest users—will be slow.

The host copy of FileMaker Pro—often called the host or server (as in client/server architecture)—is in control of all of the guests (clients).

Networking Technologies

This type of sharing is normally done over a local area network, using IPX/SPX, TCP/IP, or AppleTalk (Mac OS only). If you use TCP/IP, you can use this networking over a broader network (such as an intranet that spans many different locations); however, the relatively high volume of messages sent to and from the host may make that an inefficient topology.

Sharing Databases with FileMaker Web Companion

Web Companion, on the other hand, uses a different structure. Instead of a copy of FileMaker Pro on your computer (a guest/client) communicating with another copy of FileMaker Pro (the host/server), you use a network browser to communicate with FileMaker Web Companion (on the host/server computer).

The most significant differences in this type of sharing are as follows:

- Users (clients or guests) do not need FileMaker Pro. They only need an Internet browser.

- Because of the nature of the HTTP connection, FileMaker Pro Web Companion is not in charge in the way in which the host copy of FileMaker Pro is. Specifically, it does not keep a list of the current guests; it just answers requests (subject to security constraints) as they come in.

- There are fewer messages sent between the guests and the host, making this technique more suitable for operations involving many guests.

What you need to do to set up Web Companion is described in Chapter starting on page 141.

Networking Technologies

FileMaker Web Companion uses TCP/IP to publish data, but the FileMaker Pro network protocol can be set to any protocol in use on your network.

Intranets and extranets both use Internet technology. Intranets are self-contained networks that are normally not connected to the Internet (if they are, it is through carefully constructed gateways and firewalls). An intranet is like a small version of the Internet. An extranet is provided over a larger network (often the Internet itself), with security put in place to make certain sites appear only to designated users. An extranet appears as a self-contained network, but access to the Internet itself can be direct (rather than through a firewall or gateway).

Security Issues for Intranets and Other Networks

There are three levels of security that you can implement for FileMaker Pro databases that are shared:

1. Security via FileMaker access privileges (passwords and groups) lets you control who accesses databases. This security is implemented by FileMaker Pro and is in place at all times (if you have activated it).

2. Security via the Web Security database is used for FileMaker Web Companion. It is never less restrictive than the security implemented directly in FileMaker Pro. Do not get cute with security: if you are going to use the Web Security database, rely on it for as much security as possible and do not duplicate security with FileMaker Pro itself.

3. Many local area networks and intranets allow access only from specific locations; dial-in access may be nonexistent or limited. If you know that you will be functioning in an environment where security is provided by physical means, you may relax other kinds of security.

You can turn Web sharing on and off independently of file sharing. If both are on, you allow people to connect over a local area network as guests to a FileMaker Pro host while others connect using Web Companion to that same copy of FileMaker Pro. If you do this, make certain that your security measures are comparable in the two environments.

Scalability

As noted previously, it is much easier to think about security at the beginning of a project than at the end. Likewise, it is easier to think about scaling your database projects from the start. If you will eventually have 50, 100—or more users simultaneously accessing your database, you should probably consider not using FileMaker Pro as a host. (The File-Maker Pro Server Application can handle up to 100 users. It is a separate product.)

The decisions you make concerning networking will in turn influence how you set up your databases and their security.

Summary

Although your FileMaker Pro databases function the same way regardless of their network environment, you do have to pay attention to the different needs and capabilities of different network schemes. You also need to realize that you may need to change some of your database settings as you move from one setting to another (for example, from a physically secure intranet to the wild and woolly Internet).

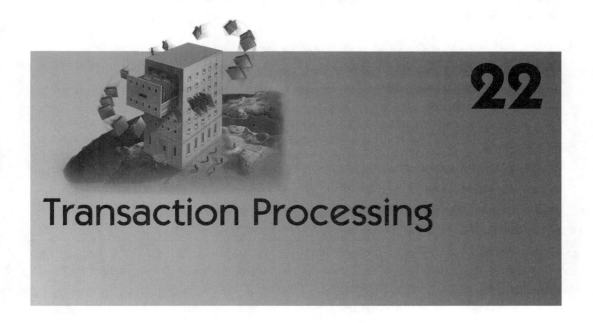

Transaction Processing

22

FileMaker Pro applications like the Shopping Cart typically involve transactions. This chapter covers some of the issues you need to think about in a transactional world. It is only the beginning of these issues—whole books have been written the subject. However, since a major use of FileMaker Pro on the Web is for database projects like the Shopping Cart example, you may want to think about some of the general issues.

The points covered in this chapter are a general definition of transactions, logs, the use of dates and times, and handling unique IDs and other data integrity issues.

Transaction Processing Defined

Transaction processing is the phrase used to describe some operations that cause something to happen to a database. Although a query can be considered a transaction, most people do not consider queries to be transactions—they do not change the database.

The definition of transaction processing provided here is an informal definition of what most people mean by the phrase. It is not a formal definition—which can be found in textbooks.

Not all operations that modify a database are considered transactions. A host of operations that are used in maintenance and housekeeping—backup, sorting, etc.—are not considered as transactions by most people.

Characteristics of Transactions

Transactions have very special meaning in the database world:

- A transaction is considered to take place at a single instance in time—although several database records may be updated at different times as part of the single transaction.

- A transaction is a unit and can be treated as such. For example, if several databases are updated as part of a transaction, a reversal of the transaction involves removing all of those changes from all of the databases.

- Transactions can typically be aborted during their processing; they also can often be reversed for a certain period of time after their completion. In either case, all affected databases should be restored to their pretransaction state.

Some databases support transactions explicitly: you can bundle a series of database calls into a transaction. If you reverse it (often called rolling it back), the database itself will take care of reversing all of the transactions. In FileMaker Pro, you need to attend to these details yourself.

Transactions Can Be Designed in Many Ways

The transaction at the heart of a shopping cart system can be designed in at least two ways.

A Shopping Transaction

You can think of the shopping transaction as starting when someone starts to shop. Each element of the transaction is the addition of an item to the shopping cart. The transaction is completed when you check out.

For physical products, the on-hand supply needs to be decremented as people add items to their shopping carts. (This is analogous to people taking items off a shelf in a store.) If the transaction is not completed, those items have to be reshelved—the on-hand quantities in inventory databases need to be restored to their pretransaction state.

A Checkout Transaction

Another structure confines the transaction to the checkout itself. Adding items to a shopping cart can be done without modifying the on-hand status in inventory databases. (This is not possible in a physical environment where people must actually place items into a shopping basket, but it is easy to do with databases.) When the transaction is processed, all inventory databases are decremented at that time.

Pros and Cons

Neither of these approaches is better than the other. In the first case, you run the risk of not letting a second customer purchase an item—even if the first customer has not paid for the item and it will ultimately be restored to stock making it possible for the second customer to have purchased it.

In the second case, you need to allow for the risk of intervening transactions so that the customer who is checking out items may need to be warned that in the time since Item X was placed in the shopping cart it has gone out of stock.

One solution that is often used by airlines is to allow a certain number of out-of-stock items to be sold—overbooking of seats. Experience has shown that a certain number of "sold" items—seats—will be returned or not used and that this buffer will usually accommodate the overbooked seats. The issue applies to more than the availability of items. What if you are changing the price of an item as people shop?

If you are designing a database project that is going to be involved with transactions, you must think about the transactions you will use. This will affect your database design as well as the way in which you implement your FileMaker Pro Web site.

This issue is sometimes referred to as the granularity of a transaction—what exactly it encompasses.

Logs

In order to manage transactions, you need a way to keep track of the parts of the transaction. Typically, this is done in a log database. Whether you define the shopping cart transaction as being at the shopping level or at the checkout level, you need to keep track of the items in the shopping cart. In the first case, you need to be able to restore them to inventory if the transaction is not completed; in the second case, you need to be able to remove them from inventory when the transaction is complete.

When the transaction is complete, an invoice is usually produced, which is the official record of the transaction. The log itself (the shopping cart) serves no purpose at that point.

Audit Trails

Logs may be designed as audit trails for what is happening in a system. You may want to keep track of items that are removed (before checkout) from a shopping cart. Audit trails may be permanent—and legal—records.

In-Process Logs

The type of log used in the Shopping Cart example is sometimes referred to as an in-process log. When the transaction is to be completed, all of its records are updated—and often deleted. If a transaction is aborted, those records may be discarded.

Dates and Times

Transactions often need timestamps as part of their information. You can use FileMaker Pro's functions to capture the current date and time, but remember that a transaction is defined as having a single moment of occurrence. For that reason, you may not want to automatically fill a database field with the current date and time—you may want to fill that field with a date and time that you will apply to all elements of the transaction.

Furthermore, remember that computer dates and times are usually wrong. There is a clock on the Web server; there is another clock on the user's computer. In the midst of any transaction, either clock may be changed. Consider computer-based dates and times to be interesting items of information, but do not rely on them for critical decisions.

Unique IDs and Other Data Integrity Issues

Rather than relying on a date and time to identify a transaction, you may want to rely on a unique ID to identify a transaction. You can use this ID in each database record so that you can reconstruct a transaction.

This transaction ID can be used in hidden fields in your CDML format files so that various Web pages all update the same transaction in your database. In many cases, this unique ID is shown in a visible field (at least at checkout time)—that is the number that you are given, for instance, to check on the status of your order.

Incomplete Transactions

It is the nature of many transactions that they are incomplete. Someone decides to leave your shopping cart Web site and do something else—perhaps walk the dog. Alternatively, the Internet connection may go down or power failures disrupt operations of the Web server or the user's computer.

What do you do about incomplete transactions? How do you know they exist?

If you have a log—a shopping cart, for example—that has not been updated for 30 minutes, does that mean that the user has lost interest? Or does it mean that a phone call has interrupted the shopping and that it will be continued in 32 minutes? You cannot even send a warning or question to the user—they may be long gone.

In designing your transactions, you must consider how you will identify incomplete transactions and what you will do. In the shopping cart example, you may want to provide the unique order ID to the user at the beginning of the shopping expedition: that way, the user can return (days, weeks, or months later) and retrieve the partially filled shopping cart. (What you do about inventory in the meantime is something you have to consider in deciding the granularity of your transactions.)

Data Consistency

Note that transaction logs by their nature are often not normalized: they contain copies of data from other databases. All of the concerns about data consistency that apply to normalization apply here (including the simple example of a price that has changed in a product database and that has not changed in the transaction log).

Summary

This chapter has provided a very brief introduction to some of the issues involved in designing transaction-based systems. It is a complex and very interesting area, and is one that you need to think about because so many FileMaker Pro-based Web applications involve transactions.

You need to consider the nature of your transactions—their scope and granularity, the ways you keep track of them in logs, how you handle dates and times, what to do about unique IDs, and the general issues of data integrity.

With this background, you should be able to create FileMaker Pro databases and to develop Web pages to access them in creative ways. That is almost all you have to worry about. The only thing left is that nagging issue of housekeeping: keeping it all running.

Maintaining Your Site and Your Databases

23

Previous chapters have dealt with FileMaker Pro Web sites and databases from the perspective of someone who can see—and deal with—all aspects of the system. In real life, only a few people have access to their Web server (which provides all Internet services), their FileMaker Pro server (which may be the same computer or may only provide database services), and to all aspects of their databases (with maximum access privileges). This chapter looks at the situation from the real-life vantage point of someone who has access only to a limited part of the picture and who must manage FileMaker Pro databases with the type of access that is available to most people.

If you do have access to the Web server, the FileMaker Pro server, and to privileged passwords, your life may be easier…for the moment. Except in very rare cases, that is a security disaster waiting to happen. If you go on vacation, does that mean the site and the database have no one to maintain them? Or does that mean that all of your security chores are delegated to someone else? Who? Just as is the case with backups of your hard disk, for most people the only way to learn the importance of security is to discover what happens when you don't have proper procedures in place.

Maintaining Your Databases on the Web from Afar

Previously, the process of moving your databases to your Web site has been treated very broadly. What actually happens when you have a FileMaker Pro Web site?

Although some people maintain their own Web server and FileMaker Pro server, for many people it is an Internet service provider (ISP) that maintains these computers and keeps the Internet and FileMaker Pro software running. Just as you move HTML pages to your Web site, you move databases to your database Web site, and the service provider does the rest.

HTML and CDML Host Computers

The actual mechanics differ from provider to provider; here is an overview of a typical installation.[1] Several computers

---

1. This installation is based on the Digital Forest site at http://www.forest.net, which provides FileMaker Pro database hosting as part of its Web site hosting for standard HTML pages.

are used to provide Web and FileMaker Pro database services. A single computer provides basic site hosting—that is, where you upload your HTML pages that have nothing to do with FileMaker Pro. This is the Web server.

Other computers run FileMaker Pro. Each of them hosts a number of client Web sites. As part of your set-up process, you are assigned your own database computer. You upload your CDML format files as well as your FileMaker Pro databases to this computer. This is your database server.

HTML files can also be uploaded to these computers, but your home page—the page to which users go when they type in your URL—is on the single HTML computer. From those pages, you can have links to other HTML pages on that computer as well as to your format files on your database computer. Dynamic URLs (those that contain FMPro) must be directed to the database computer because that is where FileMaker Web Companion is running.

If you are using Home Page, you must remember to set two different upload destinations—one for your HTML files and one for the CDML format files. Since Home Page currently supports only one FTP destination for each Web site, you must either remember to change it when you are uploading the two types of files or you must create two Web sites. Remember the power of Web links: a site for a user may be placed on many different computers (which is the case here). Decide whether you want to define your site from the user's point of view—and upload the files to several FTP destinations—or from your point of view—and split the single apparent site into its physical components. Pick whatever is easiest for you. (Hint: use the same strategy for all of your sites.)

When you establish a database account with an ISP, you will typically be given two directories to which to upload your files: one will be for the HTML files and the other will be for your CDML format files. If you are not given two directories, confirm with your ISP that both types of files are to be placed on a single computer: that is, that FileMaker Pro is running on the same computer ("box" in ISP-ese) as the Web server.

Database Directories

Inside your database directory, there typically will be three folders prepared for you. Their names may differ from ISP to ISP, but their functions are generally the same. Also, the names are usually established by the ISP: use them, but do not rename them.

Incoming Databases

This is a directory into which you place your FileMaker Pro databases. You move them into this directory using your favorite FTP application (Archie, Anarchie, Fetch, etc.).

Live Databases

At a certain moment, the manager of the database computer will move your database from Incoming Databases to the Live Databases directory. This may be done manually, but often it is done by a script that runs on the database server. It may run periodically—once a day, once an hour, or at some other interval—scanning all Incoming Databases folders and moving their contents to Live Databases. It may also run in response to explicit commands—either from the database administrator or from you.

Figure 23-1 shows the interface to Digital Forest's Database Manager, which performs this task for you.

You can select one or more databases in the Incoming Databases list to be opened by using the Open Database button. When you click that button, the selected databases are moved to the Live Databases folder and are shown in that list.

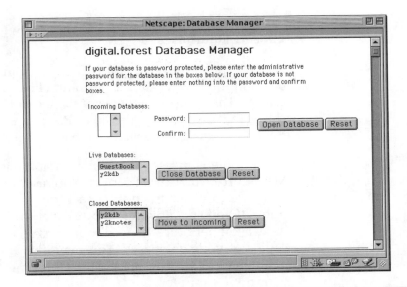

FIGURE 23-1. Digital Forest Database Manager

When a database is moved to the Live Databases folder, it is also opened by FileMaker Pro as part of this script or procedure. Remember that users cannot access databases that are not open. At the end of this process, all of the databases in Live Databases will be opened by FileMaker Pro and made ready for use.

As you can see from Figure 23-1, the interface allows you to enter a password for a database that is to be opened by File-Maker Pro. If your database does not have a default password—or if that is not the password that you want to use to open it for Web access—you provide it here. This means that the ISP does not need to know your password.

If the database server ever needs to be restarted, all of the databases in the Live Databases folder are automatically reopened by FileMaker Pro.

Closed Databases

As you can see from Figure 23-1, you can also select databases in the Live Databases list and click the Close Database button. This does the reverse of the Open Database button: it closes the database in FileMaker Pro and moves it to another folder—in this case Closed Databases.

When a file is in use (as when a database is opened by File-Maker Pro), you cannot copy it. You need to be able to close a database in order to copy it back down to your own computer. If you are allowing updates over the Web to your databases, you periodically need to do this so that you have local copies of your databases. You may also find it easier to do maintenance (see "Database Housekeeping" on page 471) on your own computer.

In this case, a shortcut is available to move a database from Closed Databases back into Incoming Databases. You would use this button to briefly close a database to allow its copying and then to move it back into production.

In most cases, if you move a new version of a database into the Live Data-bases folder (via the Incoming Databases folder), the previous version is automatically moved into the Closed Databases folder.

Variations

There may be different names for these folders and a different process involved, but this is the process that needs to be in place for you to manage your databases from a remote location (your home, office, or boat). When you are discussing establishing an account with an ISP (whether a commercial ISP or someone within your organization), make certain that you understand their terminology and procedures in this area.

Some installations may have automatic updates from a folder such as Incoming Databases; others may not have the ability to let you manually close databases or to copy old versions to your computer.

Database Housekeeping

Once you can move databases to and from your Web site, you can start to think about the housekeeping that you need to do.

Backups

Your ISP should provide you with backup as part of the service. These backups are done routinely (at least daily) for all files on the database and Web servers. They are normally not done by site or directory. In other words, the ISP takes the precautions necessary to make certain that in the case of catastrophic failure the files on a given computer can be restored from a reasonable point in time.

This backup may not be appropriate for you. There are several reasons why you might want your own backup schedule:

- You may want to keep backups from specific points in time: ends of months, years, semesters, etc.

- You may want more than one previous backup.

- You may want more frequent backups—if you have a class registration database, you may want to back it up hourly during the days of semester registration.

- You may need to place backups at a certain location for security purposes.

Know what your ISP's backup schedule is and determine if you need additional backups.

Related to backups is the question of archiving and partial archiving of data. You may want to remove old records from your online database but keep them in a backup. In the case of a guest book, you might want to periodically upload a totally empty database and to retrieve the previous one for integration with your master database on your local computer.

It is faster to do wholesale deletions of records on your local computer rather than on the database server. In doing this, however, remember not to leave a window of vulnerability in which updates to the online database are lost while you manipulate a copy of the database. That is why it is safest to upload the new database first (to Incoming Databases) and then to download the old database (from Closed Databases).

Sorting

As noted previously, sorting a database can be an expensive operation for the database server. As part of your routine maintenance, you may want to move a database to your local computer and sort it there, restoring it in its sorted form to the database server. Even if it remains only in a semisorted state, its performance will often be better at that point.

In order to fully resort a FileMaker Pro database, make a copy of the database, sort that copy, delete all records from the original database and then import the sorted records.

Data Validation and Quality

Both formal and informal database edits can be done easily with a database that you have moved off the database server. If you have to track down dubious updates, that can be done with the database offline.

Offline Databases

If you are going to be conducting database maintenance in this way, remember that you will temporarily be causing links to fail. The best way to manage this is to have an alternate home page that announces that the site is undergoing maintenance. Start by replacing your normal home page with this page, then move databases back and forth. When you are done, restore the original home page.

Thinking that you can just slip a database in or out of the database server is wishful thinking. Something will always go wrong (if only that in reaching for the telephone you knock over a cup of tea and wind up forgetting that you forgot to re-upload a database.) One of the signs of a well-run Web site is that it is not always a mess. A Web site is not your closet: it is a public area.

Summary

This part of the book has focused on the nitty-gritty of maintaining your Web-based databases. Some people do not like this part of the process—for others it is one of the more fascinating aspects of publishing databases on the Web. Whether you like it or not, the issues of security, maintenance, and transactions are critical to the long-term survival of your Web site and to the ultimate preservation of your sanity.

At this point, you have seen the possibilities of FileMaker Pro databases on the Web, you have seen how to create a site; and you have seen how to maintain your site. The last part of the book deals with the final issues: the chapters center on the people who will be using your site and your databases.

Interface and Usability Design Concerns

The Public World of the Web

Whether it is on the Internet, an intranet, or a local area network, your FileMaker Pro database is now public. The typos and misspellings in the data records are visible; the incorrect information is published. The interface to your data—your HTML pages and your CDML format files—becomes part of your data both explicitly (if you switch the "Length" and "Width" data field labels, people will receive invalid information) and implicitly (as the quality of your data is judged based on the quality of your interface).

Not just the contents of your database and Web site are public: your maintenance of them is also public. "Temporarily unavailable" is not the best response to a search request from a user.

This chapter deals with the public aspects of your Web site and your database. Although it comes at the end of the book,

477

it deals with critical and basic issues. (It requires you to be familiar with the material that precedes it.) Consider the issues raised in this chapter before you launch a Web site and before you place a database on the Web.

The principle issues to consider are as follows:

- What are you doing on the Web?

- Design issues—what your site looks like

- Letting people know about your site

- Managing problems in the public world of a network

- Handling feedback

- Dealing with registration, guest books, and gatekeepers

What Are You Doing on the Web?

The Internet is a mass medium in terms of its reach (scores of millions of people); however, its performance from moment to moment as an individual user clicks from link to link is less that of a mass medium than that of a highly personalized and individual communications medium. What an individual sees—the links traversed—is almost always a unique sequence. Indeed, with dynamically built Web pages based on database searches, the very pages that a user sees are unreproducible and ephemeral.

In addition to being simultaneously a mass and personal medium, the Internet (as is true of all networks to a greater or lesser extent) brings together people from a wide variety of backgrounds and areas. Your site will most likely be used by people who share certain interests (mountain trekking, for example) that are relevant to your site; at the same time, these people will bring different regional, cultural, linguistic, and social perspectives to your site.

What Your Site Says about You

The look and feel of a site often betray unwanted and unnecessary information about its developers and sponsors. In an international context, references to "abroad" are ambiguous or insulting. It is not a matter of political correctness to make certain that the manner in which you present your site and its information does not make people feel unwelcome: it is a matter of good manners (and often good business).

By the same token, the look and feel of a site can provide a vast array of desirable information about its developers and sponsors. A database of movies is perceived very differently if it is encountered on a site sponsored by a church, by a women's group, by a school, or by a gay and lesbian association—even if the database contains exactly the same information in each context.

It is a mistake to believe that your site's information is unaffected by its context; it is an even bigger mistake to believe that you have somehow or other managed to construct a neutral environment for your information. Its mere presence on a network makes a statement about the potential users and the information: the users are computer literate (or semi-literate) and the information is more or less public.

Being a Publisher

You are a publisher, and just as a book publisher is concerned about the look of a book's cover as well as what is inside, you need to be concerned about your site's appearance.

In addition to considering the look of your site, you have to think about some issues you may never have considered before.

Who Owns the Material You Are Publishing?

You must consider whether you are publishing information that you do not own. Where did your database come from, and under what circumstances was the information collected? The data that you legitimately can collect, index, and store may not be yours to publish electronically (even if you have the right to publish it on paper).

Watch the Export Records access privilege. It allows users to republish your database using their own copy of FileMaker Web Companion (as well as to explicitly export the records). Turning on that access privilege means—in practical terms—that you have granted all of your privileges to those users.

Publishing a database can compromise copyrights that you own. The law is still evolving in this area, but there are some rulings that say that even public information can be copyrighted in a database form: in other words, even though each item is public information, the database compendium is copyrightable.

If you feel that your project may fall into these areas, consider what precautions you need to take to avoid losing your copyright on your database by publishing it online. (A legal warning may be sufficient—consult an attorney for guidance.)

What is the Nature of the Material You Are Publishing?

This is a very tricky area. The Internet is an international medium, and laws vary from country to country with regard to issues such as pornography, violence, and other hot topics. What might be a database of chemical formulas to you could be a bomb maker's guide to someone else.

Personal information is another area that requires careful thought. The convenience of publishing the names and addresses of all students in a school may be outweighed by the problems that such publication might cause.

Is It Worth It?

With these cautions and concerns, you might wonder if it is worth publishing your databases on a Web site. The answer is almost always a resounding Yes. The fact that you can get a very nasty paper cut by slitting open an envelope doesn't mean that you should leave your billets doux unopened in the letterbox. But there is no excuse not to be aware of these issues—just as you must be aware of security on your site.

Having thought about the big issues involved with your site, you next have to focus on the particulars, such as what it looks like.

Design Issues

There is a great body of material on design issues: major works on design date to the Renaissance, and several classical texts survive. In the twentieth century, works such as *The Shape of Content* by Ben Shahn, *Interaction of Color* by Josef

Albers, and *Design of Cities* by Edmund N. Bacon, as well as Information Age books by authors such as Edward R. Tufte, Donald Norman, Marshall McLuhan, and Bruce Tognazzini have dealt with some of the issues related to form, function, content, and functionality.

The design of your site should be directed at your users: it is not what you want to put on your site, it is what people want to see and what makes it easier for them to use your site. Some people think that design does not matter, but it does: it is an integral part of your site.

Decoration versus Utility

There is a big difference between decoration and utility. As all of the authors cited previously have pointed out, decoration for its own sake is not appropriate in the information world. The Baroque Era is over; the Modern Age—like it or not—is functional.

That does not mean that things need to be ugly. Making tools usable and information understandable is done best with design that is attractive and meaningful. But avoid cute touches that are not relevant.

If you do not believe that decoration detracts from the power of a Web site, watch yourself as you visit various Web sites. Sooner or later, you will find yourself clicking on something that isn't a button. Some graphical element will appear to you to be a useful object (a button or link), but in fact it is just a piece of decoration.

What Is Your Objective?

Make certain that your site's purpose is clear. That may seem self-evident, but all too often sites are jumbles of unrelated information. Use tools like site maps and subsites to keep different parts of your site in different locations; use backgrounds and other graphics to create a common look for pages (or subsites) that have common purposes.

Home Page has a number of assistants and templates that provide good examples. Also, look at sites on the Web—those you like as well as those you do not like, those you are comfortable visiting as well as those that frustrate you.

Other Design Concerns

New design concerns crop up every day—particularly on the Web. One of the latest concerns set-top boxes—the devices that sit on top of TV sets and let you surf the Web on your TV screen. This technology is available now and may become very common in the near future.

Meanwhile, back at the TV factories, a new television technology—high-definition TV (HDTV)—is marching forward. In the United States, all television stations will be broadcasting a new HDTV signal within a period of not too many years. (For the next few years, both traditional and HDTV signals will be transmitted by various stations as this transition occurs.)

What matters to you is that someone looking at the Internet on an HDTV set with a set-top surfing device is going to be looking at a very different screen than the current computer monitor or television set. The HDTV screen has a different aspect ratio: it is much wider in relation to its height than a typical TV screen (much as the shape of a movie screen is wider than the shape of a TV screen).

For some purposes, people may start to design Web pages that are much wider than those in use today, so as not to waste the new HDTV screen space. Particularly if you are publishing your database on an intranet or extranet that you know to be populated with HDTV screens, you may want to think about new designs.

Another area to watch is that of color. Originally, the mantra was quite simple: use color, but not as a distinguishing feature. This allowed people with black and white monitors to appreciate computer graphics just as well as those with color monitors. Today, color monitors are ubiquitous, and rather than starting from a black and white design and adding color, many designers are working only with a color design.

Furthermore, many designers are now working solely on the screen: more and more corporate logos require not just color but also animation for their full display.

Of course, the rise of hand-held devices that do not have high-resolution color screens adds uncertainty to this area. Again, if you are certain that your users will be using a certain type of device, optimize your design for it.

When it comes to design, the principles of design, aesthetics, and communication are centuries old; the details of implementation change by the minute.

Not only do design details change by the minute, but they also go out of date by the minute. Experienced designers and computer users can date a computer interface just by looking at it. If your site's overall design is to last for a long time (perhaps a year), avoid the widget-du-jour syndrome.

Letting People Know about Your Site

There are two ways of publicizing your site:

1. You can place references to it on other Internet re-sources; people can place links to your site on their sites.

2. You can place these references in other media—mag-azine articles, corporate newsletters, books, etc. This is the best way to reach people who do not normally use the Internet.

In either case, you should try to achieve one goal: do not change your address. This will invalidate many Internet links and make printed references out of date.

The easiest way to avoid changing your address is to follow as many of the following guidelines as possible.

Do Not Change Your Address

Make certain that your site is (or is part of) a named domain that you control. For a modest fee, your Internet service pro-vider (ISP) can help you obtain an address like mycom-pany.com. It is a simple matter to change the Internet routing tables if you should move mycompany.com to another Internet service provider. What is particularly important is that these changes are made by you, and not by people who visit your site. All links and printed references remain intact.

In order to make this most effective, make certain that you are named as one of the contacts for your site. In most cases your Internet service provider will be named as a technical contact for the site; you should be named as the business contact. That way, you can move the site if it is necessary to move to another ISP.

Identify the Site in Relation to a Known Address

If you do not have a domain of your own (for example, if you are a department of a corporation), give out your site's address in a context that will not change. It is easy to place a button on a corporation's home page that links to your site. Then, give out mycorporation.com as your address (if necessary, telling people to click on Division X). If you give out an address like mycorporation.com/~divisions/manufacturing people may get confused.

The Site Is Part of Your Address

Once you are satisfied that you have a site address that will not change, make certain that it is part of your return address in e-mail, regular mail, and on letterheads. Although your data may be the most important data in the world, in practical terms people may consider your shakes and shingles to be interchangeable with those from another company whose Web address they happen to have in a catalog ad.

Managing Problems in the Public World of a Network

You are not alone any more. Problems—network problems, database server problems, Web server problems—can stand between your information and your users. It must be very clear who is responsible for support. It is not sufficient for users to be told that whoever they have managed to reach is not responsible: a clear path of problem management must exist.

Your Internet service provider or network administrator should be happy to sit down and discuss these issues with you. After all, it is typically the ISP or network administrator who first gets the irate telephone calls. Both of you should know what problems are likely to occur and how each of you should manage complaints about the other's problems.

You should know one another's schedules. Often, a database server is located far away from you; it may be in another time zone. The time that is convenient for you to do wholesale site maintenance might just be a time when there is no one onsite who can help if a problem occurs. Plan for such maintenance (copying of databases, opening and closing databases on the server, etc.) at a time when you know support staff is available—at least at the beginning.

Finally, prepare a short but thorough manual of procedures to follow when problems do occur. The first step in every procedure should be a clear description of when it should be invoked. It is human nature to think that the solution to a problem is just one more try away. The best network and database administrators have hard and fast rules as to the amount of time that passes after a problem is noticed before contingency procedures must be put into place.

It is wise to have an alternate home page that says the database is temporarily unavailable. This is better than letting users get an error message. Replace your standard home page with this one if you know that the database has been unavailable for a period of time—such as 15 minutes. You may have every assurance that the database will be back after 16 minutes, but it just might be 2 more hours.

Handling Feedback

In the networked world, people quickly become used to immediate feedback and response. If you have mail links on your Web pages, make certain that those messages go to an address that is monitored. The explanation that "it was Easter Sunday" won't cut the mustard when the message is from Jakarta (capital of the largest Muslim country in the world).

There are problems with monitoring mail accounts from several locations. One way is to remove your mailto links and to replace them with form-based messages that are stored in one of your databases. That way you can format the message appropriately, capture the date and time, and otherwise clean up the message before it is even sent. You can then provide limited access to that database to yourself and members of your project team. This will eliminate the problem of one person retrieving a message that no one else knows about.

Dealing with Registration, Guest Books, and Gatekeepers

Databases that contain information for which a fee is charged need to have a registration screen or gatekeeper that can collect the fee or handle password information. Other databases often have such gatekeepers. There are arguments pro and con. The most important argument in favor of such a gatekeeper is that you know who is getting to the database (more or less—people tend to type in gibberish like sdsdsddsd for their name) as well as the date, time, and number of such accesses.

The biggest argument against such a scheme is that it is one more roadblock (albeit a minor one) between the user and the information. It will certainly cut down access to your site; this may or may not be a good thing.

If you have some kind of registration screen, you can use hidden fields to pass a session ID or user ID along as the user browses your site and your databases. You can log this information—down to the mouse click. Although many people are aware that such information can easily be collected over the Web, some do not like you to do so (particularly if you sell or give the information to others). In most cases, the best approach is not to attempt to follow each mouse click; if you decide that you need that information to improve your site, a message on the registration screen that you would like to monitor activity as a way of improving the site in the future is appropriate. (If you make it an option that can be turned off, that is even better—although your statistical results will not be a random sample.)

Summary

This chapter has dealt with some of the issues you need to think about when you create a Web site and publish databases on the Web. Some of the issues can be frightening—such as copyright and pornography. The point is not to frighten you out of doing something that is positive and useful; rather, the point is to remind you not to ignore these issues. Usually, they can be dealt with very easily and you can then move on to your work.

Dealing with CGI Scripts, Other Applications, and FileMaker Pro 3.0 Databases

The previous chapters of this book have examined FileMaker Pro and its built-in Web Companion. This chapter looks at how you can create that same functionality with third-party tools and why you might consider doing so.

Even if you only use FileMaker Pro, it can be useful to understand what is going on behind the scenes, if only to be able to talk to colleagues who are using other products. The basics of what happens are very simple, and all Web servers and databases do the same things. (FileMaker Pro just makes it easier for you to do them without worrying about what is happening.)

CGI Scripts and Programs

The Common Gateway Interface (CGI) provides a specification that allows Web server software to communicate with scripts and programs that run elsewhere on the computer (or on other computers). This interface provides a standard way of exchanging information and commands with these other applications. In this way, the functionality of a Web browser can be enhanced. One such enhancement—FileMaker Web Companion—lets the Web server access databases. Other CGI software handles the processing of forms, flat-file guest books, and other typical Web site activities.

Plug-ins and Scripts

The point of the standardized CGI interface is to make it possible for products from many vendors to run and interact with one another in many different environments. Thus, as soon as you get beyond the basics of the CGI interface, you are dealing with a wide variety of configurations.

A Web server's basic functionality can be extended so that it can access other applications and files (such as FileMaker Pro databases), send e-mail, and perform other functions of use to the users of the Web server. Two common ways of extending a Web server's functionality are through the use of plug-ins and CGI scripts. Plug-ins extend the Web server functionality directly; they are typically placed in a folder that the Web server software locates as it is starting up. The plug-ins—which may be written by the Web server vendor or by other developers who adhere to the Web server's interface standards—become a part of the Web server software as it runs.

CGI scripts and programs often perform tasks similar to those performed by plug-ins, but they are accessed in a different manner. Rather than being loaded into the Web server's application, they are accessed directly via URLs. CGI scripts are often placed in a directory called cgi-bin (CGI binary). Thus, you can run a CGI script by typing in a request like

```
http://www.anydomain.com/cgi-bin/ascript
```

You can add parameters to the URL using the searchpart (this was discussed in "Searchparts and Queries" on page 212). Thus, the request shown here could be modified into the following:

```
http://www.anydomain.com/cgi-bin/ascript?name=anni
```

Some Web servers are configured to allow CGI scripts and programs to exist in places other than a standard directory; they may need to have a special suffix (like .cgi) to identify them. A Web server that handles plug-ins may recognize certain names as those of its own plug-ins; rather than running a script or program in another directory, the Web server can run its own plugged-in code.

This varies from server to server; you need to work with your network administrator or ISP to know what your options are and how you should code your requests. For example, File-Maker Web Companion—FMPro—runs as a CGI application on your Web server. Two of the third-party products discussed later in this chapter (see "Tango" on page 495 and "Lasso" on page 495) can run either as CGI applications or as plug-ins to a Web server.

Remember that Web servers change their software and that you may also move your site from one provider to another. As you do so, you may find yourself using different plug-ins or scripts; scripts that you write may need to be placed in different locations, etc. Therefore, try to avoid giving people URLs such as those shown here. Give them a URL on a standard page—your home page or a page within your site—and place a link on that page that goes to the appropriate plug-in or script. That way, if you need to change the URL, you will not confuse and frustrate your users.

Modifying CGI Scripts for Use with FileMaker Pro

You may find yourself modifying old CGI scripts. Much of the functionality that you can provide with FileMaker Pro has been provided until now with these scripts. If you are dealing with an existing site, your task will be to (gradually) replace the CGI scripts that process forms, generate e-mail, and collect data with FileMaker Pro databases and CDML format files.

Other Web Publishing Tools and FileMaker

A number of third-party tools are available to address aspects of Web publishing with FileMaker Pro databases. They can be used with FileMaker Pro 3.0 (which does not contain the Web publishing tools); one of them can also be used on Unix machines in order to publish FileMaker Pro databases in an environment that FileMaker Pro does not support directly. Four of them are discussed in this section.

Tango

Tango for FileMaker lets you use a visual development environment to create Web sites based on your FileMaker Pro databases (on Mac OS). This product is part of a collection of products that interact with various databases on various platforms.

Many people find the visual development environment easier to use than a text-based (HTML/CDML) development environment. For others, the opportunity to easily integrate Java is quite attractive. In addition, being able to use a Tango application with a variety of databases (including FileMaker Pro 3.x as well as FileMaker Pro 4.x) can be important.

Tango Server runs either as a plug-in or as a CGI application.

You can get more information on Tango at the following addresses:

EveryWare Development, Inc.
6733 Mississauga Road, 7th Floor
Mississauga, Ontario
Canada L5N 6J5

EveryWare Development B.V.
Vijfzinnenstraat 6
4201 JD Gorinchem
The Netherlands

http://www.everyware.com

Lasso

Lasso technology was purchased by FileMaker; its software forms the core of the FileMaker Pro CDML environment.

Lasso remains a separate product, however, and you can run Lasso as either a plug-in or CGI application. Lasso itself has a number of features beyond those that are included in FileMaker Pro. These include an interface to Java, additional elements that provide for more extensive programming and dynamic HTML generation, and the ability to interface not only with FileMaker 4.x databases but also with databases developed under FileMaker 3.x.

Blue World Communications, Inc.
10900 NE 8th Street, Suite 1525
Bellevue, WA 98004

http://www.blueworld.com

Cuesta

FileMaker Pro must be running in order for Web Companion, Lasso, or Tango to communicate with it and its databases. This limits your database server to a machine that can run FileMaker Pro—a Windows or Mac OS computer.

Cuesta uses the FileMaker Pro merge file format to export your database records to a Unix database (UDB) file that it can then read. This allows its other software to access that data on a Unix-based computer: FileMaker Pro need not be running.

Because this technique relies on an export of the database information, it can only be used for retrieving and browsing data; you cannot update your database data directly. Still, considering the fact that it makes it possible for you to access FileMaker Pro databases (albeit indirectly) on Unix computers, this is an interesting product to investigate.

Cuesta Technologies, LLC
695 Oak Grove Avenue, Suite 2A
Menlo Park, CA 94025

http://www.cuesta.com

Web•FM

Web•FM is a plug-in for Mac OS servers such as WebStar, Quid Pro Quo, WebTEN, and AppleShare IP. It is particularly engineered for fast performance in responding to user queries. It relies on Internet standard template files, and provides a mechanism for using HTML that you store in your FileMaker Pro database to format the resultant Web pages.

Web Broadcasting Corporation
555 Bryant Street, #386
Palo Alto, CA 94301

http://webfm.com

Living in the World of Multiple Databases and Multiple Data Managers

There are many databases and data managers in the world: one of the purposes of the World Wide Web has been to make access to information in different databases available with a minimum of difficulty. While your particular project may use only FileMaker Pro databases—may in fact use only one database—you need to think about the possibility that one day you will use more than one database and that you may need to deal with several different data managers. Saying that everything must fit into a single cookie-cutter mold is unreasonable and impractical.

SQL Databases

The de facto standard for databases on mainframes—and on many personal computers—is the Structured Query Language (SQL). SQL is a text-based way of accessing relational databases. Its databases (in FileMaker Pro terms) are called tables; its layouts (in FileMaker Pro terms) are called views.

Data is retrieved in SQL systems by using a SELECT statement: it gathers data from one or more tables (databases) and presents it in a new table with one row per record. A difference between SQL and FileMaker Pro is that each SELECT statement can express a relationship (such as where the last name field of table 1 = the name field of table 2). These relationships in FileMaker Pro are defined at the database level rather than each time you retrieve data.

The terminology is different, but the design of SQL database tables is basically the same as the design of your FileMaker Pro databases. The issues of data normalization (discussed in "The Structure of Database Data" on page 21) are absolutely the same. If you hear people talking about SQL, they are not talking a foreign language: they are talking the same language you are talking—it is just a different dialect.

Working with Other Systems

Just as your Web site may contain links to other Web sites, your links to databases may include links to your own File-Maker Pro databases as well as to databases on other computers using other technologies. The requests are all of the same sort: they specify a location and some database access software (FMPro for FileMaker Pro; for Lasso and Tango this may be either a plug-in or a CGI application; and for mainframe systems this may be yet another plug-in, CGI application, or a system like Web Objects, which converts database records to objects you can manage on Web pages).

What you know about designing databases and Web pages is applicable to any database and any Web page. Do not let turf battles, platform wars, or other extraneous issues get in your way. Forge ahead, integrating all of those databases with your Web site, providing users with information and service beyond their wildest expectations.

Summary

In addition to the FileMaker Pro software, third-party products let you integrate other databases and earlier versions of FileMaker Pro databases with the Web. The tools are there, and the technologies do the same sorts of things (in different ways).

The integration of FileMaker Pro databases and the World Wide Web is a natural step in the development of both technologies.

Appendix: FileMaker Pro Web Publishing Checklist

This appendix provides a brief checklist to help you publish your databases on the Web. It is divided into three sections:

1. **Infrastructure.** These are the steps you need to take to establish your FileMaker Pro database site. Normally, you need to do this only once for your site.

2. **Database.** What you need to do to your FileMaker Pro database to get it ready. You typically do these steps once for each database. Even if you modify the database by adding or removing fields, you rarely will need to repeat these steps.

3. **Web and General Maintenance.** Here are the steps that you go through to create and maintain your Web site. You do these as often as needed.

Infrastructure

There are two general ways of approaching the infrastructure issues: using the Internet and using an internal intranet.

Internet

- Find an Internet service provider (ISP) to host your Web site. If you already have an ISP, you can use that ISP.

- If your ISP does not support FileMaker Pro, find an additional ISP that provides FileMaker Pro hosting services. (See www.filemaker.com for a list of vendors.)

- Alternatively, if your ISP runs either Windows NT or Mac OS, the ISP can purchase a copy of FileMaker Pro (you cannot give yours away—it is good only for a single user). If the ISP is running FileMaker Pro, they need to configure is as described in the "Intranet" section.

- If you do not have a domain name (www.mydomain.com), register with Internic (www.internic.net) and obtain a domain name. (Strictly speaking, this is optional, but it will make your life much easier if you ever need to move your site to another ISP.)

Intranet

- Dedicate a computer as a FileMaker Pro server. (It can be used for other purposes as well, but performance will be degraded.)

- Install FileMaker Pro, and enable FileMaker Pro Web Companion. Establish procedures (manual or automated) for moving databases in and out of production. Remember that all files need to be placed in the Web folder. Set the port if necessary (it will be necessary if you are running a Web server on the same computer—the Web server will probably use 80; 591 is the usual choice for FileMaker Web Companion).

- Give users the IP address of this computer so that they can use it in URLs that link to their Web pages.

Both

- Design and implement security and backup procedures for hardware, software, data, power, and telecommunications. (Do this before you need it!)

Database

- Set database network sharing to Single User and Companion Sharing to use FileMaker Web Companion (File/Sharing).

- Configure FileMaker Web Companion for remote administration, logs, Instant Web Publishing (yes or no), default home page, and security (Edit/Prefer-ences/Application/Plug-Ins).

- Review scripts to run when opening and closing data-bases as well as a default password to be used on opening. Remember that the database will be opened automatically rather than by a user sitting at a com-puter (Edit/Preferences/Document/General).

Web and General Maintenance

- Create your Web site using Home Page or other tool (either graphical or text based). If using Instant Web Publishing, select the layouts to be used.

- *Test everything—including errors and failure handling.*

- Upload all files to the Web folder on your server (if using two servers, upload standard HTML files to your Web server site and your CDML format files to your FileMaker Web Companion site).

- *Test everything again when files are in place.*

- For databases that can be updated online, review the database periodically for reasonableness. Make sure that you have regular copies of the database either by downloading it or by having access to the site back-ups done by your ISP.

- Be kind to people who are struggling to use other database technologies. They have enough problems.

Glossary

book

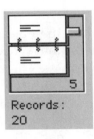

In FileMaker Pro's status area, the book icon shows you the current record (5 in this case). You can advance one record by clicking on the lower page; you can go back one record by clicking on the upper page. The records that you navigate with the book consist of all records in the database unless you have performed a Find. In that case, the book represents only the records in the current set of found records.

bookmark

The bookmark (shown at the right of the book icon above) lets you move quickly through the records in your database. You can drag it up or down to position yourself at the beginning or end of the database or at any point in between.

CDML	Claris Dynamic Markup Language. The language that you use to specify formatting commands to FileMaker Pro Web Companion. Web Companion merges CDML and HTML to produce the HTML that is downloaded to a user's browser.
CDML server	The computer on which FileMaker Pro Web Companion is running may be referred to as the CDML server.
client	An application program that relies on another program (the server) for part of its processing. Typically, the client program handles the user interaction, and the server performs the back-end processing (such as actually accessing a database). By extension, client can refer to the computer on which the client application is running, and server can refer to the computer on which the server application is running. This architecture is referred to as client/server architecture. On the Web, a browser such as Netscape Navigator or Microsoft Internet Explorer is a client; FileMaker Pro Web Companion and programs such as Apache and WebStar are servers.
controls	On HTML forms, controls are the objects with which users interact. Typically they are buttons, check boxes, radio buttons, menus, text, and images.
cookie	Information stored by a browser on a user's computer (the client). This information is stored by the browser in response to a request from the HTML page. It is subject to various security constraints and can be retrieved by other HTML pages. Cookies are used to store information such as passwords, preferences for a Web site, and temporary transaction IDs. Since cookies are stored on a user's computer, they are not available if you log onto a Web site from another computer. Cookies are sometimes considered an invasion of privacy or a possible security hazard; as a result, most browsers allow you to disable or to limit the use of cookies. Nevertheless, they are widely used.

data element	An entry in a database structure, such as age, address, or price. Each data element has a name; a data element usually has many values in a database—each value corresponds to one observation, record, or individual.
database	A collection of data that is organized for easy storage and retrieval. Databases are managed by database software such as FileMaker Pro. A database in FileMaker terms refers to a single set of data (names, addresses, telephone numbers, etc., for clients; prices, product names, part codes, etc., for goods). In some other database software, a database consists of a number of tables (where each table corresponds to a File-Maker Pro database). A database is stored in a single file.
database project	A user-created set of databases (sometimes only one) that includes layouts, reports, data entry screens, documentation, and assistance.
database software	Software that manages databases. FileMaker Pro is database software; other database software products include Microsoft Access, DB2, Oracle, and Sybase.
domain	On the Internet, a named location that corresponds to a specific IP address. Domains outside the United States end in an abbreviation of the country in which they are located. Suffixes such as edu (education), com (commercial), org (non-profit organization), and gov (government) help identify the type of domain. Thus, filemaker.com is a commercial domain, yale.edu is an education domain, and loc.gov is the Library of Congress (a government domain). In the United States, the assignment of domain names is done by Internic (www.internic.net). The domain name must be associated with a specific IP address (the address of your Internet service provider); however, if you change ISPs, you can merely notify Internic of that fact and users will still find your site since the domain name will point to another IP address.

field	A single piece of data within a record definition (also called a data element).
flat file	A traditional computer file (such as text or graphics) that does not have the indexing and fast retrieval features of database files.
form	An HTML construct that strictly speaking is a container for controls. Forms are used to enter data onto a Web page (much as paper forms are used). Data can be entered to control a FileMaker Pro search as well as to enter or edit database data. See also *table*, which is used to display database data.
format file	File containing CDML that is used as input to FileMaker Pro Web Companion. Web Companion merges the format files and standard HTML files together with data from FileMaker Pro to generate HTML files that are downloaded to the user's browser in order to display and enter FileMaker Pro data.
HTML	HyperText Markup Language. The language used to design and format Web pages. If you use a graphical Web page editor like Home Page, you may rarely see HTML itself.
HTML server	Also called a Web server. The computer on which the software resides that responds to requests from a client (browser). The HTML server may rely on additional software (such as FileMaker Pro) to produce Web pages on demand.
HTTP	HyperText Transmission Protocol. The protocol that is used to communicate between the user's browser and a Web site.
ISP	Internet service provider. An organization that provides Internet connectivity to individuals (often over telephone lines and modems) as well as to other Internet users (often over high-speed connections). The ISP may also provide a

Web server as well as FileMaker Pro hosting services (a CDML server and FileMaker Web Companion). You may use several ISPs—one for your own connectivity to dial in to the Internet and to maintain your site and another one to host your Web site and/or FileMaker Pro databases. An ISP may be a commercial organization or part of your computer and networking environment in a school or corporation.

key

A field that is used to retrieve data. Keys are usually indexed in the database by the database software for fast retrieval. Manual systems normally provide one key of retrieval (such as alphabetization by last name). Databases provide multiple keys of retrieval. Keys may be unique (such as personal identification numbers). FileMaker Pro handles keys for you automatically; to improve performance you can specify that a field is to be indexed as a key using the Storage Options dialog box.

meta-data

Information about data. Meta-data includes names of fields (as distinct from their values) and layouts.

normalization

A set of rules for structuring database data to avoid duplication, improve efficiency, and minimize operational problems.

port number

An Internet connection consists of several numbered ports. Not only do you need to connect to a specific site (such as www.filemaker.com), but you need to connect to the appropriate port on that site (such as www.filemaker.com:80). Each Internet protocol (e-mail, HTTP, etc.) has a default port number, so you often do not need to be aware of port numbers. FileMaker Pro Web Companion may require setting a special port number if you have Web serving software (using the default port 80) running on your computer.

portal

A FileMaker Pro feature that allows you to display related data from a number of records. For example, a portal in a customer record might let you display all of the items that that customer has purchased.

protocol

A formal description of the format of messages exchanged (as over the Internet). Protocols are typically defined by international standards bodies.

record

A given data instance—one student, one shopping order, etc. Each data instance consists of the data values for each of the fields in the database.

relation

A formal logical connection between records in two databases. A relation is usually based on a shared data item: the customer ID in the customer file matches the customer ID in the purchases file.

router

The hardware and software that routes messages between two network nodes. Routers are used in the Internet and intranets; they are also used to connect LANs to the Internet. A router may be a large computer or a small special-purpose box.

server

The application program that supports client software. Typically, servers do back-end processing and clients handle user interaction. By extension, server can refer to the computer on which the server application is running. A server may itself be the client of another (usually larger) server.

session

For dial-in computer users, the connection that is established over a telephone line and a modem with an Internet service provider. For other users, the connection that is established between log in of a password and user ID and log out.

SGML

Structured Generalized Markup Language. Languages that combine formatting and content in a text-based document. HTML is an example of an SGML.

site

A registered location on the Internet; a site normally has a domain name. Sites may contain subsites that may or may not be located on the same computer.

SQL

Structured Query Language. SQL is a text-based way of accessing relational databases. It has become an industry-wide standard.

stateless

Usually used in reference to HTML, stateless refers to the fact that the server does not store information about the client between transmissions. As a result, each message sent to the server must contain all of the data that the server will need to process the transaction.

status area

At the left side of FileMaker Pro windows, the status area lets you choose among available layouts. The book icon lets you navigate through the database, and status information below the book indicates the size and status of the database.

In layout mode, the status area also contains graphics tools that you can use in constructing your database layout.

The display of the status area is controlled by the status area control which is located in the bottom scroll bar of the window.

style sheet

In HTML 4.0, the ability to move some formatting information out of the basic HTML files into named styles. Styles can then be modified independent of the basic HTML pages.

table

In HTML, tables are used to organize information into rows and columns. Forms are often used to collect data from users; tables are often used to display results of database queries.

Tables are also used to format text and graphics on Web pages.

transaction

A process that may consist of a number of database accesses (retrievals, entries, and updates), but which is considered as a single unit. Checking out a shopping cart may involve updating a number of inventory records, but the checkout process is a single event.

value

An individual item of data. Data elements and fields (equivalent terms) have many values, each of which corresponds to an observation or record.

Web folder

The folder where FileMaker Pro Web Companion looks for CDML format files. It is created when you install FileMaker Pro. Do not move or rename this folder. You can create subfolders within the Web folder for each of your database projects or Web sites, but they must all be somewhere within that folder.

Web server

The computer running software such as Apache or WebStar that responds to requests from browsers for individual Web pages. Also called the HTML server. You may use several Web servers on your site.

XML

Extended Markup Language. A new SGML that allows you to describe the characteristics of information as well as its formatting. Thus, XML tags let you specify that certain information is a name or an address.

Index

Principal entries and definitions are shown in **bold**.

B

backups 471
Blue World Communications 496
body (HTML element) **196**
book 102
bookmark 102
browsers
    testing with 161
buttons 300
bw **226**

C

calculations (in FileMaker Pro) **65**
CanDelete 251
CanEdit 251
CanNew 251
capitalization (in URLs) 160
capitalization of file names 437
CDML 393–405
    data entry fields 398
    database 396
    editing 394
    email 228
    error file 396
    FMP-Include 354
    for hidden fields 396
    for submit button 399
    format file 396
    format files
        specification of 231
    layout 396
    logical operators 225
    mail requests 228
    sorting 227
    using tables with 402
CDML elements 233–275
    CDML Tool 283
    cookies 271, 274
    database 239
        encodings 240

defined **234**
file manipulation **254**
finding and sorting **261**
headers 271
if 248
    comparisons 251
    testing values 252
    variables and fields to test 249
links **255**
lists **263**
    looping through FileMaker Pro
        value lists 269
    looping through value lists 266
    selection lists **264**
looping 241
parameters for 235
range **260**
replacement **235**
    environment **236**
    See also under FMP-
CDML host computer 466
CDML parameters
    modifying 395
CDML Tool 277–287
    creating a format file for a New
        action 280
    creating tags/elements 283
    defined **278**
    templates 280
CGI **492**
cgi-bin 493
checkboxes 300
Claris Home Page
    environment 88
    FileMaker Pro assistant 92
    FileMaker Pro Reference Library 95
    FileMaker Pro tools in 91
    overview 87
    site management with 89
    uploading files 90
ClientAddress
    used for security 429
ClientIP
    used for security 429

E

-Edit **222**
eight-dot-three naming convention 437
elements (HTML) **188**
email 45
    CDML 228
    sending with Custom Web Publishing
        180
email example (forms) 307
encoding 269
    database elements 240
eq **226**
-Error 220, **223**
error handlers 346
error handling
    dynamic Web pages 346
event handlers 316
events **316**
EveryWare 495
ew **226**
Exact Delete 425
Exact Search 425
Exact Update 425
Excite 35
exporting records 430
extranet **454**

F

f (FMP-Link parameter) **256**
failure-handling
    testing 163
failures
    testing 163
Fetch 90
field definitions
    in FileMaker Pro **53**
field types
    in FileMaker Pro **54**
fields **22**

    in FileMaker Pro **53**
file manipulation elements (CDML) **254**
file names
    capitalization of 437
    eight-dot-three naming convention 437
    establishing directories 439
    testing 159
file servers 448
file sharing 448
file structures for easy maintenance 436
FileMaker Connection assistant 363–391
    files created by 385
FileMaker Pro
    calculations **65**
    choosing data types in **54**
    commands 102
    containers **62**
    data entry options **56**
    database solution commands 103
    databases
        modifying for performance on the
            Web 348
    databases described **52**
    field definitions **53**
    field types **54**
    fields **53**
    formulas **65**
    functions **65**
    globals **63**
    new record behavior compared to
        Instant Web Publishing 115
    overview 51–80
    records **52**
    security 429
        exporting records 430
        features 414
        groups 420
        logs 427
        passwords
            default 421
        related files 429
        remote administration 426
        user names and passwords 432
        Web Security databases (FileMaker

G

H

I

S

W

X

Y

About the Author

JESSE FEILER is Software Director of Philmont Software Mill. He has served as consultant, author, and/or speaker for organizations including the Federal Reserve Bank of New York, Prodigy, Kodak, Young & Rubicam, The Josef and Anni Albers Foundation, and Yale University Press among others.

His technical credits span mainframes to personal computers including machines from IBM, Apple, Burroughs, and Control Data; databases from IBM, Burroughs, Oracle, Microsoft, and Claris; object-oriented frameworks including MacApp and OpenStep; languages ranging from Fortran, Algol, and Cobol to Pascal, C++, Java, and Objective-C; as well as a host of end-user and productivity tools from vendors including Microsoft, Apple, IBM, and Claris.

He is the author of a number of books including *Rhapsody Developer's Guide* (AP Professional, 1997), *ClarisWorks 5.0: The Internet, New Media, and Paperless Documents* (Claris Press, 1997); *FileMaker Pro and the World Wide Web* (Claris Press, 1998); *Cyberdog* (AP Professional, 1996); *Essential OpenDoc* (with Anthony Meadow, Addison-Wesley, 1996), and *Real World Apple Guide* (M&T Books, 1995).

Jesse Feiler serves on the boards of the HB Playwrights Foundation, the Philmont Public Library, and the Mid-Hudson Library System. He is the 1997 recipient of the Velma K. Moore Award given by the New York State Association of Library Boards for "exemplary service and dedication to libraries."

Together with Barbara Butler, he wrote *Finding and Fixing Your Year 2000 Problem: a guide for small businesses and organizations* (AP Professional, 1997).